ARCHAEOLOGICAL DISCOVERIES OF ANCIENT AMERICA

FRANK JOSEPH, EDITOR

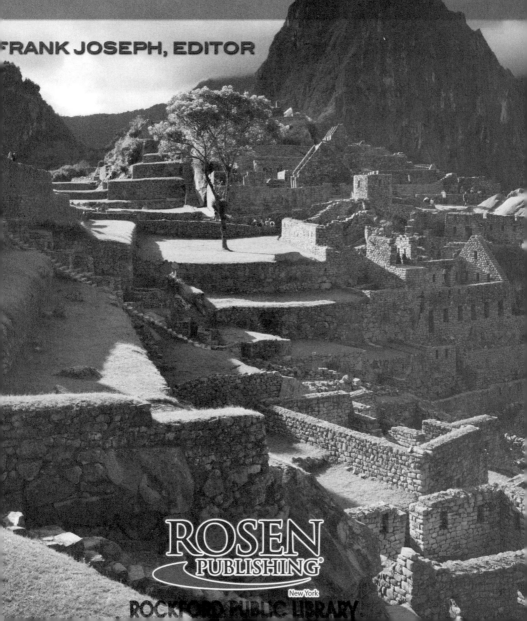

ROSEN
PUBLISHING®
New York

This edition published in 2014 by:

The Rosen Publishing Group, Inc.
29 East 21st Street
New York, NY 10010

Additional end matter copyright © 2014 by The Rosen Publishing Group, Inc.

Library of Congress Cataloging-in-Publication Data

Archaeological discoveries of ancient America/editor, Frank Joseph.—First edition.
   pages cm.—(Discovering ancient America)
Includes bibliographical references and index.
ISBN 978-1-4777-2809-3 (library binding)
1. America—Antiquities—Juvenile literature. 2. America—Discovery and exploration—Pre-Columbian—Juvenile literature. 3. Historic sites—America—Juvenile literature.
4. Prehistoric peoples—America—Juvenile literature. 5. Visitors, Foreign—America—History—To 1500—Juvenile literature. I. Joseph, Frank.
E21.5.A725 2014
970.01—dc23

2013014682

Manufactured in the United States of America

CPSIA Compliance Information: Batch #W14YA: For further information, contact Rosen Publishing, New York, New York, at 1-800-237-9932.

First published as *Unearthing Ancient America* by New Page Books/Career Press, copyright © 2009 by Ancient American Magazine.

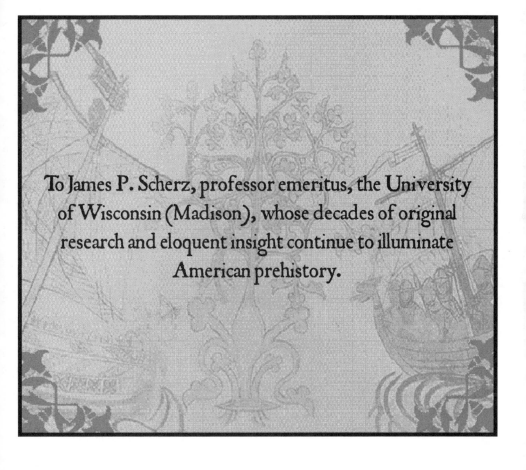

To James P. Scherz, professor emeritus, the University of Wisconsin (Madison), whose decades of original research and eloquent insight continue to illuminate American prehistory.

Contents

INTRODUCTION: WELCOME TO THE NEW HISTORY!

11

CHAPTER 1: ANOMALOUS ARTIFACTS

13

An Ancient Egyptian Statuette Found in Illinois
By Wayne May
13

Medallion Puts Buddhists in Michigan a Thousand Years Ago
By Frank Joseph
24

Ancient Michigan's Solar Eclipse Tablet
By David Allen Deal
31

CHAPTER 2: MESSAGES FROM THE PAST

39

Minnesota's Viking Runestone Is Authenticated
By Lloyd Hornbostel, Jr.
40

The Lost Inscription of Grave Creek
By Wayne May
45

The Grave Creek Tablet Is Genuine
By Ida Jane Meadows Gallagher
50

The Crespi Collection: Archaeological Fraud or Prehistoric Library?
By Dr. Warren Cook
54

CHAPTER 3: STRANGE STRUCTURES

75

Connecticut's Fifth-Century Church
By John Gallagher
75

Florida's Stonehenge?
By James P. Grimes
84

Dighton Rock: The Ancient Enigma of Massachusetts
By John Gallagher
90

CHAPTER 4: SUBTERRANEAN MYSTERIES

95

The Money Pit
By Kassandra Dycke
96

Find or Fraud of the Century?
By Philip Coppens
103

An Achievement to Rival the Pyramids
By Fred C. Rydholm
114

Underground City of the Grand Canyon
By Frank Joseph
123

Inscrutable Metallic Tablets of the Rockies
By Jared G. Barton
132

CHAPTER 5: UNDERWATER DISCOVERIES

141

A Roman-Era Figurine Recovered Off New Jersey
By Lloyd Hornbostel, Jr.

141

Has the Lost Motherland of the Pacific Been Found?
An Interview with Masaaki Kimura

144

Bimini: The "Road" to Discovery
By William Donato

148

A Rock Lake Time Line
By Frank Joseph

158

The Crystal Pyramid of Wisconsin's Rock Lake
By Frank Joseph

161

The Great Triangles of Rock Lake and Aztalan
By Frank Joseph

167

CHAPTER 6: ENIGMATIC EFFIGIES

177

The Hideous Spider Pipe of Prehistoric Tennessee
By Wayne May

177

Pre-Columbian Hebrews in Michigan
By Dr. John White

182

The Serpent and the Meteor
By Frank Joseph

183

Giants of the California Desert
By Lloyd Hornbostel, Jr.

191

Chapter 7: Lost Kingdoms

197

Found: The Pre-Inca City of Gran Saposoa
By Earl Koenig
197

The Rise and Fall of Prehistoric America
By David Hoffman
199

Utah's Nameless City of the Clouds
By Wayne May
202

Chapter 8: Forgotten Seamanship

207

Did a Sunstone Guide the Vikings to America?
By Earl Koenig
207

Sweden's Iron Age Monument to Transatlantic Voyages
By Reinoud de Jonge and Jay Stuart Wakefield
211

An Old Map and Some Chicken Bones Terrify Archaeologists
By John Gallagher
222

The Pre-Columbian Connection: Ancient Transatlantic Ships
By James P. Grimes
225

How the Portuguese Out-Foxed Columbus
By Dr. Gunnar Thompson
234

CHAPTER 9: BONES, SKULLS, AND DNA REWRITE HISTORY

245

Inca Skeleton Unearthed in Scandinavia

By Earl Koenig

245

Genetics Rewrite Pacific Prehistory

By Peter Marsh

247

Ancient American Coneheads

By David Hatcher Childress

254

Who Were the First Americans?

By Frank Joseph

265

GLOSSARY

270

FOR MORE INFORMATION

272

BIBLIOGRAPHY

275

INDEX

284

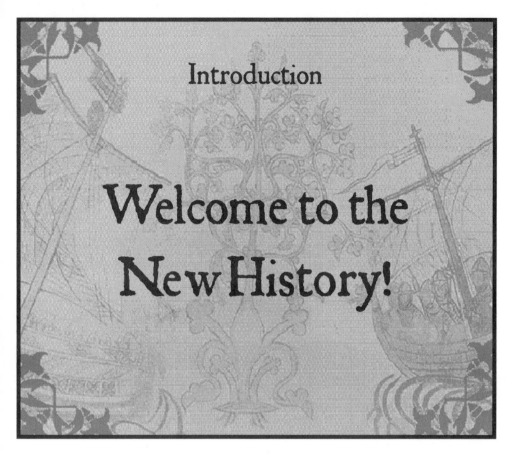

Introduction

Welcome to the New History!

At most, what Americans know of their country's prehistory is that Asiatic nomads wandered out of Siberia across an Alaskan landbridge sometime during the last ice age into our continent, where they eventually became tribal Indians. Cut to Columbus planting the Spanish flag on the beach at San Salvador 12,000 years later, and that is just about everything they have learned from teachers and television.

Aiding and abetting such public ignorance are mainstream scholars. Their vested professional and financial interests uphold the fiction of early America as isolated from the rest of the outside world in a kind of impervious cultural vacuum. This academic dogma has absolutely dominated consensus reality where our real origins are concerned. Maverick researchers or independent investigators who question official versions of the past are shunned, their careers threatened and sometimes ruined, their reputations held up

Archæological Discoveries of Ancient America

for ridicule. However, with inexorable advances in technology—from DNA to ground-penetration radar—the high-handed neglect or effortless suppression of contrary evidence is no longer possible. Accordingly, we live in an Age of Breakthroughs that is demolishing Ivory Tower isolation, while broadening the panorama of prehistory.

These fundamental changes are tracked in popular science format for everyday readers such as ourselves. And some of its latest, most dramatic finds have been collected for this book in 37 articles by 22 writers. Whether PhDs or avocational antiquarians, they are indeed "unearthing Ancient America." In so doing, they have identified its prehistoric conquerors—Vikings in Minnesota, copper-barons in Michigan, Templars in Newfoundland. Castaways unintentionally spread their Roman coins off New Jersey's shores, etched celestial navigation glyphs into a Massachusetts boulder, and stashed their Roman Era treasure in an Illinois cave.

Their lingering, if until-now unacknowledged effect on our national identity has been the victim of academic censors, the true scoundrels in this lost narrative of the past. If nothing else, it is a tremendous story—the epic of many peoples who, together, and sometimes unaware of each other, formed buried foundations on which we have been standing for countless generations.

CHAPTER 1

Anomalous Artifacts

M *ainstream scholars scoff at the very notion of ancient Egyptians sailing to our shores. Yet, a ritual grave object could be physical proof of visitors to the American Midwest from the Nile Valley some* 2,600 *years ago.*

AN ANCIENT EGYPTIAN STATUETTE
FOUND IN ILLINOIS

By Wayne May

News occasionally surfaces of persons claiming to have uncovered a dynastic Egyptian presence in prehistoric America. Unfortunately, their "proofs" for pharaonic visitors here are, at best, theoretically possible, or, at worst, patently erroneous. Far less often, a piece of exceptionally persuasive evidence emerges.

An Egyptian statuette allegedly removed from an ancient burial mound in Libertyville, Illinois.

Little is known of the object's modern origins, save that it was found in Libertyville, Illinois, some 20 miles (32 kilometers) north of Chicago. During the time of its discovery in the early part of the 20th century, Libertyville was a sparsely populated, agricultural community with only a few dirt roads, in sharp contrast to the sprawl of upper-class suburbia that mostly blankets the area today just off the I-94 tollway. But before World

War II, only several dozen families—mostly farmers—were spread over some 12,000 acres (49 square km) of largely pristine prairie.

As a young man, the discoverer (whose widow has requested anonymity for her late husband) developed an abiding interest in collecting Indian artifacts—mostly arrowheads—he found in the vicinity of his home. But the richest sources for prehistoric materials were along the banks of the Des Plaines River and nearby Diamond Lake. Otherwise seldom visited, its 5-mile (8 km) shoreline featured a number of Indian burial mounds he rifled for whatever grave goods might be dug out. These were usually limited to small pipes, spools, bones, flints, and other typical items.

From one earthwork, however, he allegedly extracted a most atypical statuette. He never attempted to have his discovery professionally evaluated, and showed it to only a few fellow collectors, perhaps for fear of criticism, either for having removed the object without informing the archaeological authorities in Chicago, or because such finds were automatically condemned as the forgeries of conmen trying to defraud money from collectors. Time passed, and, by the turn of the 21st century, his assemblage of more conventional Native American artifacts reached prodigious proportions. Only then did word of the strange statuette reach me, and I was able to purchase it.

The well-crafted object stands 9 inches (23 centimeters) high, weighs approximately half a pound (227 grams), and appears to have been sculpted from a single piece of off-white soapstone. It portrays a man wrapped in a kind of body-stocking, from which his emerging hands hold a shepherd's crook in the left and a flail in the right. The flail was an agricultural tool used in dynastic times by Nile Valley farmers to separate wheat from chaff by beating stacks of grain on a stone floor for threshing. Pharaohs were commonly depicted in sacred art holding such a device as the emblem of judgment: separating the good from the bad subjects. The shepherd's crook stood for political guidance over his flock (people).

The Libertyville figure wears a stylized wig behind the ears, together with a long beard. Beginning at the waist and descending to an area corresponding to the ankles are eight lines of hieroglyphic text, with a single, additional line composed of four glyphs running top to bottom from the ankles to the unexposed toes.

Other than what is probably some minor erosional damage at the front-left side between the hand holding the flail and the top line of script, the object is in perfect condition. Small accumulations of white material in some of the glyphs, and particularly between the vertical lines of the wig, are perhaps residues of clay. More puzzling is the appearance of dark orange pigment found mostly on the wig, but also in the eyes of the face, and in some of the glyphs and the horizontal lines separating them. The ochre-like coloration may have been caused by an unknown powdery substance ritually sprinkled on the figure prior to burial, or caused by reaction with the soil after interment.

The artifact's overall workmanship is exceptionally fine. Particularly outstanding are its hieroglyphs, which, for their individually crafted details, betray the hand of a master scribe intimately familiar with his subject. Everything about the object, quite obviously, bespeaks Pharaonic Egypt. So much so that its provenance may be easily traced to a specific dynasty; namely, the 26th Dynasty, or "Saite," after the Nile Delta city of Saiis, where the royal house was founded in 664 BCE, enduring for another 139 years. This era brackets a time frame when such images were portrayed wearing the body-stocking described earlier; numerous, comparative specimens are displayed at Britain's Fitzwilliam College, in Cambridge.

The figure's identification as an *ushabti* is no less apparent. Ushabti were small statuettes placed in ancient Egyptian tombs to act as servants for the soul of the deceased. Imbued with ceremonial magic during his or her funeral, the figures were supposed to come alive after the mummy had been sealed inside its tomb. The term *ushabti* means "the answerer," from the verb *wesheb*, "to answer." Inscriptions on a 26th Dynasty ushabti typically read, "If it is decreed that Osiris [the god of resurrection] is to do work in the Afterlife, cast down the obstacles in front of this man. Behold me whenever you are called. Be watchful at any moment to work there, to plow the fields, to carry water. Behold me whenever called."

Another commands, "Oh, ushabti, allotted to me! If I be summoned or detailed to do any work which has to be done in the realm of the dead; if, indeed, obstacles are implanted for you therewith, you shall detail yourself for me on every occasion of making arable the fields, of flooding the banks. 'Here I am!' you shall say." If the Diamond Lake object is indeed an ushabti, its hieroglyphic text almost certainly carries a similar message, or other analogous lines from Chapter 6 in *The Book of the Dead*, a collection of sacred texts aimed at guiding the human soul successfully through the terrors of death into the Afterlife; it was likewise interred with the deceased.

As mentioned, the Libertyville object stands 9 inches (23 cm) tall, the same height for most ancient Egyptian ushabti. They were made in a variety of media, including stone, wood, and faience (from a glass-ground paste), so the fact that the Northern Illinois specimen is soapstone means nothing.

For all its apparent authenticity, there is a problem with this find. Although most ushabti were meant to stand in as servants for the deceased in the Afterlife, a few of the statuettes represented his or her own soul-essence. The Diamond Lake figure appears to represent one of these ritual personifications of the grave-owner's soul, and therein lays the rub.

Archæological Discoveries of Ancient America

The Northern Illinois item clearly depicts supreme royalty, which means it belonged in the tomb of a king. All mummies of the 26th Dynasty's nine monarchs are accounted for in Egypt, so the Libertyville ushabti could not have come from the burial of a Saite leader who somehow ended up in America.

Even though it does not bear a cartouche encircling the name of the king to whom it was consecrated, the figure's hands grasp the crook and flail, emblems of the highest authority. In Egyptian temple art, a cartouche was a stylized loop of rope knotted at one end to contain two of Pharaoh's names. Although many royal ushabti, such as those belonging to the famous Amenhotep III, are more easily identified by the inclusion of a cartouche, others possessed none, such as several "answerers" serving the still better known Tutankhamun.

Yet the Diamond Lake statuette did not necessarily have to come from the grave of a king. Similar images were available for general purchase, even by common people, to be interred with their own burial, as a means of continuing their veneration of the king. Pharaohs were, after all, considered gods before and after death. It is therefore conceivable that such an ushabti could have been carried in an ancient ship that made landfall in North America, even though its owner was not the pharaoh himself. If the Libertyville find does indeed represent such a ruler, then its inscription cannot call upon the ushabti to serve the deceased, but rather, according to other, more relevant passages in Chapter 6 of *The Book of the Dead*, it enables the soul of the person interred to honor his or her god-king. This would have been particularly important for anyone venturing far from the land of his or her birth.

Ancient Egyptians traveling beyond the Nile Valley always carried religious symbols of their homeland with them in case of death. Burial outside the holy land of Egypt was thought to imperil the human soul, which could not find its way to the Afterlife, itself hardly more than an idealized version of Nile Valley civilization. Hence, a 26th Dynasty ushabti personifying the royal soul of Egypt discovered in distant Illinois fits the arrival of an ancient Egyptian who required just such a religious object in the event that he or she died too far away for burial in native ground.

What makes the Diamond Lake object's Saite provenance especially cogent was one 26th Dynasty ruler in particular. In 610 BCE, Wehimbre Necho became Pharaoh Necho II, and 10 years later commissioned the first known circumnavigation of the African continent, as documented by the sixth-century Greek historian Herodotus, in his famous *Histories*. An expedition of Phoenician ships with mixed Punic-Egyptian sailors was commissioned and fitted out in July, successfully docking at the Nile Delta in the opposite direction from which they disembarked three years earlier. They returned minus a few vessels with their crews, who were driven out to sea, probably as they entered the Canary Island current. It sweeps off North Africa's west coast near the Canary Islands to run straight across the Atlantic Ocean and into the Gulf of Mexico. It also brought Christopher Columbus to the New World more than 2,000 years after Necho launched his own maritime enterprise.

The Diamond Lake item's identifiably Saite configuration, together with Necho II's contemporary Atlantic expedition, suggest that the figure is indeed a 26th Dynasty ushabti. It probably belonged to an Egyptian crew member in one of the Phoenician ships swept across the ocean by the Canary Island current, depositing his vessel in the Gulf of Mexico at a place along the southern coasts of North America. Somehow, his ushabti came into the possession of native Indians, who learned at least enough about the statuette to understand that it was a valuable grave good, judging from its alleged discovery in a burial mound. The little "answerer" passed, perhaps as a trade item, from hand to hand up the Mississippi Valley, until its last owner interred it in the Northern Illinois earthwork, where it was found in the first decades of the last century.

Of course, Necho's sailors could have sailed all the way up the Mississippi River to the western shores of Lake Michigan, which are just 5 miles (8 km) inland from Libertyville. There, the corpse of one of his crew members was buried, along with his ushabti, under a simple mound of earth. Before the installation of "wing-dams," little more than 100 years ago, raising the river's current to 7 miles per hour (11 kilometers per hour), the Mississippi was sluggish to the point of stagnation, and easily navigable by sailing vessels, particularly if they had the advantage of summer winds blowing up from the south. As late as Mark Twain's day, canoeing up the Mississippi was a popular pastime. In any case, either scenario tends to emphasize the object's Saite identity.

Such interpretations, though perhaps credible, are undermined by the entirely anecdotal account of the Diamond Lake object's removal under undocumented, unscientific conditions by an anonymous, amateur artifact collector. The exact location and time of its supposed discovery are unknown. Beyond the few, sketchy, unverifiable details of its early-20th-century origins, all investigators are left with to establish its true identity are the elements of the item itself. They are, however, compelling.

Suspicions that the find may have been a relic from the Chicago World's Fair, which took place in 1930, or some similar, recent source, are doubtful, because the artifact was not mass-produced; it is handmade. The glyphs particularly, as already cited, are exceptionally well done—not the usually sloppy workmanship seen since the fall of Dynastic civilization, and superior to most modern replicas.

I also mentioned the apparent residue of dried clay and/or pigment of some kind. If these materials or stains are the organic substances they appear to be, they might lend themselves to radiocarbon testing, which could at least provide a time frame for the item's burial, if not its manufacture. A reliable date before the 19th century would help establish its historic authenticity. In fact, the Diamond Lake item is presently undergoing examination by a certified antiquities investigator. Until he has made his final determination, the jury is still out on Mr. X's find. For the present, at least, it is an attractive, intriguing object that may yet turn out to be far more valuable than its inherent beauty.

Dr. Gunnar Thompson writes, in his encyclopedic *American Discovery: The Real Story,*

> "Insatiable curiosity and the growing demand for copper were the driving forces behind Egyptian voyages to America. Egyptian pharaohs demanded knowledge of foreign kingdoms, and they dispatched explorers across the oceans in search of new worlds, exotic imports, and metal ores. Copper was the *sine qua non* of their dreams to build a lasting memorial to Nile civilization. According to the oldest Egyptian legends from the early third millennium BCE, explorers and geographers knew about continental land to the west beyond the Atlantic. The land was thought to be the resting place of the sun, and so it was called both 'the Abode of the Sun' or 'the Land of Immortals.' It was also referred to as the Underworld, because on the spherical Earth it was situated beneath Egypt on the opposite side of the globe. As early as 2600 BCE, pharaonic fleets sailed into the Atlantic Ocean, returning four years later. No report has survived to reveal what the voyagers discovered across the seas. Later records tell of similar expeditions without reporting any results. The funeral text of Pepi II (dated 2180 BCE) claims

Archaeological Discoveries of Ancient America

the pharaoh sailed across the 'Two Parts of Heaven' manned by 'inhabitants from beyond the western horizon.'"

Dr. Thompson's observations demonstrate the possibility, at least, of Egyptian voyagers to North America in Dynastic times. He was supported by Dr. Barry Fell, another unconventional scholar, who uncovered evidence for an ancient Egyptian written language among Native Americans. At Harvard's Widener Library, he, with the help of a fellow researcher, located copies of 300-year-old papers composed by a Jesuit missionary in Canada's eastern provinces. The priest had apparently put together a teaching aid for his Micmac Indian students, who copied out the Lord's Prayer in hieroglyphs. On closer examination, about half were recognizable hieratic, a simplified form of Egyptian hieroglyphs. More surprisingly, the Micmac characters corresponded to the meaning of the Egyptian glyphs. Dr. Fell concluded that someone familiar with Egyptian hieroglyphic writing very long ago had contrived the Micmac writing system of hieratic symbols.

More evidence for Egyptian influence in pre-Columbian America surfaced in the Michigan tablets during the 1840s. Most of these inscribed artifacts display an unfamiliar written script that nonetheless include several Egyptian hieroglyphs. Additional examples of Nile Valley effect on prehistoric America came from Burrows Cave in southern Illinois. Of the 7,000 inscribed stones removed from it since 1982, few bare traces of Egyptian hieroglyphs, although many do depict persons dressed in Nile Valley garb. Josiah Priest, in his book *American Antiquities: Discoveries in the West*, was one of two mid-19th-century explorers who documented the rock art illustrations of similarly costumed men and women adorning the walls and ceiling of a site now known as "Cave in Rock State Park," again in southern Illinois.

These varied collections of evidence support archaeological probabilities for the Libertyville ushabti. Similar examples have been found elsewhere in the Americas. According to Mariano Cuevas, in his 1922 *Historia de la Nación Mexicana*, "An incident along the line of our inquiry [into contacts between Mexico and Egypt], which no Americanist can ignore, has been the fortuitous discovery of two statuettes. Their discovery was made a few years ago, in August, 1914, in a rural parish of His Excellency the Archbishop of San Salvador, the Reverend Father Velloso.

Professor Miguel Angel Gonzalez was conducting precise excavations in the City of Acajutla in the Maya area near the farthest limit of the railroad line. These excavations, which were undertaken at the request of the aforementioned archbishop, resulted in the uncovering of two precious artifacts. One has to keep in mind that many similar objects have been encountered by ignorant natives and subsequently ruined. At this same site, according to the Central American historian Garcia Pelaez, who was later Archbishop of Guatemala, there existed in antiquity a city that was very grand and important.

"The most important fact of the statuette is that it represents a sarcophagus or mummy of a male. It gives all the appearances of resembling an Egyptian statuette. If we make a closer inspection and focus our attention on the headdress, we notice a typically Egyptian beard beneath the point of the chin. More than anything else, the inscriptions on both statuettes have Egyptian features, such as the classical ellipse or cartouche on the male statuette. We are led to conclude without the slightest doubt that these are Egyptian. They are similar to statues in pictures by Champolion, mark for mark. They have demotic characteristics and hieroglyphs identical to those found on classical Egyptian monuments, which also have analogous ellipses. Because of all these characteristics, which are comparable to features of artifacts in the Cairo Museum, we are able to confirm assertions that we have established the certain Egyptian heritage of these statuettes.

These Mexican counterparts of the Illinois statuette not only tend to support its identification as an ancient Egyptian ushabti, but also suggest that our continent was indeed visited by travelers from the Nile Valley around 600 BCE.

The fortuitous rediscovery of a strange, coin-like object on a remote island in Lake Superior led to its surprising identification after more than 70 years of controversy. But no one could have guessed that the weird images appearing on either side confirmed its origins in an ancient holy city halfway around the world.

MEDALLION PUTS BUDDHISTS IN MICHIGAN A THOUSAND YEARS AGO

By Frank Joseph

In 1983, James Scherz, professor of environmental studies and civil engineering at the University of Wisconsin (Madison), was shown a photograph taken by Dr. Pat Carmody, in L'Anse, Michigan, of an unusual medallion. About 1.75 inches (4 cm) in diameter, it had been found some 2 feet (.6 meter) beneath the surface 55 years before by a man digging foundations for a building on the Lake Superior island of Isle Royale, near the Canadian order.

The obverse side of the object represented a man or statue seated in the entrance of a pyramid flanked on either side by palm trees before an audience of observers. The perimeter of the object was surrounded by 79 dimples. A hole pierced the medallion at its top, perhaps for a small chain to be passed through, allowing the coin-like item to be worn around the neck.

Although found in Michigan, the scene depicted on this medallion places its manufacture in medieval India.

Reverse of the Michigan medallion.

The reverse featured the image of a radiant lion holding a scimitar in its right, extended paw at the center of a heart with wishbone surrounded by 69 dimples. In a space between these and another 79 dimples appeared the raised letters of (to Scherz) an unknown Asian script resembling Tibetan or Indonesian examples with which he had a passing acquaintance. He guessed that the medallion "was produced by pouring some yellow metal alloy into a mold." Unfortunately, its metallurgical testing was not possible, because the artifact had apparently vanished with its last known owner in 1986. All Scherz had to go on was the photograph. It particularly intrigued him, not only for its Asian imagery, but because of the circumstances of its discovery at an important place in the prehistory of North America.

Around the turn of the fourth millennium BCE, Isle Royale suddenly became the center of a colossal copper mining enterprise that came to just as abrupt a halt 2,800 years later. From hundreds of pit-mines stretching for some 50 miles (80 km) across Michigan's Upper Peninsula, an unknown people excavated a minimum of half a billion pounds of the world's highest-grade copper. No less mysteriously, this enormous yield disappeared without a trace. The mines lay mostly dormant throughout the following centuries, until they were reopened from 900 CE to 1300 CE. Professor Scherz wondered if the strange medallion could have had something to do with Isle Royale's prehistoric miners, long suspected (at least by unconventional investigators) of overseas' origins.

Beginning in the late 1980s, he republished a drawing of the missing item in several papers. Nothing was heard of it again until March 2003, when Mr. Paul Tolonen, of Tularosa, New Mexico saw Professor Scherz's illustration of the medallion. Recognizing the object, Mr. Tolonen telephoned magazine publisher Wayne May to explain that, in 1929, his uncle found the medallion, and, before his death, passed it on to Paul, who still owns it. The vanished artifact had resurfaced! Mr. Tolonen was kind enough to share a photograph of the object, the first ever published of the Isle Royale find.

But what does it mean? Is it an authentically ancient discovery, or a modern souvenir of some kind? If it is genuinely prehistoric, how did it get to a remote island in Lake Superior? How old is it, and from where did it come? What is the significance of its imagery? When Professor Scherz showed the Carmody photograph to university colleagues, they dismissed the medallion it depicted as a "coin made by modern Masons." To confirm their opinion, he contacted several Masonic scholars, who assured him it was under no circumstances associated with Freemasonry.

Some students in his class from various Asian lands agreed that the figure seated in the pyramid's entrance was unquestionably Buddha. "Raj, a PhD student in surveying from Nepal, where Buddha was born, recognized the letters," Professor Scherz recalled, "and translated the script [on the medallion] as pertaining to some honored leader. But there are no palm trees [as depicted on the face of the object] in Nepal. When shown to Tibetan monks associated with the Dalai Lama visiting Madison in 1989, they themselves could not read the ancient script, but said that the piece was likely made at the great Buddhist temple at Borobudor, in Java." About 10 years later, a pair of Maya elders visited Wisconsin, and Professor Scherz took the opportunity to show them the Carmody photograph. "Although the more knowledgeable elder could speak no English, he immediately responded through an interpreter that the piece was a temple medallion from Borobudor."

A comparison of the minted image reveals that it was obviously meant to portray the pyramidal stepped temple of Borobudor, the Temple of Niches, as recognized by the Tibetan monks and Maya elders. The structure is actually a *stupa*, the ritual center of a monastery, monumentally expanded into five square and four circular terraces rising one upon the other to form a three-dimensional *mandala*, or cosmic diagram. Its location in tropical Java explains the presence of palm trees depicted on the temple medallion.

The reverse is more difficult to interpret. The lion with rays streaming from his back, a scimitar in his raised, right paw, is a political symbol traditionally associated with royal families from old Ceylon (today's Sri Lanka) across southeast Asia. The heart-and-wishbone containing insignia indicates that the royal family is someone's "heart's desire." Partially decipherable script surrounding this emblem appears to describe Raj's "honored leader" as a Buddhist from Borobudor. The medallion may have been issued as a commemorative device to worshippers at the great temple he patronized with financial support. Whoever originally possessed the artifact must have come from Java. But when did he or she arrive in North

Archaeological Discoveries of Ancient America

America? According to Professor Scherz, "the coin could not have been made before 200 BCE, for about this time Buddha was first represented in statue form by missionaries who took Buddhism to China, Southeast Asia, and islands such as Java. Before that date, Buddha was symbolically represented by lattice-like gates." Buddhism did not predominate in Java until the ninth century.

In *American Discovery* (218), Dr. Gunnar Thompson reproduces a relief carving from Borobudor's Temple of the Niches dated to this period. It shows a three-masted ocean-going galley about 100 feet (30 m) long. According to Thompson, "Buddhist records of a fifth-century pilgrimage from Ceylon to Java report vessels large enough to carry 200 passengers.... It was not unusual for [ninth-century] crews to sail thousands of miles on the Indian Ocean. Pacific crossings, though hazardous, were not beyond the capability of either ships or seamen" (220, 221).

Actually, the temple building depicted on the Tolonen medallion is not Borobudor's Temple of the Niches, but the Mahabodhi Temple at Bodh Gaya in northeastern India. This proper identification is important, because it makes sense of the Buddha figure prominently portrayed on the token: The Mahabodhi Temple marks the place where the founder of Buddhism, Siddhartha Gautama, achieved enlightenment. "Mahabodhi" refers to the *bodhi* or *pipal* tree under which he reached illumination, and is the most important place of pilgrimage for Buddhists around the world; hence, the crowd of robed figures and the prominence given to trees depicted on the token.

The temple was completed during the seventh century CE, but has been subsequently embellished and renovated. Although the structure depicted on the Tolonen Medallion is unmistakably the Mahabodhi Temple, it differs markedly from the building as it appears today. Missing is the stupa, a bell-like shrine added to its summit sometime in the early 16th century CE. The Isle Royale object could only have been minted before the stupa was put in place, and therefore brought to Michigan in pre-Columbian times. Our conclusion is underscored by an archaic script on the token's obverse side. Professor James Scherz's foreign exchange student from Nepal, the Buddha's birthplace, had difficulty reading the script, and was only just able to effect a loose translation, indicating significant change in the written language throughout the course of several centuries. Linguistic and architectural considerations join local prehistory to suggest that the Isle Royale object was manufactured between 750 CE, when the Mahabodhi Temple was completed, and 1300. An early-14th-century speculation is inferred for the end of our date parameters, because that period marks the final termination of copper mining at Isle Royale in pre-Columbian times.

A duplicate of Mahabodhi was built in Pagan, the old capital of Burma, during the late 12th century CE, but this is not the same structure appearing on the Tolonen Medallion. Its reverse features a lion-with-sword symbol historically associated with India.

The artifact appears to be an authentic medallion or token issued by some royal patron of the Mahabodhi Temple. Perhaps a Buddhist missionary brought it from India to Isle Royale, where it was lost sometime between 900 CE and 1300 CE, a period framing the last epoch of the Upper Peninsula's copper-mining enterprise. Bodh Gaya lies just 75 miles (121 km) from the Ganges River, which connects to the Bay of Bengal, allowing access for a transoceanic traveler.

If our conclusion, based on the Tolonen Medallion's internal evidence and contemporary Michigan history, is correct, it establishes that seafarers from the distant subceontinent were visiting North America's source of mineral wealth long before Columbus was born. Such a scenario is not altogether far-fetched. Professor Scherz's Nepalese student, Raj, told him that, "another name for Buddha in [his] country was *Fue*. When Catholic missionaries came to the Athapaskan Indians of Canada, the natives tried to tell the French that they were followers of Fue. The missionaries described the Athapaskans as *Gente de Fue* ('People of Fue,' not knowing what *Fue* meant). Other native peoples similarly referred to as *Gente de Fue* are also found in French monastery records from the 1600s, as far south as Greenbay, Wisconsin. But the wars between the Protestant British and Catholic French in the 1600s (really part of the Thirty Years War in Europe) erased any further reference to the Fue in the region."

Among the most vilified evidence for overseas visitors in the Upper Midwest during the fifth century are several thousand clay tablets dismissed by conventional archaeologists since the 1800s as part of a transparent hoax. But when a particularly intriguing example fell into the hands of David Allen Deal, the entire collection was suddenly cast in a new light.

Deal was especially qualified to examine a particular example of what seemed to be an astronomical device of some kind, because he had already determined that an ancient carving in Colorado signified a Saturn-Jupiter conjunction on August 8, 471 CE, *as published in* Celtic America. *Another book,* In Plain Sight, *described his interpretation of an Arkansas petroglyph that again defined a conjunction of Jupiter with Saturn, this time adjacent to the star Wasat in the constellation Gemini, as it appeared on March 30, 710* CE. *His conclusion was verified by computer experts, one of whom remarked, "Nothing we found disputed Deal's proposals."*

David Deal is a practicing, professional artist and designer, a fact that, he says, has done "nothing to detract from my ability to interpret design and intent. In fact, that is what I am paid to do, to create such imagery and allegorical designs, designs that represent ideas, products, and themes graphically, sometimes with great subtlety." Thus equipped, he proves that astronomers from the Old World were at work in America some 15 centuries ago.

The Copts whom Deal mentions were early Christians in Egypt who blended Gnostic mysticism with the original teachings of Jesus. As such, they were singled out for special persecution by the Roman Church around 400 CE, when some Copts fled for their lives into foreign lands. Their descendants still flourish in modern Egypt.

ANCIENT MICHIGAN'S SOLAR ECLIPSE TABLET
By David Allen Deal

On September 3, 1896, a slate tablet was unearthed at what is now called Rolland Township, Isabella County, in Michigan. Ironically, an artifact that gives evidence of Old World visitors who predated Columbus by more than a thousand years was found in a county that was named for Columbus's own benefactress, Queen Isabella of Spain. The slate tablet has been categorized as fake by authoritative archaeologists. It nonetheless possesses internal evidence that dates a previously unknown and unwanted community of Egyptian Christian (Gnostic) Coptic mound builders who created thousands of slate, copper, clay, and stone artifacts, not to mention a considerable collection of earthworks.

Much has been written about this Coptic connection, first by Henriette Mertz, in her 1980 book, *The Mystic Symbol*, and later by this author-investigator in many articles and research papers. Our conclusions came from slightly differing points of reference, but we agreed on the basic fact that Coptic Christians were in North America around the fourth century CE, regardless of academic and professional disbelief. The Michigan mound builders were called *Tallegewi* by the Leni Lenape, otherwise known as the Delaware Indians, and that name is certainly Hebrew. In Hebrew, *tel* means a hill or mound (*tel-y* is plural), and *gew-y* signifies "my nation" or "nations" (plural again). So, *tely-gewy* in Hebrew indicates "mound nations." And that is what they were. The Coptic people merely moved in with the previous Old World inhabitants who were all a bit like them, "people of the book."

Archaeological Discoveries of Ancient America

To explain the presence of Copts in prehistoric Michigan, Henriette Mertz cited logic and historical records of Christian pogroms and persecutions in the Mediterranean area after the Roman emperor Constantine had codified his beliefs at the Council of Nicea in 325 CE. She correctly stated there was a "50-year period of mass-migrations out of the Mediterranean in the fourth century." She also could see a strong (and obvious) Egyptian influence in these artifacts, and, because the Copts were Egyptian in large part, she made logic her tool and came to, not surprisingly, accurate results. Ms. Mertz was not burdened by the academic bias and dogma that disallow such ancient intercourse or movements of people across the Atlantic. Nor is the present writer.

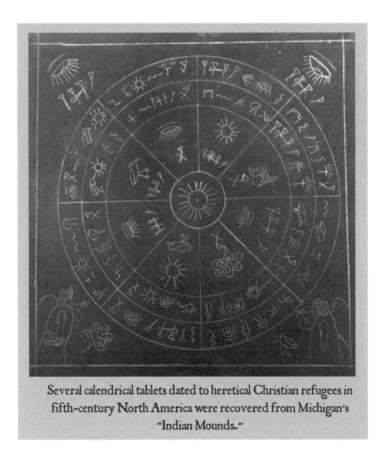

Several calendrical tablets dated to heretical Christian refugees in fifth-century North America were recovered from Michigan's "Indian Mounds."

Early in 1991, Evan Hanson of Beryl, Utah, sent me the Xerox copy of a single page from a book in the Etzenhouser collection, showing the largest of the so-called Michigan tablets excavated from the state's numerous mounds beginning in the 1840s. It showed a particular artifact that showed an apparent rendering of the Old Testament Flood, a common theme found throughout the tablets, identified as "Plate 36 Black Slate, Etzenhouser Collection," subtitled "Roland Township, Isabella Co. Mich. Sept. 3, 1896."

An ocean migration 1,600 years ago must have been tortuous, which is perhaps why so many depictions of the Flood of Noah are found among the Michigan artifacts. Having recently endured such a crossing themselves, and thus being empathetic towards the biblical character, their artists must have thought it well to emphasize that part of the Bible's history. Nothing else would explain such an emphasis on Noah's Flood among the Michigan Coptics.

Hanson guessed that the particular artifact in question represented a meteor he believed was responsible for the biblical Deluge. I saw something altogether different, however: a solar eclipse panel. I had previously deciphered fundamentally similar imagery in New Mexico at a place known as Hidden Mountain, where I was able to coax a very specific reference from a Hebrew-inscribed boulder: September 15, 107 BCE, the earliest recorded date in North American history. So archaeo-astronomy was not something new to me when I saw the Michigan artifact.

Some months after Hanson's Xerox arrived, I visited the tip of Baja, California—Los Barriles, to be precise—to observe a total eclipse of the sun on July 11. It was a magnificent seven minutes of totality. People from around the world were there: Japanese, French, Germans, and others. Small solar observatories of concrete were constructed nearby to solidly mount their equatorial telescopes and cameras. A carnival atmosphere prevailed, except for the Guatamalans and Oaxacans there for work. They were terribly nervous when the trees cast shadows filled with crescent spots of light, and the summer day began to cool off. During the eclipse, the goats came down from the hillsides, and chickens, caught unaware, huddled in open ground, covering their brood for the seven-minute night. Flowers closed, while pregnant Mexican women stayed indoors for fear of angering the sun-god during his "nuptials" with the moon-goddess. They were afraid that, if they looked at the event, they might go blind. Well, they had that part right, of course. It was amazing, from an anthropological point of view, how basic and superstitious some supposedly modern people really are.

I was at Los Barriles primarily to verify that one could readily see first-magnitude stars and planets during totality, because this was a major point in my analysis of the Hidden Mountain petroglyph, and was, in fact, a point of contention brought up by one of my critics. My personal, empirical observations there proved that what I had previously written about the 107 BCE eclipse had been correct: Planets and first-magnitude stars are, indeed, visible during totality. This became important to my later analysis of the Michigan solar eclipse tablet.

The following November, I reported my findings about the Michigan tablet in the annual *On SITE* journal of the American Institute for Archaeological Research. The design of the tablet included a typical Hebrew 13-month calendar, and made a case for the design being a depiction of a solar eclipse I predicted would be found somewhere between 350 CE and 650, a time envelope determined by historic events in the eastern Mediterranean. I chose this period for the same reasons Henriette Mertz had: because Coptic theological doctrines portrayed in the artwork were in disfavor following the Roman Church's Nicean Council of 325 CE, after which the Coptic immigrants would have left for America. During my continuous examination of the Michigan tablet, I was drawn to the meteor or comet depicted on it, in front of the eclipse, obviously having something to do with the entire event.

I asked Richard Shanaberger to run a conjunction check on *Voyager*, a computer application able to find solar eclipses with ease. "What are the coordinates of the location for the eclipse?" he asked. Not 15 minutes after I gave him the grid coordinates for the township of Rolland, Michigan, he called back to ask, "Is July 27, 352 CE good?" Well, it was perfect. A total solar eclipse passed, as I had predicted, on the morning of July 27, 352 CE, directly over the place where this artifact was found in Michigan some 15 centuries later. The date lay within the envelope that I had estimated, and at the correct time of the month. But why was that meteor or comet shown flying in from the west, at a point in time when the eclipse was not yet fully developed? That needed more research.

I went to University of California–San Diego library to review orbital data and possible dates for Halley's Comet, found that it was nowhere close to July 27, 352 CE. Then I remembered the Leonid shower I had witnessed as a child back in 1949. I returned to the books and discovered that the night of July 27–28 is a period of maximum intensity for the annual Delta Aquirid meteor shower. That was it! I had found the answer with a double verification. Not only were the year and month correct, and as predicted, but I had also discovered that the meteor I suspected was now explained. Its answer provided extra dating proof that sent it over the top. The meteor shower was at its annual two-day maximum during the eclipse. Observers in fourth-century Michigan not only witnessed an eclipse of the sun—a somewhat rare occurrence—but were also treated to a massive meteor shower visible only during the eclipse, or for two nights of the 27th and the 28th. This is what they inscribed on the tablet. It was a rare event, indeed.

Archaeological Discoveries of Ancient America

Later investigation showed why the meteor is shown on both tablets flying east. The Delta Aquirid meteor shower always comes from the direction of Aquarius, which is west of Cancer, where the eclipse occurred. The meteor passed over before the eclipse was full, and on each tablet it is shown at this stage of eclipse. It was obviously drawn this way because that is what the fourth-century observers saw. This research of a single piece from the vast body of Michigan artifacts has established the time, or at least a moment within time, that the Coptic Christians were in North America's Upper Midwest.

We do not know when these people abandoned Michigan, if they were killed off by the feathered enemy portrayed on their tablets, or they were absorbed into the native population. But we do know that for a moment in 352 CE they were here, their transplanted society intact, because they recorded it in stone. They witnessed a spectacular and unique solar eclipse. One cannot really comprehend the beauty and majesty of a total solar eclipse unless one has witnessed it in person. Until you have witnessed one, you are an eclipse innocent, and completely ignorant of the feeling of awe it engenders.

Now, one must ask the professional skeptics, how could this accurate piece of scientific information be reproduced on a so-called fake tablet? It is precisely and scientifically correct, and is based on information not widely known back in the late 19th century. In this small tablet and its mate, we see a unique window to the past. We see a precise moment in time observed by little-known people who recorded this astronomical event. This is no mere fake. It is an authentic and true ancient American relic of an odd people who lived here. It has been analyzed in a scientific manner and proven to be so.

However, it is only one representative of a larger body of related artifacts uncovered all over Michigan and neighboring areas, found during a period from about 1840 to 1910. These ancient artifacts must be considered, and fairly evaluated with an open mind. Of course, there have been cases of fraud in all areas of archaeology. There even may be some cases of fraud among the Michigan relics. But good investigative science should be applied, not dogma—not disdain before investigation.

Herbert Spencer once wisely said, "There is a principle which is a bar against all information, which is a proof against all arguments, and which cannot fail to keep man in everlasting ignorance—that principle is contempt before investigation."

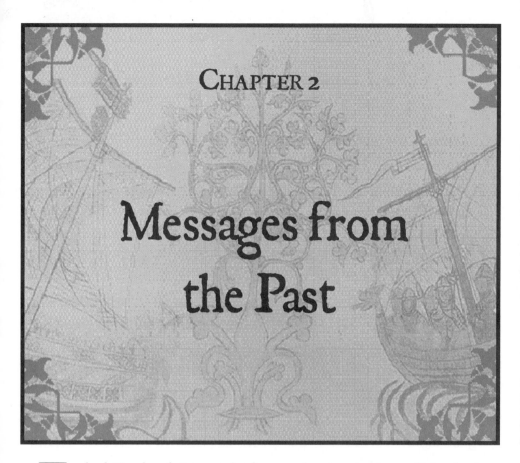

CHAPTER 2

Messages from the Past

L loyd Hornbostel, Jr., was the director of engineering for applied technology at the famed Parker Pen Company (Beloit, Wisconsin). He earlier received a degree in geology from the University of Wisconsin (Madison), part of a professional background that lent authority to his articles for Ancient American from its first issue in 1993 until his death 14 years later. Long a believer in the possibility of Viking cultural impact on North America, he was particularly thrilled to report on new tests conducted by his geology colleagues firmly establishing the archaeological authenticity of a famous boulder inscribed by Norse seafarers to Minnesota.

Lloyd's article presents the latest word on this highly significant artifact, which must henceforward be regarded as incontestable proof of 14th-century Northmen in America's Upper Midwest.

MINNESOTA'S VIKING RUNESTONE IS AUTHENTICATED

By Lloyd Hornbostel, Jr.

"This is it," declared Richard Nielsen before a gathering of fellow investigators and newspaper reporters at Minnesota's Kensington Community
Center. "The smoking gun that proves it's medieval." The Houston oil-
industry engineer referred to a rectangular boulder covered on two sides
with carved runes—glyphs used more than 10 centuries ago by the Vikings.
But the runestone Nielsen described differs from the dozens left behind
by the Northmen in Norway, Denmark, or Sweden, because it was found
some 120 miles (193 km) northwest of Minneapolis, Minnesota.

On November 8, 1898, Olof Ohmann accidentally unearthed the
202-pound (92 kg) monolith while clearing a field with the help of his
son and neighbors at his farm in a rural Kensington community. The
6-inch (15 cm) thick, 36-inch-long-by-15-inch-wide (91 × 38 cm) slab was
firmly entwined in the roots of a 40-year-old poplar. With great difficulty,
Ohmann and a neighbor, Nils Flaaten, cut the granite specimen free,
and realized at once that it predated their time. Modern Europeans had
not yet settled in west-central Minnesota during the 1860s, when the tree
roots had begun to grow. The curious discovery was sent to the University
of Minnesota, in St. Paul, where geologists declared that the boulder was
graywacke granite, a kind of hard feldspar.

Linguists found translating the runic inscription challenging, because
it was in medieval Swedish, although their original version has been given
a finer rendering by Nielsen. It reads, "We eight Goetalanders and twenty-
two Northmen are on this acquisition expedition far west from Vinland.
We had properties near two shelters one day's march north from this stone.
We went fishing one day. After we came home, I found ten men red with
blood, dead. Ave Maria, save us from evil! I have ten men by the sea to look
after our ships fourteen days' travel from this site. Year of the Lord 1362."

The runic text describes an expedition leader from 14th-century Scandinavia in what 500 years later became the state of Minnesota. There, he and his fellow Swedes suffered casualties in clashes with local Indians. The inscription mentions that the Norse arrived via "Vinland," which researchers believe was somewhere along the coast of Maine, or Labrador, where a thousand-year-old Viking settlement at the archaeological site of L'anse aux Meadows is located. The "island" cited in the runestone text seems at first contrary to the farmland on which the monolith was found. But during the year carved on one side, the 50-foot (15 m) knoll where Ohmann made his discovery was standing above a higher water-table that formed a shallow lake in central Minnesota.

Geologist Scott Wolter explains how the
Kensington Runestone is an archaeologically
authentic artifact inscribed by Norse explorers
in Minnesota before Columbus officially
discovered the New World.

Archaeological Discoveries of Ancient America

But internal evidence such as this was ignored when, shortly after it was found, the Kensington Runestone was blasted by journalists and scientists as a transparent hoax designed to simultaneously boost tourism and Swedish-American prestige. Olof Ohmann had the misfortune of being a Swedish immigrant, and his ethnic background was used by skeptics to accuse him of forging the inscription, thereby twisting history for his own ethnic advantage. Although this accusation was to dog him for the rest of his life, he continued to insist he had not fabricated the runestone. Nor did he ever financially profit from it, even when he sold the artifact for a few dollars to Hjalmar R. Holand, nine years after it was found. The sympathetic scholar championed the Kensington Runestone for the next five decades with published books and popular lectures.

Holand's persistent efforts gradually penetrated academic obduracy, convincing a new generation of researchers that the discovery was authentically medieval; so much so that it was set up in a place of honor at Washington, D.C.'s famed Smithsonian Institution in 1948. The Kensington Runestone, declared its director, "is probably the most important archeological object yet found in North America." In March of the following year, it went back to Minnesota, where it was ceremoniously unveiled in St. Paul as part of the state's centennial celebration. It was set up half a year later in Alexandria, Minnesota's, Runestone Museum, where it is still on public display.

During the latter half of the 20th century, however, mainstream animosity toward the runestone resurfaced. In 1986, Erik Wahlgren spoke for conventional wisdom when he asserted, "[F]rom the very beginning, the Kensington inscription was recognized by linguistic scholars on both sides of the Atlantic as a simple, modern forgery." Either he was unaware of or uninterested in the unanimous conclusion of Scandinavian linguists who stated 30 years before that "the Kensington inscription" was authentic

14th-century Swedish. Professional naysayers such as Wahlgren are almost consistently aided and abetted in their denigration of contrary evidence by mainstream journalists, who enjoy ridiculing independent investigators, regardless of their professional credentials, as "crackpots."

A case in point was Richard Nielsen's public announcement that the latest scientific testing has confirmed the Kensington Runestone's medieval origins. Instead of greeting the news as an important breakthrough in American prehistory, Jim Ragsdale, reporting on December 12 for St. Paul's *Pioneer Press*, urged readers to consult Chapter 29 of *Vikings: The North Atlantic Saga*, "a debunking of the Kensington Runestone and similar finds." This same source was exposed by Michael Zalar in the *Journal of the New England Antiquities Research Association*, when no less than 37 errors of fact were identified. Even the Smithsonian author of the deeply flawed chapter admitted to at least 10 of them.

Part of the smoking gun Nielsen mentioned were weathered grooves in the artifact's carving examined by Scott Wolter, a St. Paul geologist and director of Alexandria, Minnesota's, Runestone Museum hired to determine the object's prehistoric authenticity. Although unable to determine precisely when the text was made, Wolter established that it was inscribed centuries before the first modern Europeans settled in Minnesota. His studies further showed that modern scratches atop the original runes had been carved hundreds of years earlier, as indicated by residue of oxidation surrounding each glyph.

Skeptics such as Wahlgren claim that particular words, numbers, grammatical marks, and individual letters of the Kensington Runestone were modern additions introduced during the 19th century. For example, they cited the English *fromm* in the inscription as a word not used by 14th-century Scandinavians. But Nielsen discovered medieval Swedish manuscripts in which *fromm* may be clearly read.

Archaeological Discoveries of Ancient America

Wahlgren and company declared that a J found on the Kensington Runestone was an obvious fake, as the Norse never had a rune for that letter. Here, too, Nielsen demonstrated their false assumption by producing several 14th-century runes for the letter J.

Skeptical linguists faulted the runestone's text for its occasional umlauts, because such punctuation was not introduced until the 17th century. Nielsen revealed, however, that double dots over various letters are not umlauts, but grammatical conventions common in the 1300s. No less importantly, he proved that the Kensington Runestone was written in a Swedish "e"-dialect, a variant form found exclusively in parts of Sweden's southernmost region—contrary to Olof Ohmann, who spoke only an "a"-dialect, a form confined to rural areas northwest of Stockholm. Moreover, the inscription describes Goths from Gotland, where the "e"-dialect was spoken.

The incised text features 11 medieval rune forms unknown to scholars at the time Ohmann found the stone, although these same forms, including abbreviations, were found in Scandinavia during the following century. All of the stone's grammatical anomalies have traced back to Gotland during the High Middle Ages.

These and hundreds more facts have been compiled in a new book, *The Kensington Rune Stone: Compelling New Evidence.* Its publication shifts the burden of proof back onto the skeptics, who will be hard-pressed to debunk such overwhelming evidence. Until they can successfully defend themselves from the weighty counter-argument so convincingly presented by Richard Nielsen and Scott Wolter, the Kensington Runestone must be henceforward accepted as a monument left behind by Norse explorers in what much later became the state of Minnesota 130 years before Columbus began his search for the New World.

>—+—◆>—○—<◆—+—<

The discovery 170 years ago of a tablet inscribed with an ancient Old World text should have rewritten American history books. Instead, the priceless find was condemned by officials as a fake, shamefully discarded, and forgotten by all but a few "antiquarians." Here is the story of this remarkable find, hard evidence for Hebrew refugees arriving in West Virginia during the early Roman Era.

The Lost Inscription of Grave Creek

By Wayne May

In January 2006, I visited the grandest earthwork of its kind in North America. At 62 feet (19 m) high and 240 feet (73 m) across at its base, Grave Greek Mound towers near the Ohio River, about 10 miles (16 km) south of Wheeling, West Virginia. Seeing this immense earthwork in person was the fulfillment of an old dream, and the local museum proved to be an enlightening experience in itself. Especially interesting was a showcased replica of the famous "Grave Creek Tablet" captioned with a surprisingly impartial text that suggested the controversial object excavated from the mound may have had overseas origins after all. The original tablet was a sandstone disk about 1 7/8 inches (4.8 cm) wide and 1 1/2 inches (3.6 cm) high, and inscribed on one side with an inscrutable, though apparently Semitic text.

West Virginia's Grave Creek Mound.

Archaeological Discoveries of Ancient America

As Huston McCulloch of the Midwest Epigraphic Society writes in the *Journal of the New England Antiquities Research Association*: In 1868, the inscription belonged to the collection of E.H. Davis, before being purchased by the Blackmore Museum (now part of the British Museum, which states that "the Grave Creek Stone is not at present in the Museum's Squier and Davis collections. ...Davis made a plaster cast of the stone and deposited it in the Smithsonian Institution's National Museum of Natural History.... The NMNH in fact has *four* casts of the stone. It is not known where the stone itself is today."

According to late-19th-century antiquarian E. Thomas Hemmings, in his book *West Virginia Antiquities*, "Grave Creek Mound is the preeminent archeological monument in West Virginia, and the largest conical earth mound in the New World. West Virginia geological and economic surveyors carried out two phases of field investigation here in 1975 and 1976, followed by extensive laboratory analysis. This project, conducted under terms of an agreement with the Department of Natural Resources, is the first systematic, archeological work at Grave Creek Mound since it was penetrated by tunnels in 1838."

Core drillings revealed carbon material circa 250 BCE, and scholars estimate that approximately 3 million basket-loads of earth—equivalent to some 57 tons (52 metric tons)—were required to erect the 70-plus-foot-high (21 m) mound. It was encircled by a moat or ditch, its purpose unknown, save perhaps as a ceremonial barrier to ritually define sacred burials. As with many similar sites, other peoples came and went, leaving their mark on this vast area long after the original builders vanished. Archaeologists refer to them as the "Adena," who belonged to the Early Woodland Period, from around 1000 BCE to 100 BCE.

Certainly the most controversial item associated with the mound is the Grave Creek Tablet, which was unearthed from inside the earthwork itself. Mainstream scholars "know" the object must be "an obvious fake" because it carried an inscription. Archaeological dogma holds that no written language existed in the Americas before the arrival of modern Europeans. Despite academic insistence, however, some independent investigators point to a number of Adena artifacts that at least suggest that an ancient syllabary of some kind existed in ancient America. These include the Bat Creek Stone, the Ohio Decalogue Stone (an apparent Hebrew prayer-stone dating to the third century BCE), the Wilmington Tablet (a highly sophisticated design), and an estimated 2,000 Michigan Tablets (likewise enumerated by Deal). Although university-trained research-ers acknowledge the pre-Columbian provenance of at least some of these objects, their identification as script is not deemed worthy of consideration.

In 1885, newspaper publisher J.P. MacLean described in an article entitled "The Grave Creek Stone Was Real," just what early investigators found when they dug into the earthwork:

> An excavation was made towards the center at the north side of the mound, 10 feet (3 m) in height and 111 feet (34 m) long along the original surface of the ground. At the end of this ditch was a vault 12 feet (4 m) long by 8 (2.4 m) wide and 7 (2.1 m) deep. Upright timbers had been placed along the sides of the vault which supported other timbers thrown across which served for a roof. Over these timbers had been thrown loose stone, such as is found in the neighborhood. The timbers were rotten and the stone had tumbled into the vault. In this vault were found two skeletons, one of which was surrounded by 650 beads composed of sea-shells, and a bone ornament 6 inches (15 cm) long. From the top of the mound a shaft was sunk, and at the depth of 34 feet (10 m) from the bottom another vault was found, containing a

skeleton surrounded by over 2,000 discs cut from shells, 250 pieces of mica, 17 bone beads, and copper bracelets and rings weighing 17 ounces (482 grams).

It was in this vault that the inscribed stone was found on the 16th of the following June (1838). From a letter written to Mr. P.P. Cherry, March 7th, 1878, by Mr. Tomlinson, it would appear that the stone was found at the end of a second drift which was excavated from the side of the mound to the upper vault. After striking the second vault the men from the first vault drilled upward until the second fell to the bottom. The inscribed stone is an oval disc of white sandstone nearly circular in form, about three-fourth's of an inch thick, and an inch and a half in diameter.

On one of the flat surfaces are engraved three lines of unknown characters. That the stone or tablet was deemed of some importance by the owner is proven from the fact of its having been entombed with him. It may have possessed, to him, some mysterious importance in his journey to the future state of existence, and hence a charm to protect him from the evil influences that might beset him. No doubt was ever cast on the authenticity of this stone until nearly ten years after its discovery.

Ever since, professional skeptics have not lamented the Grave Creek Tablet's disappearance.

West Virginia University's Website succinctly expresses the mainstream science party-line: "Today, most archaeologists consider the tablet to be fraudulent, because similar examples have never been found...."

Wrong! In 1922, a farmer working his field near Morristown, Tennessee, plowed up a stone similar in size to the Grave Creek Tablet, covered with precisely the same inscription, symbol for symbol. The farmer knew nothing of its West Virginia twin, nor made any effort to profit from his accidental discovery in any way. Since then, two more stones—one in Ohio County, the other near Braxton Creek, West Virginia—were found emblazoned with identical written characters incised on the Grave Creek and Morristown Tablets, though here, too, their discoverers made no claims to fame or fortune, and, in fact, were ignorant of the controversy.

The Grave Creek Tablet is physical proof that voyagers from the ancient Old World did, after all, cross the vast ocean to successfully establish themselves in what would much later become West Virginia. Their surviving mound in West Virginia is therefore more than a sepulcher for the long-dead, but a monument to the pre-Columbian discovers of America.

The Grave Creek Tablet's archaeological authenticity and actual significance were publicly disclosed at 2007's "Ancient American Conference" (Wilmington, Ohio), by renowned West Virginia epigrapher Ida Jane Gallagher. She revealed that the written text was commensurate with a form of paleo-Hebrew contemporary with the construction of the earthwork itself in 250 BCE. Likewise appropriate for a burial mound, the brief inscription is a mortuary statement, referring probably to one of the two men interred in the structure more than 22 centuries ago.

She cites the work of Dr. Barry Fell (1917–1994), professor of invertebrate zoology at the Harvard Museum of Comparative Zoology, where he was "an accomplished and respected marine biologist," according to his Wikipedia biographer. Applying his scientific expertise to the decipherment of pre-Columbian inscriptions, Dr. Fell found that many of them resulted from contacts between Native Americans with overseas visitors from the ancient Old World.

Archaeological Discoveries of Ancient America

A native of Beckley, West Virginia, Ida Gallagher is a retired schoolteacher in English, journalism, and history, with a BS and MA in education from West Virginia University (1952, 1955). She likewise served as college academic counselor at C.W. Post College, and assistant to the Dean of Women at Adelphi University. With the publication of numerous articles and photographs in newspapers, popular magazines, and scholarly journals, she is a member of the New England Antiquities Research Association, the Ancient American Artifact Preservation Foundation, Early Sites Research Society, and the Epigraphic Society.

THE GRAVE CREEK TABLET IS GENUINE

By Ida Jane Meadows Gallagher

The Grave Creek Tablet, an oval, grayish sandstone tablet, started a great debate, because three lines of unknown alphabetic characters were inscribed on one side of the object. One hieroglyphic sign beneath the alphabetic inscription resembles a cross with elongated arms, with the profile of a bird's head on the end of the right arm and a dot under the left arm. One horizontal line is incised beneath the cross.

Modern re-creation of the Grave Creek Tablet. The original disappeared during the last century.
Photo © by Ida Jane Meadows Gallagher

50

Soon after the Grave Creek Tablet was discovered, numerous, unsuccessful attempts were made to decipher and read the inscription. The result was that some people poked fun at a variety of translations, which cast doubt on the tablet's authenticity. David Diringer's recovery of ancient Iberic vowel values in 1968, however, enabled Dr. Barry Fell to make the first sensible translation, published in 1976. He identified the alphabet as South Iberic (from Roman Era or pre-Roman Spain), and translated the three lines on the Grave Creek Tablet reading from right to left in the Semitic manner:

"The mound raised on high for Tasach.

This tile

His queen caused to be made."

Donal Buchanan, author of a definitive work on the language, "The Decipherment of Southwest Iberic," confirmed Fell's decipherment with minor changes in the wording: "Tumulus in honor of Tadach. His wife caused this engraved tile to be inscribed."

Years of controversy about the authenticity of this tiny tablet followed. On-site accounts of the artifact's removal from the mound should disprove rumors describing the tablet as a fake, that it was "planted" with the burial of a single male in the upper tomb of the earthwork. When it was excavated, the Grave Creek Tablet was generally recognized as a genuine artifact.

Eyewitnesses to its discovery made the following statements.

Dr. James W. Clemens, a respected Wheeling, West Virginia, physician, wrote the earliest known account of the discovery of the tablet. He and Wheeling newspaper publisher J.E. Wharton watched the mound excavation. Clemens's account was published shortly after the tablet was found. It stated, "Abelard Tomlinson, Thomas Biggs, myself and others were present when the stone was discovered with the copper bracelets and shell necklace."

At this time, Dr. S.G. Morton was writing *Crania Americana* when he asked Dr. Clemens to visit the Grave Creek Mound and send him a report on the skulls found in the structure. Clemens reported the following information to Morton: "In this vault a large skeleton was found, with a necklace composed of perforated shells, two copper bracelets and a curiously inscribed or hieroglyphic stone, the characters of which are distinctly traced in parallel lines. These curiosities were all found together, near the skeleton, the stone is now in my possession, and I have had an exact facsimile of it taken." Unfortunately, Morton's book did not include any reference to the inscribed tablet; his work was devoted exclusively to the study of skulls of ancient man. The omission nonetheless bred serious controversy.

In 1846, Ephraim George Squire published a booklet in which he argued that, because *Crania Americana* made no reference to the Grave Creek Tablet, the most remarkable artifact found in the mound, the object must be fake. Squier suggested that the motive for faking the tablet was to attract visitors to the Grave Creek Mound museum, which required a small admission charge. Squire's innuendo was a serious affront to the Tomlinson family, who owned the mound and operated the little museum.

Distinguished etymologist Henry R. Schoolcraft entered the fray. He angrily characterized Squier's accusations as "offensive to the truth." Others took sides pro and con until rumor overcame truth. Today, most professional archaeologists generally regard the Grave Creek Tablet as a hoax. Yet its story actually demonstrates how uninformed statements were perpetuated by successive writers and archaeologists who failed to check out the facts. Events associated with the discovery and decipherment of the Grave Creek Tablet show how innuendo and repetition of false information can cast doubt on an authentic artifact. Researchers must assemble factual information before announcing new finds. It is difficult to correct errors previously accepted as truth.

Critics of the find accused Abelard Tomlinson, who was in charge of opening the mound, of fraudulently producing the Grave Creek Tablet. But in 1876, Tomlinson clearly recalled finding the artifact: "I was carefully removing the dirt, which was mostly of decayed timber, when I uncovered the inscribed stone. The inscription being up, it took my attention. I examined it; found it to be the work of the ancients; I then placed it with the other relics."

Peter B. Catlett helped with the excavation of the mound. "I am the one that found it first," he testified in 1878. "It was not in its original bed when first found, it was taken out of the stone arch in a wheelbarrow and emptied outside.... As for anyone placing the inscribed stone there [planting it], it could not have been done."

According to J.E. Wharton, the Wheeling newspaper editor who accompanied Dr. Clemens at the mound excavation, "In the forenoon, they struck the center of the vault and bought out decayed wood.... Among the dirt was bought out the inscribed stone and picked up by one of us from the loose dirt [Catlett?]. A fraud was impossible.... When I first saw it, it was being handed to Dr. Gans with some of the earth still clinging to it."

But who was responsible for the brief text? Was it a visiting scribe or a native Adena Indian who learned the South Iberic alphabet from an overseas tutor? Research suggests that the ancient Iberians followed Adena trade routes and may have had extensive contact with the prehistoric inhabitants of North America. In any case, the archaeological authenticity of West Virginia's Grave Creek Tablet is certain, even if the identity of its author is not.

Archaeological Discoveries of Ancient America

Mainstream scholars continuously belittle claims for overseas visitors to the Americas before Columbus for lack of any material proof. But an abundance of physical evidence persuasively arguing the arrival in Ecuador of ancient Phoenicians and/or Libyans has been at hand for nearly 50 years. Preserved throughout decades of selfless service by an Italian priest, the Crespi Collection is persuasive testimony to regular contacts between the Old World and the New thousands of years ago.

Before a large number of its treasures were lost, they were sought out by Dr. Warren Cook, who, prior to his untimely death in 1989, was among the brightest lights of unconventional science. Professor of history and anthropology at Vermont's Castleton State College, he earlier obtained his MA and PhD at Yale, where his doctoral dissertation, "Floodtide or Empire: Spain and the Pacific Northwest," won the coveted Bolton Prize for best book of 1973. What made Dr. Cook's quest in Ecuador all the more remarkable was his physical incapacity: He was crippled with polio since childhood. Read in the context of the man's self-evident erudition and personal challenges, his description of these remarkable artifacts is all the more valuable.

THE CRESPI COLLECTION: ARCHAEOLOGICAL FRAUD OR PREHISTORIC LIBRARY?

By Dr. Warren Cook

Weakened by acute bronchopneumonia, Padre Carlo Crespi's valiant heart stopped on the evening of April 30, 1982, one month short of his 91st birthday. As the old priest's memory dimmed in his last years, so did hope of learning about some of the most remarkable artifacts ever turned up in the Americas.

I first heard of the Crespi Collection from Barry Fell, who showed me a slide, taken in Cuenca in 1976 by Brigham Young University historian Dr.

Paul Cheesman, of what has come to be called the "Masinissa Plaque." Projected and briefly interpreted by Fell during his evening address at the "Ancient Vermont" Conference at Castleton State College in 1977, portions of it were pictured and discussed in his *Saga America* (1980). He believed that the gold-colored, roller-stamped, rectangular metal plaque, with a perfectly round hole cut from its center, announces the death of Masinissa (King of the Libyan-Egyptians, known to have died in 148 BCE) and the ascension of his son to the throne of a united Egypt.

Another Cheesman slide of a gold-like plaque from the same collection, showed at the top a bird with outstretched wings, and beneath it two bearded, hooded, priest-like men carrying staffs. On either side, in grid-like panels of script, Fell pointed out letters in a variety of Cypriot, spelling "Ku-kul-ka-n" and "Ko-et-tse-tse-ve-ko-atl," telling of a mission to a land called "sunset" and discovery of "Tla-o-lee" (the Aztec name for maize). I recognized the correspondence to the Maya Kukulcan and Aztec Quetzalcoatl, white-skinned, bearded Central American deities or culture heroes.

But both names on a single plaque, and from South America!

John Cole, then-instructor in anthropology at Hartwick College, Oneonta, New York, immediately assailed Fell from the floor of the conference for using artifacts from the collection of a man "who is relatively well-known in Ecuador as somebody who is very confused about what he collects, and has spread the word that he will buy anything if it looks impressive."

Subsequently, Dr. Cheesman showed me additional photos he had taken of the Crespi relics, which obviously did not fit into the known parameters of Andean archaeology. Because Cuenca, anciently Tomebamba (*tumi-pampa*, "plain of the knife" in Quechua, language of the Incas), functioned as northern capital of the Inca Empire under three monarchs, it is not an unlikely place for antiquities treasured from past millennia to surface. Because my specialty is Andean culture history, and I have been researching Inca religion since 1947, I felt a responsibility to see the Crespi collection for myself, and have its significant components adequately photographed in color by Warren W. Dexter.

Given the difficulties inherent in photographing and studying the Crespi Collection, and my Andean experience and linguistic advantage, Dr. Cheesman and I drew up a plan of action: a between-semesters, three-week visit to Cuenca, accompanied by Mr. Dexter. Cheesman would meet us in Cuenca. Another "Ancient Vermont" Conference attendee, Charles Hepburn, had a Pennsylvania friend (Donald Rasmussen) with a contact in Cuenca (Dr. Alfonso Serrano), from whom he was able to learn up-to-date details about the state of the aged Padre's precarious health and the collection's current accessibility.

Brought out of the Ecuadorian jungle by Christian Indians, this plaque, magnificently wrought in gold, appears to depict a high-ranking astronomical priest, as indicated by his bishop-like garb and serpent symbols among stars. Although the object has a somewhat Phoenician appearance, glyphs squared in the floor are not Punic and are unlike anything known in archaeology. Holes at the top of the plaque suggest it was mounted on a wall, possibly of a temple.

In late December 1977, Warren and I had reservations to Guayaquil when a call from Hepburn warned that, because of his increased frailties, Crespi no longer had a key to the rooms with the most important portion of his collection. The call from Serrano to Rasmussen to Hepburn to Cook aborted our trip—and saved Cheesman's life, in that he cancelled his reservation on a flight from Guayaquil to Cuenca, which, as it turned out, crashed against an Andean mountaintop, killing all on board.

In the months that followed, reports from Cuenca did not improve prospects of access to the controversial assemblage. Word came in 1979 that the old man was at death's door, and the collection in peril of dispersal. The urgency of recording on color film anything that remained became even more imperative. Eventually, knowing only that Padre Crespi was reportedly still alive, Warren Dexter and I arrived in Guayaquil on June 15, 1981. After four hours of fearful careening in a speedy fulgoneta, a van whose driver seemed more like a pilot flying too low brought us up through the clouds, over the Continental Divide, and down into the exquisite valley of Cuenca.

The city, of 111,000 residents in 1974, lies on a tributary of the Amazon River in a fertile basin high in the Andes. In the bustling capital of Azuay province, and not far from its center, is a flat-topped hill called Puma Pongo ("Puma Gate"), reputed to be the site of the palace of Tu'pac Inca Yupanqui, who added southern Ecuador to his Tawantinsuyu ("The Empire of the Four Corners of the World"). His son, Huayna Capac, and grandson, Atahualpa, were born there.

At 2,576 meters (about 8,000 feet), Cuenca is sufficiently high that breathing deeply is a constant task for visitors unaccustomed to such altitudes. Our modest hotel was less than a block from the Museo del Banco Central, the provincial museum owned and administered by the Ecuadorian Treasury Department's Central Bank. As we soon learned, the Banco Central had purchased the Crespi Collection, and everything deemed worthwhile had been transferred to its local museum, where Director Licenciado Rene Cardozo and his helpful staff extended us every possible assistance.

The evening of our arrival, Alfonso Serrano was ill, but the very next day his wife took us to meet Padre Crespi. We found him in the confessional bearing his name-plate, just to the right inside the Church of Maria Auxiliadora's front entrance. The 90-year-old priest greeted us eagerly, in heavily Italian-accented Spanish, breaking away from a dozen men and women of every age and social class clustered around him, and we went out to the sidewalk. He seized me by the lapel, then rambled on about things crowding his mind, all the while acceding to a constant stream of persons who came up, knelt, and kissed his hand, saying "Dime su benedicion, santo Padre!" ("Give me your blessing, saintly Father!") Senora Serrano had introduced me as a North American professor who had come to study his collection, to which he responded vehemently: "Ay, eso me lo han robado todo!" ("Ay, they have robbed me of all of that!")

Not once during the ensuing 15 minutes did I succeed in turning the conversation to anything pertinent to his collection. The kindly old man had a warm sparkle in his eyes, obviously enjoyed foreign visitors, and was robust of voice, but it was evident that arteriosclerosis had robbed us of the chance to learn from him anything relevant. Later that day, Richard Boroto, director of the bi-national Centro Cultural Abraham Lincoln, a Latin American organization aimed at facilitating cooperation with the United States in matters of mutual cultural importance (such as the protection of archaeological treasures), acquainted us with which way the bull went through the pea-patch, so far as local authorities were concerned. Searching out these authorities, we soon pieced together a pathetic picture for New World history. Some of its nuances may never be clarified, even for those closest to the scene. But knowledge of the man associated with the collection is crucial to evaluating the significance of its anomalous items.

Carlo Crespi Croci was born in Legnano, near Milan, Italy, on May 29, 1891, but not into a family of dukes, as some have said. His father, Daniel, a farm administrator, opposed the boy's priestly vocation, but his mother, Luisa, was supportive. Third among 13 children, at age 5 he began to assist a local priest. In Milan and Turin he attended schools run by the Salesians, an order founded in 1856 by John Bosco to care for poor and needy teenagers, using a system of education based on reason, religion, and kindness. Those values are the key to understanding the course of young Carlo's subsequent concerns.

At 15, he became a novice in Foglizzo (Turin), and was ordained in Verona at 26. Four years of study at the secular University of Padua, with a thesis in anthropology, gave him a master's degree. A dissertation about a previously unknown aspect of Paduan fauna earned him a doctorate in natural sciences in 1921. Subsequently, he obtained doctorates at the same university in music and engineering. All of these would be evident in his subsequent achievements.

Crespi came to Ecuador for the first time in 1923, not as a missionary, but to gather scientific data and artifacts for an international missions exposition to be held in Rome, from 1925 to 1926—material he subsequently exhibited in New York City, from 1928 to 1929. Having returned to Ecuador in 1926, in 1931 Crespi was assigned to a Salesian mission at Macas, in Ecuador's Oriente, or Amazon region. His jungle stint was brief, and the following year he returned permanently to Cuenca. In 1933, he commenced the five-year labor of constructing the Instituto Cornelio Merchan, an imposing, four-storied boys' elementary and trade school, becoming its first director. Crespi once told a journalist that his impulse to create a museum came from having encountered an ancient potsherd (a pottery fragment) during excavations for the foundation of Cornelio Merchan. The same interviewer then asked him, "Is it certain that Padre Crespi has been sold things that have no scientific value, that they swindle you?" To this he answered: "En somma, permitame. Esto no lo ponga. Todavia hay en Cuenca mucha gente que pasa hambre. Y el P. Crespi lo sabe." ("In summary, permit me, don't put that down. In Cuenca there are still many people who experience hunger. And Padre Crespi knows.")

While serving at Macas, Crespi filmed *Los Terribles Shuara del Alto Amazonas* ("The Terrible Jivaros of the Upper Amazon"). As an educator, he was devoted to the use of motion pictures, importing some 40 of them. He loved to explain, beforehand, what his charges were expected to perceive. Woe betide the boy who fell short of the Padre's expectations! Watching over them with a bell, he didn't hesitate to rap on the head any lad who didn't behave appropriately. He was both feared and loved, and the bell is now a cherished relic. It is legend how it was never too late to knock on the street-level outside window of the Padre's quarters, for him to go out and administer the last rites to someone in his parish. "Ya voy!" ("I'm going!"), he would always answer, and moments later be underway, it having been his habit to retire fully dressed, on newspapers spread out over his bed.

Carlo Crespi had a passion for learning and creativity. His former secretary, Imbabura-born Padre Luis Flores Haro (who began serving in Cuenca in 1951), tells how Crespi over and over would say, "Siempre quise que mis niños comprendan bien las cosas." ("I always wanted my boys to understand things well.") Crespi published numerous musical works of his own composition, and formed the best band in Ecuador. Several of its members are currently illustrious members of the Musical Conservatory of Cuenca. He is credited with introducing skill-mastery into Cuenca primary education. He founded the Agricultural School (1931) in Yanuncay, a Cuenca suburb, and nearby the Instituto Orientalista of Cuenca (1940), which prepares young men for ministry in the Amazon region. On average, Crespi had to worry about feeding some 2,000 students daily. Countless mothers with children came to him each day seeking means to survive, a practice that we observed Padre Flores still maintained.

In 1962, Colegio Cornelio Merchan burned to the ground. Although a room holding some of the best of the collection was destroyed, the majority was spared, in the old wing that remains today. On the ruined site, Crespi and his brethren in time erected the present Church of Maria Auxiliadora.

Padre Crespi never lacked local recognition for his accomplishments. Ecuador awarded him a medal in 1935, the mayor named him "Illustrious Son of Cuenca" in 1956, and that same year the Ministry of Education gave him another medal. In 1974, a Cuenca street was named after him, as has been the new school being built with funds from the sale of his collection to the Museo del Banco Central. In January 1982, scant months before his death, Italy conferred on him the Medal of Merit of the Republic, and Cuenca again declared him its adoptive son. Crespi's kind deeds, throughout the decades, had earned the nonagenarian a secure place in the hearts of people of all classes. A taxi driver, hearing us discuss him, volunteered that "every family in Cuenca will want to accompany him to his grave." Dr. Ezequiel Clavijo, an archaeologist and legislator from Cuenca, told me, "All Cuenca will overflow with tears the day that Padre Crespi dies. One time I was with him," Clavijo continued, "when a woman came up with an obviously bogus object for sale, and he pulled several coins out of his cassock and bought it. When I told him it lacked any value, he said, 'I know, but they don't have any other means of living.'" A similar incident was reported by Dr. Carlos Ramirez Salcedo, of the University of Cuenca, one of Ecuador's most respected archaeologists. "When my father passed away in Italy," Crespi once told a compatriot, "he left me a legacy, and I could think of no better way to use it than by salvaging their ancient treasures from greedy traders and black marketeers."

It was the Padre's penchant for using such funds as available, as a form of charity, to buy anything and everything offered to him that led to the fate that has befallen the collection. Apologists say he wanted to keep sources of valuable relics from drying up. Flores told me Crespi frequently said his purchase of potentially idolatrous objects was a concern "that the people not have them in their houses, and thus I liberate them from fetishism." According to Flores, countless small amulets were acquired thus throughout the years, but all had now been disposed of, "where they will never be found," he informed me zealously.

Flores tells how Crespi, long after his priestly labors were finished, would stay awake three or four more hours, reading history and archaeology. From such study, and from the Egyptian, Babylonian, and Phoenician appearance of some of the objects in the collection, decades ago Crespi arrived at the conviction there had been ancient Mediterranean contacts with Ecuador. The more his views met resistance, the more dogmatic he became on the subject when guiding visitors through his collection.

The consensus opinion of Ecuadorian archaeologists was that Cuenca artisans, always noted for their skill and inventiveness, began to bring the Padre objects particularly crafted to suit his predilections. Many tons of sculpted stones, great piles of embossed metal sheets, 1,300 paintings, numerous polychrome statues, and countless pieces of pottery, whole and in shards, created severe problems by their very volume, for conduct of the school, by clogging rooms, lining balconies, and littering courtyards.

Obvious to everyone, even to Crespi himself, much of his stuff was of recent fabrication. Matters worsened when Erich von Daniken's *Gold of the Gods* (1972) held that Crespi's strangest relics came from an extensive network of tunnels stacked with 2,000 to 3,000 metal plates bearing ancient inscriptions, in the province of Morona-Santiago, not far east of Cuenca, but difficult to access. Juan Moricz, a Hungarian and naturalized Argentinian, allegedly had stumbled upon them in 1963, and von Daniken claimed to have been taken there in 1972. Subsequently, a government-backed expedition failed to find anything of importance in the "Cueva de los Tayos," the suspected site. I talked with Cuenca archaeologist Juan Cordero Yniguez, who had been to Los Tayos, and saw nothing to warrant give the bird-dung-littered cavern any further attention. Others claim that Moricz, who in 1981 still lived in Zamora, had never disclosed the actual cave in question. But official disappointment blighted local enthusiasm, and, in Cuenca, von Daniken is regarded as a liar and fantasist. Following publication of *Gold of the Gods*, Flores says so many foreigners came by Maria Auxiliadora to see Padre Crespi that it became something of a nuisance.

In March 1979, Crespi was struck low by illness, received the last rites, and for a time lay near death. The old man's constitution was strong, however, and a prostate operation eventually put him back on his feet. In January 1980, nonetheless, commenced the implementation of a decision made when he was helpless. For 13 million sucres ($433,000), the Museo del Banco Central purchased the Crespi Collection, with an option to select or reject as its experts saw fit. With its proceeds, the Salesians are now constructing a new school, appropriately named "Carlo Crespi." But the money is already exhausted, according to Padre Flores, and $200,000 more will be needed to finish the basic physical plant. The school will readily accommodate the 640 boys now in primary grades, but an additional $66,000 would be needed to build a second story over one wing for a gallery to appropriately display what remains of Crespi's collection.

When the process of selection began in February 1980, as best as could be managed, the old priest was shielded from seeing his treasures removed, but at times, "se puso bravo" (he went into a rage). Sorting had to take place behind locked doors to keep him from interrupting. Dust hung thick in the air, as ceiling-high tiers of Inca jars, metal-sheathed statues, and embossed plaques were lowered to the floor. Participants in this labor claim they still cannot shake off respiratory ailments from the experience.

Specialists were appointed to separate the wheat from the chaff: Dr. Gustavo Reinoso Hermidia, of Cuenca, and Dr. Olaf Holm, director of the Museo del Banco Central of Guayaquil, were the archaeologists charged with sorting ceramics and stone, respectively. About a third of the ceramics proved valuable, by Reinoso's estimate. They range over every Ecuadorian ceramic period excepting the earliest—Valdivia—and include hundreds of truly superb examples. Some 8,000 pieces, plus countless shards, were transferred to the Museo for cataloging, storage, and eventual exhibition. To the same repository were removed about 1,300 paintings—colonial 19th century—as well as numerous old polychrome religious statues of all sizes.

Except for about eight giant stone seats from Mante, a few headrests, and perhaps a dozen other stunning pieces, the balance of the lithic material—many, many tons—was judged worthless. In this, all local authorities seem to have concurred. Because uncounted hundreds of stones congested corridors and potential classrooms, the way the Salesians opted to dispose of them was to give them to any and all takers. Dr. Reinoso told me that, on one occasion, upon entering a patio, he saw fresh cement being poured over an area filled in with carved stones. The hundreds of embossed metal plates and three-dimensional metallic objects, all of them rejected, were moved up to the old school's fourth-floor attic.

This was the situation Warren Dexter and I encountered upon arriving in Cuenca. Seeing the superb pre-Columbian pottery, valuable paintings, polychrome sculpture, and the few remarkable stones in the Museo del Banco Central immediately increased our respect for Crespi as a collector and preserver of art. Reportedly, nothing had been taken to Quito. Museum authorities had no knowledge of the whereabouts of the other stone, metal, or ceramic objects left behind, and welcomed our investigative efforts, collaborating in every way. Through the museum we were introduced to Padre Flores on June 22, and were escorted to the fourth-floor attic where the remnant of metal objects and ceramics left by the Banco Central's experts were scattered in total disarray. Warren was allowed time solely for a few overall pictures that, when printed, showed a number of significant pieces that escaped our notice under such hasty circumstances. Then, from his own quarters, Flores brought down into the courtyard three of the objects he said Crespi had treasured the most:

1. A "Zodiac Plate" with a grid of 56 symbols embossed on a 51×13-inch (130 × 33 cm) oblong sheet of remarkably unoxidized copper alloy, which Fell considers Paphian script accompanying the corresponding Zodiac signs.

2. A rectangular Pyramid Plaque, embossed on the same type of burnished alloy, bearing a panel of lettering across the Pyramid's base that Fell identifies as "neo-Punic" script, but that translates meaningfully in Quechua tongue, in a dialect of Ecuador.

3. A large brownish-black ceramic jar bearing symbols identified by Fell as Cypriot, but translating meaningfully in Quechua. As for the hundreds of stones that had been given away, no records were kept, but Flores recalled some of the destinations:

    a. Cuenca's Cuartel Cayambe, a closely guarded army base.

    b. The impressive new multi-million-dollar Artepricticas furniture manufacturing plant in the country at Zuchay, not far south of Cuenca.

   c. The Colegio Agronomico Salesiano.

   d. The Colegio Grientalista Salesiano in Yanuncay, a suburb south of Cuenca.

   e. The Colegio Nacional Kleber Franco Cruz, in far-off Machala, near the Peruvian border (whence a big truckload had been taken when two science teachers there, former Crespi students, learned that they were being given away).

Enumerating this list is easy in hindsight, but extracting it from informants, and then finding, gaining access, and photographing the stones involved weeks of detective work, diplomacy, and travel, including a wild goose chase to a nonexistent Colegio San Juan Bautista, in Loja, spending 21 out of 42 hours in a bus on an incredibly torturous, bumpy, and muddy road, over three successive Andean ranges. With much assistance from a number of very kind people, we ascertained there is no likelihood that any of the schools in Loja have any of the Crespi stones, and that particular trail is cold.

The other reputed destinations, however, all paid off. Once into zealously guarded Cayambe, we found 40 or so large sculptures, many of them monstrous in their demonic conception. Discounting several obviously modern confections of wood, cement, and plaster of Paris, most of the remainder in their ugly but vigorous force suggest idols described in Jose de Arriaga's *Extirpacion de la Idolatria* (Lima, 1611), when priests in Peru were dismayed to find such statues secretly built into Christian chapels or hidden deep within underground chambers, still receiving Shamanistic cult-worship. Upon consulting stone sculptors at work near Cuenca, we learned that similar-sized carvings would require a minimum of three weeks apiece for one artisan to complete. Each is a unique, albeit grotesque, artistic creation of some vivid imagination.

The owner of the Artepracticas factory at Zuchay, reportedly one of the wealthiest individuals in Ecuador, had selected for an intended exhibit a particularly interesting group of large, flat stones bearing rectangular grid patterns, each square containing characters similar to those on metal plaques and headpieces translated by Fell from Cheesman photographs, which we were unable to locate. Stones from the Crespi Collection doubtless migrated elsewhere in the Diaspora of 1980, and may turn up in due time, particularly if there is local publicity as to their potential importance.

There was less interest in removing from Maria Auxiliadora the school's embarrassment of metallic objects. Several huge plaques, recognizably bogus, had been used to sheath a kiosk. With the exception of a few metal plaques at the Colegio Agronomico, the rest that we saw were in the fourth-floor attic, to which Warren and I were admitted a second time, on the eve of our departure, and then only in response to my despair at departing without having had further opportunity to assess the accumulation.

In one attic room we found a score of bronze castings, some of them recognized from Cheesman photos. Fell has suggested they were ancient Phoenician-Cypriot copies of religious and historical motifs of various earlier Middle Eastern civilizations, fabricated as trade gifts with overseas customers! One may depict Cleopatra, bitten in the breast by an asp (implying a date post-30 BCE); another may be David carrying Goliath's severed head (a dent in the monstrous brow supports such an interpretation). One portrays a Syrian bird-headed genie (Nisroch) and the Tree of Life. Accompanying the bronze plaques, cast by the lost wax process, are several rough castings of the same motifs. From their pitted surfaces and imperfections, as well as the fusing of motifs from several distinct cultures, I suspect them to be of local artistry, showing the difficulty of emulating such a complicated technique without firsthand instruction, and guided solely by observing the imports.

Archaeological Discoveries of Ancient America

From the dust-covered objects littering the floor of one room, Padre Flores lifted a small hoop that he particularly treasured, the emerald- and gold-encrusted crown from the image of Maria Auxiliadora, so damaged by the fire of 1962 that only the padre's personal memory would have distinguished it from the other clutter.

We saw the fantastic metal-sheathed statues described by Hugh Fox and Pino Turolla: the man in armor with modern false teeth, and a curved-tailed beast for which, Flores assured me sorrowfully, Crespi paid the equivalent of $5,000—yet was obviously worthless. Flores named the fabricator, a still-living Azuay artisan.

Crespi had shown compatriot Pino Turolla a drawer full of paintings that the friar claimed were by old masters: Leonardo, Rafael, Cimabue, Botticelli, and Tintoretto—40 or 50, and, for all Turolla could tell, they were genuine.

When asked how they came to be in his possession, Crespi responded, "My order is one of the oldest in Italy. Many of our founders were sons of great Italian families, families that go back to the Renaissance and before. Their families had these paintings. But times were very troubled in Italy then, and they were gathered together by our order and brought here for safekeeping."

Italian-born Padre Virgilio Berassi of the Instituto Orientalista Salesiano of Cuenca, when asked about this, told me he never saw any old masters, but Crespi was fond of making such wild claims, and never let visitors get very close to any of his treasures. Crespi called many of the metal pieces "gold," and brought them out one at a time, but never let anyone else heft them. Numerous objects photographed by foreigners and alleged to be gold, turned out, upon our inspection, to be of burnished, presumably copper alloy. These contrasted notably, however, with the tarnished surface of crudely designed pieces, some of which bore, upon the reverse side and in English, the modern manufacturer's annealed trademark.

One famous artist represented in the Crespi Collection was Francisco de Goya, by a tapestry woven in Madrid from one of his early paintings: The museo values it at $10,000. The Crespi canvases, with few exceptions, seem to have been painted in America by little-known artists, albeit often of considerable quality. In the 1960s, he had been officially prevented from shipping a collection of colonial canvasses to Italy, presumed for sale to support his beloved school. Expertly restored, they are now the pride of Cuenca's Casa de Cultura. No charges were brought against the padre, and our inquiries disclosed that, prior to the incident, the government's attitude toward protecting such things was not as sensitive as it is now, and unrestored old paintings were often purchased and taken abroad without hindrance.

The old friar had a standard spiel: Visitors would hear how one of the Pharaohs had left Egypt and traveled up the Amazon to settle in southern Ecuador. Inquiring around, Turolla was told that Crespi had collected books and pictures of Egyptian, Phoenician, and other Old World cultures, gave them to the natives, and said: "If you ever find anything like this, bring it to me, and I will reward you."

The father superior in Cuenca, Pedro Lova, confessed to Turolla that Crespi's "voluminous and ever-growing collection, and his strange ideas, were an embarrassment both to him and to the order." From the vast quantity of obviously bogus items, Turolla concluded that Crespi "was living in a dream world of his own creation."

Cuencan authorities, prior to our visit, were convinced that Crespi's anomalous objects most likely were copied from illustrations from foreign sources. But, since Turolla's time, local esteem for the quality of much of the material in his collection had vastly improved. That many authentic Andean treasures were mingled with the dross is testified by the superb selection now in possession of the Museo del Banco Central for which the government was willing to pay $433,000.

Fox, Turolla, and previous Cuencan opinion notwithstanding, some of Crespi's unique relics should be considered authentically ancient on the basis of internal evidence. Who in Ecuador would be capable of counterfeiting inscriptions in Cypriot or Phoenician, for which no published sources are known to exist? That the Padre obtained them from Europe is improbable, considering that some of them translate in Quechua. The many large slabs at Zuchay, bearing recognizable Cypriot letters within grids, are so heavy as to discount the modern-import theory. The inference is that at some time in the past, Andean artisans had access to knowledge of a variety of Mediterranean scripts.

It would appear that first-millennium BCE navigators had trade contact with native sovereigns of the Cuenca region, their likely objective being the abundant gold of that area. The date of the Masinissa Plaque, 148 BCE, corresponds archaeologically with a handsomely decorated Ecuadorian ceramic type called Cerro Narrio, about whose culture and political structure little is known, because it long preceded Canari and Inca traditions. On the last day of the time we had available for research in Cuenca, the Masinissa plaque still had not turned up. Padre Flores did not recall ever seeing it, but both Dr. Gustavo Reinoso and Dr. Benigno Maio, editor of *Revista de Antropologia*, remember commenting upon its Egyptian quality—although they considered it completely anachronistic, and all the metal sheets "only worth melting down."

Now, on the eve of our departure, with Padre Flores's blessing, Reinoso was enthused about rummaging through the fourth-floor attic in search of it. If still there, he was certain he could find it. In Quito, we showed our color prints from the Crespi Collection to architect Hernan Crespo Toral, nationwide director of the museums of the Banco Central. He, too, remembered having seen the Masinissa Plaque—the size and shape, with its hole, of a 3-inch-by-5-inch (8 × 13 cm) back of a rounded desk blotter. Although it is unique, he felt certain that many had been manufactured as gifts for Cuenca's doctors earlier in the 20th century, and one ended up among Crespi's stuff.

As to how it could bear three types of exotic yet translatable script, he showed no real concern, falling back upon the assurances of his authorities that all of Crespi's objects not selected out for the museum were of recent fabrication.

One scholar's modern ink blotter holder is another's trilingual proclamation of stunning historical import! And then the artifact itself gets lost! Both men have integrity. Wherein lies the truth? Without informing him of the importance of his answer, I called Paul Cheesman upon returning to Vermont and asked him to recall the size of the Masinissa plaque. His response: It was approximately 4 by 8 inches (10 × 20 cm) in size, with a 1 1/2-inch (4 cm) hole. Dr. Cheesman's understanding was that Crespi knew the name of the man on whose farm it had been found, that he had it made into an ink blotter holder, and that upon the man's death it had come into the Padre's possession.

We could not locate the elephant stela photographed by J. Manson Valentine and published by Charles Berlitz (1972) either. Crespi had said it was found during construction of Cuenca's airport. It bore Libyan script of the finest style, which translates, "The Elephant that supports the Earth and therefore is the cause of the Earthquake." That it once existed is beyond doubt, and that anyone in Ecuador prior to 1972 could have counterfeited it stretches credulity.

Archæological Discoveries of Ancient America

To some extent, dismemberment of the Crespi Collection stems from the zealous padre's own conduct. He was eager to have foreign investigators take pictures, but seldom brought out the same important piece twice. Because of the bogus items, professional archaeologists paid him no attention. Judging from his cagey treatment by our predecessors, had we arrived there in 1978 as originally planned, we probably would have fared no better. In 1981, Padre Flores permitted us to take careful color photographs, albeit during very limited time. We were too late to see some of Crespi's other significant artifacts, which may be lost forever. Again, this is the consequence of Carlo Crespi's idiosyncrasies. His brother Salesians had scant reason for confidence that any of the anomalies were genuinely important. Examining Fell's translation of the elephant stela, Padre Flores—the closest to Crespi—still had his doubts. "Don't you think," he asked me, "that an artist could consult a book and copy that?" What book, I asked, because it is unknown even to Libya's most prominent scholars?

It would appear that, many years ago, Crespi concluded that his favorite pieces were genuine and of ancient Mediterranean derivation, yet disinterred locally. A man of impressive learning, he realized that his treasures reflected some kind of contact with the Old World. Convinced of this, deservedly so, and with the prospect that more evidence ought to be forthcoming, he began the practice of indiscriminate collecting, in the belief that it kept his sources flowing and truly served his parishioners, while relieving them of objects that he judged idolatrous.

His clever behavior tantalized foreign scholars, but prevented close inspection of what was worthwhile. As a consequence, everyone began to doubt his judgment. Before the aged priest was willing to give up his mortal shell, illness pried loose his grasp upon the incredible accumulation. Only that which fit the present consensus paradigm of Andean cultural history was taken into government custody. Much of the rest was scattered to the wind, and may be beyond recovery.

Day after day, the owner and employees of Cuenca's Foto Ortiz graciously interrupted their normal, busy routine to develop Mr. Dexter's pictures within a few hours' time, which greatly assisted me in demonstrating to Ecuadorian scientists that portions of the collection left behind by the Museo del Banco Central or scattered far and wide merited protecting until further studied. His color prints raised the level of awareness of the issue among local authorities, and became a factor in their evolving perception of Ecuador's remote past.

Padre Flores's plan for a gallery at the new school to display the Crespi relics that remain in Salesian hands is worthy. Hopefully, it will find the monetary support it merits, but Flores was subsequently named director of the Don Bosco school in far-off Quito, where he took up residence in August 1982, thus further weakening the link between the anomalous artifacts and their past.

The Museo del Banco Central plans to excavate Puma Pongo, site of the Inca palace in Cuenca, and construct a museum there to store, study, and display what it purchased from the Salesians. Such a dig, if thorough, would be very valuable. The ideal physical location of Tomebamba was appreciated by Inca monarchs, and excavation there promises to disclose much about their predecessors, who presumably would have taken advantage of the prominent hill as well.

Crespi was not the first to acquire metal artifacts in Cuenca of the exotic style in question, as shown by a BBC program screened on American Educational TV in the spring of 1981, called "Treasures of Buckingham Palace," which included a supposedly gold crown very similar in aspect to a Crespi example. The Lord Chamberlain's Office confirms that it was the gift of President Gabriel Garcia Moreno, in 1854, and reportedly excavated in Cuenca.

Archaeological Discoveries of Ancient America

A single comparable artifact found tomorrow in an archaeological context could vindicate Carlo Crespi's perceptiveness, if not his judgment. That the old padre had acquired some of the most anachronistic objects in New World archaeology is evident. That they were disinterred in or near Cuenca—ancient Tomebamba—seems very likely. Whether still available or known only through photographs, they have cracked open a bit wider a door slammed shut when Rome destroyed Carthage and then subjugated the Libyan-Egyptians, obscuring from us a significant chunk of knowledge of the past.

As the taxi driver had predicted, tens of thousands of Cuencans of every age and social condition participated in the vigil that followed the beloved priest's death, on a Friday, until his funeral the next Sunday. Carlo Crespi's enduring concern had been for the less fortunate in society. In his final illness, suffocating with pneumonia, his voice reduced to a whimper, he still repeated anxiously, "No dejen llorar a los ninos. Donde está el nitio que llora? Ayuden a los niños que sufren." ("Don't let the children cry. Where is there a child crying? Help the suffering children.")

It is not as an antiquarian that Padre Crespi will be remembered in Ecuador, but as a saintly man, a pastor never too busy or too tired to attend to the needs of the humblest of his flock.

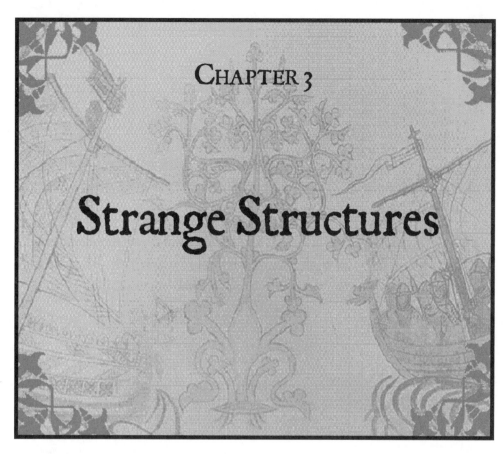

CHAPTER 3

Strange Structures

B efore his death in 2007, John Gallagher (no relation to Ida Jane
Meaows Gallagher) preferred to think of himself as "a historical detective."
With a BA in history from Fordham University, New York City, he was
epigrapher consultant for the American Institute of Archaeological Research in New
Hampshire. As such, he was eminently qualified to describe the ruins of a sacred
structure built by early Christians in New England shortly after the fall of the Roman Empire. His credible examination of this revealing site is unique, because it
has been thoroughly ignored by mainstream scholars.

CONNECTICUT'S FIFTH-CENTURY CHURCH
By John Gallagher

In the stillness of Cockaponset State Forest, southern Connecticut,
near the town of Guilford, masterfully carved from solid rock, stands North

Archaeological Discoveries of Ancient America

America's oldest Christian church. Recent epigraphic evidence found here suggests that it is 1,500 years old and linked to a voyage of Christian Byzantine monks who fled from North Africa during the fifth century, in the wake of Vandal invasions. Greek and North African inscriptions, Greek cupule patterns in the form of *Chrismons* (monograms of Christ), baptismal fonts, a *cathedra* or throne, candelabras, and an altar have been found at the site.

These items indicate that it was a place of worship, an early Christian church. The artifacts are illuminated by Libyan Arabic texts found at Figuig (Hadj-Mimoum), a remote oasis in eastern Morocco, in 1926. They tell of a voyage undertaken by North African Christian monks sailing "toward the setting sun," to "Asq-Shamal," the "Northern Land," suggestive of North America. A diffusionist scholar, Frederick J. Pohl, who studied the Figuig inscriptions during the 1960s, placed the monks' arrival in North America at about 480 CE.

He was told of some strange carvings on stone in the Connecticut woods, and obtained the services of a local physician as guide to their location. The author of several books describing Norse voyages to America, Pohl anticipated Viking origin for the Connecticut inscriptions. Seeing them in person, however, he knew at once that they were not 10th-century runic, but belonged to something entirely different and much older. Seeking clues from the immediate environment, he noticed that a nearby cove suitable as a landfall for ships was visible from the inscriptions.

When I first met an older Frederick Pohl at his home in Brooklyn, New York, in 1976, he asked me to go to the site, look it over, and see what I could make of it. For two and a half years thereafter, I regularly visited the location, gathering information, taking photographs, and making drawings, followed by long hours investigating source materials in public and university libraries. Together with Pohl, I sought out the opinions of other experts in pre-Columbian matters. Their insight combined with diligent, independent research, revealed the Guilford location as an early Christian church and baptismal site of Byzantine Greek North African origin. Epigraphic evidence identified its construction or carving by Christian monks who voyaged to Connecticut from North Africa in the mid-fifth century.

To understand the origins and reasons behind this 1,600-year-old undertaking, something about the history of the early Christian Church during this period is needed. By 430 CE, more than 600 bishops operated across North Africa, mostly in Tunisia, where Christianity sank its roots in the Dark Continent at the ancient Phoenician port city of Carthage. From its beginning, the new faith was a tale of violence and heresy. Under emperors Decius (249 to 250), Valerian (257 to 259), and Diocletian (245 to 313), many Christians everywhere were arrested, tried, and executed on charges of theological or political subversion, because they characterized the deities of all other faiths as "devils," and called for the downfall of the Roman state.

Meanwhile, fanatic followers of Manichaeism, Montanism, Pelagianism, and a dozen other, largely forgotten heresies, fought bitterly between themselves for control of Christianity. Among them was Arianism, after a late-fourth-century Alexandrian priest who preached against the alleged divinity of Jesus. Arius claimed that the Christian Holy Trinity was a descending Triad with only the Father as the True God. Jesus was considered the Son of God, but only by way of grace and adoption, and was neither co-equal nor co-eternal with the Father. Because they stressed the human nature of Christ, Arius and his followers were condemned as heretics by the Councils of Nicea in 325 CE, and again 56 years later in Constantinople.

Even so, Arianism spread throughout the Germanic tribes of Northern Europe. Fleeing from other barbarians, the Vandals crossed into North Africa after 400 CE, remaining there for more than a century, until 534 CE. Meanwhile, saints Basil and Augustine had introduced the *cenobitic*, or "common life," form of monasticism into North Africa, the latter forming his rules for monks as early as 388 CE. North Africa was by then ruled by six Vandal monarchs, three of whom (Geiseric, Huneric, and Thrasamund) vigorously persecuted their fellow Christians in the Roman Catholic Church. Huneric dispatched many bishops in an attempt to purge monasticism from North Africa. Geiseric drove many monks from the deserts and mountains of eastern Libya in the latter part of the fifth century. Only after Roman Emperor Justinian sent his General Belisarius to conquer the Vandal army in 534 CE were non-Arians able to safely return to North Africa.

Destruction wrought by the Vandals and the end of these "years of trouble" by the "trousered men" (in other words, Vandals) was vividly described in the Figuig inscriptions by a monk who returned to his homeland after the Vandals' defeat. He also described the voyage of fellow ascetics to North America: "In the name of the hermitage of the fraternity now dispersed abroad, by oath sworn to Christ the Lord, the testimony of an eyewitness who has returned home by ship, that has put into the seaport, now in his homeland, a second time. Ended are the years of trouble by the trousered men."

The author wrote of destruction by fire, looting, and the eventual escape of the monastic community "toward the setting sun," to Asq-Shamal, or the Northern Land, in several ships. "Across the void of waves," guided by a "cross-staff" by which to sight positions of the sun and presumably the stars, and using calculations known only to their helmsman, they crossed the mid-Atlantic Ocean. After months at sea, they made landfall in an unknown country, then "ventured into the wilderness." The inscription refers to a "north and west course from Morocco."

At the southern Connecticut site, 96 holes, or cupules, have been found. All are in the form of Chrismons, or monograms of Christ and the Blessed Mother Mary. Some are also acrostics in the shape of a fish spelling out in abbreviated Greek letters a theological statement about Christ. An acrostic is a verse or arrangement of words in which certain letters in each line, such as the first or last, when taken in order, spell out a word or motto. The Guilford holes or cupules were used for candle-like objects known as tapers. The cupule pattern of holes drilled into the rock face of an apparent altar spells out the ancient Greek Christian ICXCOYC, an acrostic for *Iesous Christos Theos Yios Soter*, or "Jesus Christ Son of God Savior." Appropriately, it is in the shape of a fish, an early Christian symbol for Jesus and baptism. When Christianity was an underground movement in Rome, its followers recognized each other by each sketching one half of a fish, connecting the two sides together to form a Chi-Rho, the first two letters in Greek for Christ's name (XP for XPICTOC, or "Christ"). The likeness of a candelabra has also been found at the Connecticut site, carved into the right side of the large rock outcropping referred to as the "altar." It is adjacent to the fish cupule pattern.

The candelabra features 14 holes, which were used to hold candles or tapers, with a seven-level plinth or base below. The 14 holes incised into the horizontal surface of the altar niche spell out the Greek letters *IC* with a ligature of Byzantine style above it. *Ligature* refers to a written character containing two or more united or combined letters, such as *ae*. *IC* are the first and last letters of the Greek word *IHCOC*, *Iesous*, or "Jesus." The Byzantine-style ligature above these letters, also composed of holes, binds the two letters *I* and *C* together to form the name of "Jesus." The plinth or base of the candelabra is Doric Greek in style.

Archaeological Discoveries of Ancient America

Also found at the site is another cupule pattern that spells out the Greek letters *MP*, the first and last letters of the Greek word *meter* or "mother," here referring to the Blessed Mother Mary. These two forms can be seen in the former Byzantine Cathedral of Sancta Sophia in Constantinople, presently a mosque. They were uncovered by archaeologists presently engaged in restoration. The modern name of Constantinople is Istanbul, now part of modern Turkey. Flanking the mosaic of the Blessed Mother Mary and the mosaic of Christ are the letters *MPOY* or *meter theou*, "Mother of God," in Greek. On the mosaic of Christ are the Greek letters *ICXC*, In Byzantine Greek form with a ligature above it, the translation is *Iesous Christos*, or "Jesus Christ." These examples date from the ninth century, but the others can be seen in Rome's fifth-century Santa Maria Maggiore, as well as from other churches of the period.

Found also at the Connecticut site are two extremely impressive baptismal fonts; one rectangular, the other in the shape of a flame, representing the Holy Spirit. The flame-shaped baptismal font is carved into a large rock outcropping that also contains the letters *FPBC*, probably an abbreviated form for the Latin words *Fons Pro Baptisimus Catechumen*, or "Font for the Baptism of Catechumens." Incised into the flame-shaped baptismal font are nine holes for candles. Eight holes, when containing lighted candles at Easter, could have represented the eighth day after the Crucifixion: the Resurrection, the beginning of the New Era, also signifying a second (spiritual) birth for baptized Christians. The flame shape represents the Holy Spirit received at Baptism.

The ninth hole in the middle of the font stands for the Paschal candle, symbolic of Christ. Here, the elderly were baptized by effusion, or the pouring of water over their heads. The rectangular baptismal font a short distance away was used for the ablution of infants who were lowered into its waters by a priest while baptizing them in the name of the Holy Trinity. The three times they were lowered into the font represented the three days Jesus remained in the tomb before his resurrection; the rectangular baptismal font represented Christ's tomb. A similar ceremony probably occurred at the nearby cove, where adults were baptized by being lowered into the waters three times, in the name of the Father, the Son, and the Holy Spirit.

A beautifully crafted symbolic carving representing overflowing water and fishes protruding from the waters lies nearby. It is symbolic of the newly baptized Christians (who were known as "little fishes") emerging from the waters of eternal life after being baptized. Another carving forms a rock seat or throne in which the bishop or abbot sat while conducting a confirmation ceremony, presiding over the newly baptized Christians and the baptismal ceremony itself. Carved into one of the rocks is a four-petaled flower signifying the Christ and the newly baptized Christians.

Like Jesus, believed to have flowered from the stem of Jesse and David, the newly baptized Christians were intended to bloom and flower into holy Christianhood. Such imagery was suggested by an Old Testament passage announcing the arrival of Jesus from the house of Jesse and David: "He will flower from the rod [Nazareth] and the stem [house] of David and Jesse." An inscription carved in two languages has also been recovered from the site. A scholar requesting anonymity believes one is in Mi'kmaq, an Indian tongue of Nova Scotia, whereas the other is Greek as was spoken in Cyrene, Libya. In his translated interpretation of the inscription, the Lord is the eternal father of his children, humankind; the Redeemer has ascended into Heaven, and sits at the right hand of the Father. A word appearing in the text, *Chrismon*, or *ICYTH-XPICTOC* ("Jesus, Son of God, the Messiah") is an abbreviated form in accord with the Byzantine and North African Church of the Vandal period.

Archaeological Discoveries of Ancient America

A Roman Catholic priest of New York City, Father John O'Connor, has identified the Guilford inscription as a paraphrase of the Epistle of Saint Paul to the Romans (Chapter 8, Verses 14–17, and also Verse 34). The writing style is fifth-century Greek, just when the Vandals invaded North Africa, where Lybian Cyrene was one of the oldest Christian bishoprics. Some 100 miles or more to the east, also in Libya, lay Adrimachidae, from which some of the Christians who made the Connecticut carvings are believed to have originated, based on linguistic affinities between the Greek spoken there and that represented in the Guilford text.

Others who contributed to the inscription, as the Figuig decipherment or inscription proves, were from Morocco. Because the Vandals' powerful navy controlled the western Mediterranean, these and other early Christian groups from North Africa must have endured an arduous journey to the sea coast of Morocco before attempting to cross the mid-Atlantic Ocean. Inscriptions, acrostics, and symbolic carvings found at the Connecticut site are evidence for the arrival of these Orthodox Christians from the persecution of Arian Vandals in Libya. Ruins of the church they built confirm their landfall in America a thousand years before the official arrival of Christianity with Christopher Columbus in 1492.

>—I◆>—O—<>I—<

The accidental excavation of a 38-foot-wide (12 m) stone platform during demolition of a Miami apartment building at Florida's Brickell Point brought to light something absolutely unlike anything else of its kind ever found throughout the Americas. Although officials attempted to identify the Miami Circle with a local tribe, such a connection is as unlikely as it is baseless.

Because Tequesta Indians formerly inhabited the area, Establishment scholars concluded these indigenes were responsible for the site. They were persuaded by numerous shell tools, axe heads, shark teeth, and other items of aquatic origin found within the archaeological zone that matched known Tequesta artifacts. Their association with the stone platform was underscored by radiocarbon dating of retrieved organic elements, including charcoal from fires and human teeth, all of which affirmed a period commensurate with Tequesta occupation of the location: circa 200 BCE. Both this time frame and the fact of the former tribal inhabitants were deemed sufficient to explain the Miami Circle's provenance.

But equating these datable materials and Tequesta-like artifacts with the Miami Circle requires a prodigious leap of faith, because the shell tools, charcoal, teeth, et al. might just as well have been left behind by a different people who occupied the site after its original builders no longer resided there. The physical evidence proves only that Tequesta Indians once resided at Brickell Point. Nothing, in fact, has been found to specifically link the Tequesta to the stone platform; their relationship is a complete assumption. A closer look at the site reveals they could not have been its creators.

The site was laid out in a perfect circle cut evenly into the limestone bedrock, bordered by 24 identical, uniformly spaced oval holes, which may have originally held posts, as some investigators believe. If so, then the Miami Circle begins to resemble a calendrical structure similar to counterparts among the standing stones of Neolithic Western Europe. Indeed, the regular placement of 24 holes is a self-evident doubling of that supremely cosmological number, 12—applied to the 12 months of the year, the 12 hours of the day, the 12 houses of the Zodiac, the 12 Greek and Norse (that is, Indo-European) gods, the 12 gates of the celestial city in the biblical Book of Revelation, and so on, and so forth—all referencing the heavens.

Furthermore, the Tequesta never exhibited the considerable organized labor required to create the Miami Circle. They were nomadic hunter-gatherers chiefly interested in chasing alligators through the Everglades, not megalithic astronomers charting the heavens. Nor did they possess the tools—let alone the precise measuring instruments—necessary to lay out, much less build the stone platform. Their own domiciles were actually inferior to those set up by other tribes, and, if they were responsible for the Miami Circle, it was their only such construction, and far superior to anything else they ever made—an unlikely proposition. Nor were they particularly interested in astronomy, unlike perhaps the creators of the Miami Circle.

Although none of this information can tell us who the creators were, it does at least rule out the Tequesta, while strongly suggesting transatlantic influences from the ancient Old World.

(Note: The so-called Brickell Point Site was listed in the National Register of Historic Places on February 5, 2002.)

FLORIDA'S STONEHENGE?
By James P. Grimes

In early 1998, a 50-year-old apartment building in the waterfront heart of downtown Miami, Florida, was completely razed to make room for a modern, $100 million, twin-tower apartment complex/shopping plaza with 600 apartments. This 2.2-acre (8,903 square m) prime property, now vacant, is on the south bank of the Miami River where it empties into Biscayne Bay (which connects directly with the Atlantic), and is completely wedged in by the river, skyscrapers, and high-rise hotels. This land has recently yielded a large, prehistoric site that is holding all of southeast Florida's interest: a deeply carved, stone circle platform that some are now calling "Miamihenge" or "Biscaynehenge."

A routine survey of the site by local archaeologists in August of 1998, turned up enough artifacts and ancient evidence to justify a closer look at the property and a formal dig by Miami-Dade County. As the archaeologists' study progressed, they were amazed to uncover a 38-foot (12 m) diameter, perfect circle (including many post holes, cut-outs, and basins) deeply cut into the limestone bedrock natural to the property. The excavation is continuing and has burgeoned into a major archaeological find.

The site has proven to be a single massive structure carved directly into the limestone by some unknown people long before Ponce de Leon visited here in the early 1500s. The making of the circle had to have been a major undertaking, requiring knowledge of stone carving methods, proper tools, and considerable manpower. It has 300-plus vertical post-holes cut deeply into the stone on its surface and around its perimeter, plus a series of 20 well-designed cavities or basins cut out across its surface. The rock was been cut down to a depth of at least 4 feet (1.2 m) around the circle's exterior by its originators.

On-site investigation is being conducted by the Miami-Dade County Historical Preservation Division under Robert S. Carr. Operating on a financial and manpower shoestring, they are also working against time: The developer gave them until he got his building permits from the City of Miami to complete their study. These permits were issued by the City of Miami, leaving the future of the location in jeopardy. Excavators got off to a slow start because of funding and manpower constraints, to say nothing of the unexpected size and complexity of the find. At first, they assumed they were only investigating the remains of a 19th-century Miami pioneer's home or business. But soon the broader implications of the circle became evident.

Some historical Indian artifacts have been found, together with the skeletal remains of a 5-foot (1.5 m) shark buried in one of the cavities. Any conclusions about the site would be premature, but general consensus holds that the circle was carved about 2,000 years ago. Most investigators believe that the circle was built by the ancient Tequesta Indians, who inhabited much of southeastern Florida from 500 BCE until they were virtually wiped out by disease and wars in 1763 CE.

Conventional guesses for the purpose of the structure include an animal pen, a fort to guard the river entrance, a chief's house, a meeting place, or a celestial platform or calendar. The perimeter holes range in diameter from 6 to 12 inches (15 to 30 cm) , and could have been used for a fence, lodge poles, or, as some think, observation posts. Two holes face due north with single holes at the other cardinal points. One hole faces east and has a discernable "eye" with a stone pupil carved in it, underscoring the structure's identification as an observatory. Large, well-carved cavities and cut-outs across the structure would seem to indicate it was built for specific, deliberate purposes.

Artifacts found include stone tools, shells, beads, and broken pottery. Some of these could have been left by later inhabitants many years after the circle was built. Two basaltic stone axes not manufactured in Florida (they are from neighboring Georgia) are anomalous finds at the site.

Several curious facts have come to light about the Miamihenge. For example, the property was surveyed by unnamed archaeologists as long ago as the 1940s, before the old apartment building was erected. They found artifactual materials at the location, but the results of their work appear to have been lost. Several reports about the structure were published between 1950 and 1975, but these publications have been out of print for more than 20 years. Noted anthropologist and archaeologist Dr. J. Manson Valentine, then-curator of the Miami Museum of Science and History, now deceased, wrote in 1959 that when engineers were digging the foundation for the old building they found a 30-foot-in-diameter (9 m) cylindrical shaft on the property and investigated it: "Enigmatic square holes, apparently of considerable age, appear in the reef rocks of our Florida Keys, and a perfectly cylindrical shaft 30 feet (9 m) in diameter, had been sunk in ancient times near the mouth of the Miami River. After excavating it to a depth of 60 feet (18 m) without finding a bottom, the engineers lost their curiosity and filled in the hole over which now stands an apartment house. The above were definitely not the workings of Indians."

A detailed search of Dr. Valentine's papers could not turn up his sources of information. But a previously unpublished letter to a friend in his own handwriting (June 2, 1966) provided a few more details: "Your information regarding the obliteration of ancient landmarks and records by the encroachment of modern tourism is unfortunately too true. At the mouth of the Miami ('Maya' = great + 'imi' = water, referring, no doubt, to Okeechobee in Caloosa language) River, there was a perfectly round hole of 30 feet (9 m) diameter cut into the native rock. Seeking a firm foundation for an apartment house which now straddles the site, a drag-line went down 60 feet (18 m) without touching bottom. In the Keys, I have photographed perfectly square holes mysteriously fashioned in the reef rock at a very early time."

Investigators of the 1950s and 1970s who knew and wrote about the Miami site believed, with Dr. Valentine, that outsiders, not local Indians, created the circle. They had good reasons for their conclusion: Even if the Tequesta Indians are in fact responsible for its construction, they never made another one, nor anything even remotely similar. Researcher Charles Berlitz, in *Mysteries From Forgotten Worlds*, believed:

> Other evidences of what may have been harbor-works prior
> to the discovery of America existed in Miami on the south shore
> of the Miami River in the shape of a large circular hole near the
> "prehistoric" beach line, expanding down in a perfect circle cut

into the beach rock for about 60 feet (18 m), the sides showing indications of tool marks. It may be noted that circular inner harbors were a mark of Carthaginian harbor construction. Whatever it was, it is now filled in, and what may have been a prehistoric harbor work is concealed under an apartment house across from the Dupont Plaza. Another ancient construction, a canal also showing tool marks on the reef rock walls, is still traceable underwater at Key Largo, Florida.

The Dupont Plaza is directly across the Miami River from the site now being excavated.

Altantean theorists have long argued that Miami is a site for the sacred Temples of Atlantis: Florida was named *Phaeacea* during one of the Phoenician occupations when Loucothea-Tanith was the temple goddess. The Egyptians did indeed appear to have been there earlier when the temple was dedicated to the god Min—hence the name *Bimini*. The renowned British Atlantologist Edgerton Sykes, in his *Atlantean Journal* article "Atlantis in America," located the site exactly: "The Temple of Miami is now buried underneath the foundations of a hotel or office block; that on Bermuda has vanished; the Temple of Isis and Rephthys on Haiti still awaits rediscovery."

The future of the dig is unsure, however. The site's developer has his building permits and wants to start construction. He has been very supportive of the survey so far, providing funds, allowing access to Carr and his people, and building a fence around the acreage. He even paid for guards to protect the site. But after his five-month wait, he understandably wants to proceed with his building project, valued at more than $100 million: a twin-tower complex with a parking garage between. The circle is located precisely where the garage is supposed to be built. Various groups, including local

Indians, the Smithsonian, and the Sierra Club, are taking up arms against the developer to preserve the site.

Daily protests are held to save the site. City of Miami officials claim they have no legal recourse against the construction, as the archaeologists have completed a mold of the circle. An attempt was made to cut the circle loose from the bedrock and move it to a safe storage area, but the stonecutter got bad vibes, and refused to cut it into the 28 pieces as planned. The developer says he is still interested in saving the monument. As of this writing, he, politicians, and scientists have gotten together to see what, within reason, can be done to preserve this mysterious link to our past.

The Miami Circle has become *the* popular topic in Miami, where conversations are usually no more controversial than the weather. There are almost-daily reports about it in area newspapers, on television, and on talk radio. The last time I visited the site there were four TV station trucks to cover a group of demonstrating Indians. The circle could be of particular interest for diffusionists, because its location in a protected harbor at the mouth of a river is an ideal spot for a trading station, and carbon-14 dating could coincide with the voyages of Carthaginian or Roman navigators. The platform may be a trading station/fort established for protected commerce with the natives. Maya beads have been found as far north as an island off San Sebastian inlet near St. Augustine, so the location might be a result of visitors from Yucatán. A Maya Shaman at the site believes the Miami Stone is the first of four more examples to be found.

In any case, let us hope this discovery can be saved for the future.

From the days of Cotton Mather to our time, the richly adorned face of a New England boulder has perplexed and challenged would-be interpreters of its bizarre imagery. But by carefully reexamining the confusion of glyphs within an astronomical context,

Archaeological Discoveries of Ancient America

John Gallagher may have discovered the real identity of their scribes and deciphered an elusive message encoded in celestial symbolism.

DIGHTON ROCK: THE ANCIENT ENIGMA OF MASSACHUSETTS

By John Gallagher

In 1630, a band of religious immigrants arrived by boat in Massachusetts: the Puritans. With increased immigration, their numbers grew to survive the harsh, cold winters. While walking in the woods, and along the rivers of Massachusetts, the pious newcomers found boulders adorned with strange carvings and inscrutable writing resting on the left bank of the Taunton River near what is now the town of Dighton, Massachusetts. Some of its puzzling images suggested the cartoon-like figures of animals, although skillfully interconnected. Running alongside and in between these forms appeared to be letters and words in an unknown script.

Early-19th-century illustration of the Dighton Rock.

The Puritans asked their most respected clergyman, Boston's Cotton Mather, to decipher the puzzling artifact. Because of extreme conditions—ice in winter, summer's high tides, and autumnal mud—the rock could be examined close-up only on rare occasions, sometimes only for a few hours a day. But Mather got lucky, and was able to personally copy the inscriptions and figures, sending his illustrations on to linguists at the Royal Society in London. The people of New England are still waiting for a response.

The Dighton Rock that Cotton Mather studied weighs 40 tons (36 metric tons) and is formed of gray-brown crystalline sandstone of medium to coarse texture. At 5 feet (1.5 m) high, 9.5 feet (3 m) wide, and 11 feet (3.3 m) long, and formed like a slanted, six-sided block, the surface covered with inscriptions has a trapezoidal face inclined 70 degrees to the northwest. About 13,000 years ago, the boulder was deposited on the left bank of the Taunton River by glacial movement and the melting of an ancient icecap. In 1951, the Massachusetts Legislature expropriated 49.5 acres (200,319 square m) of land adjacent to the rock for the purpose of creating a park. Just 12 years later, the rock was removed from the river by a coffer dam. Still later, additional land was purchased, and in 1974 the boulder was housed in a new museum at the Dighton Rock State Park near Berkeley, some 40 miles (64 km) south of Boston and about 15 miles (24 km) slightly northeast from Providence, Rhode Island. There, sheltered in a glass case, it is today protected from erosion, rising tides, and graffiti.

Since Cotton Mather became fascinated with it in the early 18th century, countless scholars and laymen alike have become similarly enthralled with Dighton Rock's challenging glyphs. Skeptics continue to denigrate the Dighton Rock as a hoax, but generations of local Indians insist that its imagery—to which they have never laid any claim—was in place on the boulder long before the Puritans arrived in 1630. No less importantly, Iberian-Punic—the written language that identifiably appears on it—defied translation until the 1970s.

The Dighton Rock images comprise an astronomical text inscribed by Iberian-Punic speakers; in other words, Phoenicians from Spain.

A prominent example features the horns and face of a bull formed by the Iberian-Punic letters *TR* for Taurus, "the bull." Another recognizable symbol is in the shape of a fish with its mouth open, signifying Pisces. These and related characters are astronomical signs identified with constellations in the night sky. Still others appear on the boulder: an eagle (Aquila), a wolf (Lupus), a rabbit (Lepus), a snake (Serpens), a crab (Cancer), a cat (Leo), a hunter (Orion), and a ram (Aries). Another 10 figures amount to 20 constellations in all depicted on the Dighton Rock. It is clear, then, that it possessed some astronomical or astrological significance for its ancient artists.

Most of the animal forms are constructed with letters in the Iberian-Punic alphabet. In other words, each letter takes on the shape of the animal itself in something known as a *rebus*. These Iberian-Punic letters form the head and horns of a bull, just as *LP* was configured into the face and long ears of a hare for Lepus. The rebus of a young horse, its upraised leg formed of the Ibero-Punic letters for "foal" (*FLS*), occurs on the left side of the rock to symbolize the constellation Equuleus, which may be observed between the eastern and southeastern sky in the month of August, next to the constellation Pegasus and directly above Aquarius. With a few exceptions, however, the constellations do not appear on the rock in their proper celestial positions, but in random order. They are joined by the Iberian-Punic word for "ladle" or "spoon," which might symbolize Ursa Major, the Big Dipper.

Evidence of yet another script is found on the boulder in the form of five white dots above a horizonal line for the word *aw-wa*, or "one who shouts" (an announcer?) in Numidian/Tifinag, a language spoken in North Africa (Morocco-Libya) during the Roman Era. *Aw-wa* was Numidian/Tifinag for the constellation Bootes.

Throughout the centuries, the Dighton Rock has been linked to Egyptians, Etruscans, Romans, Hittites, Vandals, Vikings, Indians, Atlanteans, the Lost Tribe of Israel, and medieval Portuguese. It is none of these. The letters on the stone are clearly Iberian-Punic, as it developed by 500 BCE. The Phoenicians carried their Punic language into Spain nearly a thousand years earlier, when it was adopted by the Iberic natives as their own variant: Iberian-Punic. And Dighton Rock is not the only specimen of this script found in North America. Other examples include West Virginia's Adena Stone, the Aptuxcet Rock in Central Vermont, and the Davenport Tablet in Davenport, Iowa. Language experts, beginning with the renowned epigrapher Dr. Barry Fell, have dated these inscriptions from roughly 600 to 200 BCE.

Archaeological Discoveries of Ancient America

None of this, however, begins to explain why anyone from ancient Spain would have bothered with a transatlantic voyage to Massachusetts, nor what they intended by inscribing so many astronomical symbols on a boulder at the Taunton River. A closer look suggests an answer: Of the 20 brightest stars in the heavens, 13 appear on the Dighton Rock, including Polaris (the North Star) and Sirius, the brightest star of all. A particularly revealing rebus spells out *BDCU*, which means to "serve Cetu," the whale in the constellation Cetus. These hints suggest that the artists who adorned this lonely boulder were seafarers, who etched prominent signs of their celestial navigation on its surface, thereby making it North America's oldest known star chart.

First came Iberian-Punic-speaking voyagers from sixth-century BCE Spain, followed by North African sailors, probably during the early Roman Era, as indicated by the appearance of two distinct written languages at Dighton Rock. These separate syllabaries imply that it was not inscribed by hapless castaways. Instead, what long afterward became Massachusetts must have been repeatedly visited by sailors from the ancient Old World—southwestern Europe and Numidia—who would have come, as the French and English later would, for the abundance of furs they obtained in trade with ancestors of the local Wampanoag tribes. As such, Dighton Rock joins the growing collection of physical evidence on behalf of transoceanic mariners, who left their imperishable mark on the emerging prehistory of our continent 25 centuries ago.

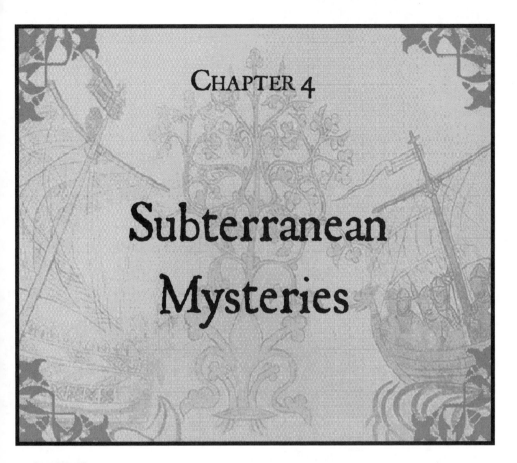

CHAPTER 4

Subterranean Mysteries

T here are always two sides to every story—the exoteric and the esoteric; the public and private version of events. No organization more exemplified this double conception than a group of men known as the Knights Templar. They were ostensibly commissioned to guard pilgrimage routes from Europe to the Holy Land, beginning in the early 12th century. But the warrior-monks simultaneously carried out covert excavations at Jerusalem's Temple Mount, from which they derived the name of their semi-secret order. What they found there has been the source of controversy ever since. In any case, the original nine Templars soon after amassed a great fortune.

Its sudden disappearance coincidental with that of the Templar fleet led a Canadian investigator to a small island off the eastern shores of her country. A resident of Comox, British Columbia, Kassandra Dycke may not only have found a lost treasure, but also proof of Western Europeans in America a century before the official discovery of our continent.

THE MONEY PIT

By Kassandra Dycke

When the Knights Templar were being rounded up for arrest in France under King Philip IV in 1307, 18 ships were allegedly loaded with unknown cargo at La Rochelle, and set sail for the West, never to be seen again. It has been suggested that the cargo was in fact the vast treasure of the Knights Templar, and maybe even the Holy Grail itself. Their destination? Rosslyn Chapel in Scotland. Or perhaps the Baron of Rosslyn, Prince Henry Sinclair, carried it with him to his "Castle at the Cross," now being unearthed near the village of New Ross, Nova Scotia. Templar wealth might now be connected to one of the greatest treasure hunts of all time.

Its story begins in 1795 with a curious teenager. On a lazy summer afternoon, Daniel McGinnis wandered onto the eastern shore of Oak Island in Mahone Bay on the east coast of Nova Scotia. As with most details surrounding his history, whether or not he lived on this island at the time is unclear. In any case, he noticed something strange during his hike. In a grove of oaks—trees not otherwise encountered along the Nova Scotia coast—he came upon a clearing of old stumps among new growth. A circular depression in the ground between 7 and 13 feet (2.1 and 4 m) in diameter was overhung by a heavy, old branch apparently affixed at one time with a tackle block. These subtleties in the natural environment sparked the lad's sense of adventure. Having grown up surrounded by local lore of pirates and their buried treasure, he quickly rounded up a couple of friends, and soon they were digging in the depression for lost loot.

The soil was easy to move, as though the shallow pit had been dug and refilled, although its walls were a hard clay. After removing about 2 feet (.6 m) of earth, the boys uncovered neatly laid flagstone of a kind not native to Oak Island. At 10 feet (3 m), they discovered a platform of oak logs, rotten on the outside, with ends firmly embedded into the clay walls. At 25 feet (8 m), worn out by their labors, which produced no further discoveries, they called it quits, but never forgot their adventurous excavation.

Seven years later, grown up now, McGinnis and his pals attracted the attention of various investors to form the Onslow Company and fund renewed digging. Returning to the island, the young men unearthed another oak-log platform, a layer of charcoal, and one of blue putty. At 90 feet (27 m), they hit a large, peculiar stone 24 by 15 by 10 inches (60 × 30 × 25 cm), and weighing about 175 pounds (79 kg). They hauled it to the surface with some difficulty and were perplexed to observe that, like the flagstone found in 1795, the boulder was not native to Nova Scotia, but resembled dark Swedish granite or fine porphyry, olive in hue, and particularly hard. The broad surfaces were smooth, with strange writing etched onto one side. The text—apparently a kind of code, not a foreign language—made no sense to anyone at the time, but someone later claimed to have deciphered it to read, "Forty feet below, two million pounds are buried." Henceforward, the site has been known as the Money Pit.

The original inscription has long since disappeared, however, and surviving copies are generally regarded as unreliable at best. The stone itself was eventually embedded in the fireplace of a private home, until it was removed in 1865 by A.O. Creighton to his bookshop window. He used it as a gimmick to attract buyers of shares for yet another treasure-seeking enterprise: the Oak Island Eldorado Company. In 1935, Harry Marshall, son of one of the bookshop owners, recalled that, as a boy in the 1890s, he could no longer see any inscription, it having apparently faded by that time. The stone was used as a door-stop, and subsequently vanished when the shop was sold.

Just beyond the 90-foot (27 m) level where the stone had been found, Onslow Company excavators encountered water oozing into the pit.

Archaeological Discoveries of Ancient America

Overnight, to the great devastation of the treasure hunters, the pit filled to its 32-foot (10 m) level with salt water that could not be lowered with any amount of bailing. The following year, they sunk a second shaft alongside the Money Pit to 110 feet (34 m), and planned to tunnel over to an envisioned "treasure." However, as soon as they got close, water from the pit began to pour in and submerged this shaft as well. They gave up.

Throughout the years, a long parade of hopefuls have come to the island, confident and eager, inevitably leaving depressed and broke. No fewer than 29 shafts now dot the island, all to no avail. Many of the shafts had been sunk in an effort to block the water that had proven time and again to thwart all attempts. In 1850, the Truro Company, headed by mining engineer James Pitblado, uncovered the source of the mysterious water. Just 500 feet (152 m) from the pit lay Smith's Cove, which he discovered was, to the amazement of all, an artificial beach. Beneath the top layer of sand and gravel, a 2-foot (.6 m) layer of coconut husk and eel grass, native to the Caribbean and often used as ship's dunnage, was found covering a 145-foot (44 m) stretch of beach. The original layer of clay had been removed. A coffer dam was built in the bay by the company to allow further excavation, during which they discovered a most curious thing: Five well-constructed stone box drains fanned out across the beach, converging to a point at a flood tunnel heading up the hill toward the Money Pit.

The men were excited, realizing that for anyone to have gone to the great trouble of booby-trapping the pit with such a complicated system of flood tunnels must have been trying to conceal a very great treasure indeed! They began dismantling the drains, but their coffer dam was destroyed by a higher-than-usual tide, and funds were lacking to build a new one. They turned instead to sinking a shaft in the hope of intercepting the flood tunnel and blocking it. Upon doing so, they found that the Money Pit could be drained somewhat, but not enough to allow further digging. It was later learned that another flood tunnel ran from the western shore of the island.

The Truro Company treasure-hunters drilled five holes in the pit to 112 feet (34 m), bringing up evidence of similar layers that had already been encountered, such as oak and spruce, putty, and coconut husk. But they also drilled through two 20-inch (51 cm) layers of loose metal that made a distinct noise when the drill pressed through, and was sandwiched between layers of oak. The auger, though, was not properly equipped to bring up the pieces, and only three small links of gold chain were retrieved. Perhaps the most significant find of its kind occurred when Pitblado removed something from the auger following a drilling, inspected it, and pocketed it, unwilling to show anyone what it was. He promised to share it at the next board meeting, but didn't. Shortly thereafter he applied to the Province for treasure rights on Oak Island. Unfortunately, Pitblado died soon after, as did the secret of what he found that day.

The treasure hunt resumed under the Oak Island Association of Truro, leading to the most significant setback. Following the example of previous attempts to dig parallel shafts and tunnel over, they met with identical failure, as water burst through, filling the shaft. However, in this instance, as the water entered, something shifted in the Money Pit itself in a fearfully dramatic fashion. As the secondary shaft filled, the Money Pit rumbled and gurgled furiously as it sucked down all of the excavators' materials, including 10,000 board feet (24 cubic m) of lumber from the cribbing. It appeared that the bottom had fallen out of the pit. Cores taken following the cave-in revealed only mud and stone where before there had been carefully constructed layers of various materials.

The Money Pit quest appeared to have come to an abrupt end, but its saga was far from over. In 1893, the Oak Island Treasure Company was

Archaeological Discoveries of Ancient America

formed, its members drilling additional core samples. And what they found opened up a whole new chapter of speculation concerning possibilities at the bottom of the shaft. At 171 feet (52 m), the drill hit an iron barrier and could go no further, so the operator pulled it back up to the surface. Embedded in the auger from 154 feet (47 m) was a small piece of parchment, upon which the letters *vi* were clearly written in black India ink. Since that intriguing find was made, no further discoveries have come up from the pit itself, though related artifacts continue to engage treasure-hunters. In 1897, a Captain Welling found a stone triangle on the beach. Its significance has been much disputed, some arguing that it was a kind of marker pointing to the Money Pit. Whatever its purpose, from descriptions and photographs it appears to have been deliberately constructed with large, carefully placed stones. Sadly, the whole thing was destroyed by the heavy machinery of treasure-seekers in the 1960s, who also, quite absurdly, built a causeway from the mainland to the island, thereby allowing access for such heavy machinery.

Other rocks that appear to have had a clear purpose were found elsewhere on the island. At least two stones with drill holes, approximately 2 inches (5 cm) deep, were discovered in positions that may correspond somehow to Captain Welling's triangle. Throughout the course of several years, Fred Nolan, an island resident, recovered a vast number of conical stones on his property. Their significance seemed beyond comprehension until 1992, when he realized that they indicated a very large, strangely shaped stone. When laid out on a grid, they correlated precisely with a large cross measuring 720 feet (219 m) by 867 feet (264 m), intersecting at a tidy 90 degrees. Another discovery of some significance on Nolan's property was buried beneath one of the conical stones forming the cross. Previous to realizing its significance, another treasure-hunter dug up an old, wrought-iron, pot-bellied stove buried beneath it. Several old coins have been found in the vicinity of the Money Pit, the most interesting specimen being a copper coin dated to 1317 found in 1887.

Further curiosities have been found in Smith's Cove where the box drains were discovered. Treasure-seekers there dammed the beach to discover the remains of an arc-shaped, wooden structure with notches cut into it at regular intervals and marked with Roman numerals. Later, a tourist walking the beach picked up an ivory or bone boatswain's whistle that may date to Elizabethan times.

For more than two centuries, numerous diggers have come to the island seeking their fortune. The lucky lost merely their life's savings; 10 of the less than fortunate lost their lives. And nothing of real value has been recovered. Questions remain: What is (or was) the Money Pit? When was it made, and by whom? Proposed solutions range from pirate's treasure and Shakespeare's lost manuscripts to Basque fishermen, Havana gold seized by the British, Louisburg's lost treasury funds, Inca sailors, and so on, and so forth. But all fall short of any plausible theory.

The most credible explanation may have begun to emerge in 1972, when Joan Hope purchased a home in New Ross. Only after moving in did she learn that the property covered the ruins of what appeared to be an old castle. No one took her suspicions seriously, so she began excavating the site herself. To her surprise, she unearthed a 14th-century Scots-Norse castle with grand towers, a main gate of pillars, and an old well nearby. Since Hope began digging, she has brought to light numerous artifacts, including a large stone with strange markings. Her discovery caught the attention of some investigators who believe it may mark a castle built by Prince Henry Sinclair, the Baron of Rosslyn, home of the now famous Rosslyn Chapel.

Sinclair is widely believed to have been a central figure in the Knights Templar, and his exploits at sea during the late 14th century were recorded in the design of the Chapel itself. He was said to have constructed a fortress at the center of an island overseas, known as the Castle at the Cross. New Ross sits at the center of Nova Scotia, along Gold River, which empties into

Archaeological Discoveries of Ancient America

Mahone Bay. A second river runs north of New Ross and empties into the Bay of Fundy's Minas Channel. At the mouths of each of these rivers are two islands with groves of red oak, one of those islands being our Oak Island. Furthermore, local Mi'kmaq native oral tradition tells of this settlement, and also relates in some detail that the king of these people, affectionately called Glooscap, wintered in the area of Advocate Harbour across Minas Basin, where he built a ship for his return voyage.

While sailing along the coast of Massachusetts, so theorists speculate, one of Prince Henry's men died. Sir James Gunn was buried under a grave marker carved with the figure of a knight bearing the Clan Gunn insignia on his shield. Known as the Westford Knight, the image appears on an inconspicuous glacial boulder surrounded by a small chain fence in Westford, Massachusetts, along the side of Depot Street, just north of the town center. Interestingly, a 14th-century cannon of Venetian design was recovered from the bay at Louisburg, Cape Breton, and is on display there. Sinclair's navigator hailed from just that very region.

Evidence has been presented to make quite a convincing case that Sinclair was in fact residing in Nova Scotia sometime around 1398, and would have entered the region by the mouth of Gold River, passing directly by Oak Island. He is known to have wintered in the north across Minas Basin, which he would have entered by passing the only other island known to have featured a stand of oaks. The cross on Oak Island, with the unique stone at its center, could correspond to Sinclair's castle at the cross. The Money Pit itself may have been constructed by Sinclair, but later modified, which would account for the tropical coconut husk and recent clearing around the pit. Certainly, an undertaking as long-term and complex as the Money Pit would have created enough of a hubbub to be noticed by nearby residents who fished and traveled regularly in Mahone Bay, had it been constructed merely 40 years before its discovery by McGinnis, as is suggested by the age of the growth in the clearing in 1795.

Whether or not Sinclair had anything at all to do with the Money Pit is debatable, but it seems likely that he had some affiliation with the island. What was initially pursued as simple pirate's treasure may in fact be physical evidence of far greater worth; namely, material proof that Western Europeans arrived in North America 100 years before Columbus.

As some indication of the international debate generated by a North American site known as Burrows Cave, Dutch author Philip Coppens threw new light on this hotly contested enigma in a 2007 article for Ancient American. *The editor-in-chief of his own magazine in Holland,* Frontier, *he previously broke the story to the outside world of the existence of ancient pyramids in China. Far afield from this archaeological scoop, he also uncovered new evidence used by a 1994 U.S. government inquiry into the death of President John F. Kennedy concerning assassin Lee Harvey Oswald. Coppens here applies his acknowledged investigative skills toward solving a no-less-controversial mystery similarly potent enough to radically change the way we view the past.*

FIND OR FRAUD OF THE CENTURY?
By Philip Coppens

Burrows Cave is a site in southern Illinois alleged to contain the tomb of a king from North Africa in the first century CE. In Version I of its discovery, Russell Burrows, a local treasure-hunter, accidentally found the subterranean location along a branch of the Little Wabash River, a tributary of the Ohio, near his hometown of Olney in 1982. Searching for pioneer relics, he was surprised to stumble upon a shallow depression leading into an underground corridor like nothing else known in rural Illinois. The passageway was lined with oil lamps and had several chambers on either side, the ceiling black from smoke.

Archæological Discoveries of Ancient America

In Version II of our story, Burrows deliberately created a hoax, claiming to have discovered a tomb from which he sold faked stone artifacts of his own making, all of them copied from various archaeology books. Either way, his find has become famous for its large numbers of inscribed stones, often emblazoned with the profiles of distinctly African, Egyptian, European, and Native American men and women (mostly men). At first sight, many appear crude, the work of an amateur or someone trying to meet an imminent deadline. Preliminary analysis of the writing with which many of the artifacts is adorned revealed a mix, if not a mishmash, of various styles, words, and languages professional linguists dismissed as "obviously fake"—*obvious* being their preferred word used to underscore what *they* know is fake, while amateurs are fooled by it. Obviously.

Engraved in marble, this image of a male figure in ancient Egyptian attire is one of approximately 7,000 such artifacts removed from the Illinois cave.

Just a year after his supposed discovery, Burrows placed a selection of retrieved artifacts on sale in a local antique shop. But if he was responsible for personally fabricating the entire collection, it is clear he made many more than he could have ever sold. Moreover, not until 1997 did he actually begin to cash in on sale of the by-then dubious objects. If Burrows wanted to get rich by manufacturing fakes, his hoax was obviously ill executed. But the cave is more than just a collection of inscribed stones. Burrows claims to have found and removed many gold artifacts from it. These do indeed appear genuine, though they feature the same alphabet soup of mixed-up scripts. One can only wonder why a fraud, if Burrows were indeed one, would promote his "find" with gold, which is costly to obtain.

It is true that there are conflicting stories about this gold. Swiss author Luc Bürgin claims that Burrows removed huge quantities of gold from the cave, had it melted down, and then sold it, depositing a grand total of 15 million U.S. dollars into Swiss bank accounts. If true, then Burrows did indeed get his hands on tremendous amounts of gold, which he sold for its monetary, not archaeological, value. Skeptics contend that Bürgin was merely repeating "information" from a fellow researcher and possesses no real evidence for his assertion.

Others assert there *was* no gold; that it has never been seen. That, quite clearly, is not correct. I have myself seen color photographs of such gold items with Burrows; some are available for viewing on my Website. Other cave-deniers argue that his "gold" was actually lead finished off with gold paint to make it look real. If they are correct, then Burrows merely created these fakes to fool archaeologists, amateur scientists, and the media, and so he could never allow the objects' direct contact or testing. But it would also have meant that he could never have regarded the gold objects as part of a quick money-making scheme. In short, this conclusion contradicts accusations that Burrows tried to profit from a hoax.

Incised marble profile of a non-Indian wearing ancient Old World headgear and pectoral from Burrows Cave in southern Illinois. A glyph at the bottom (VII) signifies Alexander Helios, Cleopatra the Great's son. The vertical line of four characters in Numidian, a written language current in North Africa during the Roman Era, probably spells out the name of the person portrayed here.

Burrows claims to have come upon a human male skeleton in the cave's first crypt. Moving on to the second chamber, he noticed that it enclosed a funeral bier with the remains of a woman and two children. A golden spearhead lay in the woman's ribs, where the heart would have been. Skulls of nearby children showed signs of perforation, suggesting that they and the woman had been murdered when the male (her husband?) died.

Altogether, Burrows counted a dozen crypts. The central chamber, containing a golden sarcophagus, was closed by a stone too heavy for him to roll away alone. The walls of this room, including the ceiling, were profusely decorated. The golden sarcophagus, he remembered, resembled the ancient Egyptian mode, as evident in the deceased's hairstyle, as well as the crossed arms over the chest, with the hands holding an ankh. Burrows reported that he pried open the sarcophagus, which contained human remains and a death mask, likewise Egyptian in appearance. Although of tremendous value, comparable to the golden sarcophagus of Tutankhamun, it was too ponderous for removal without the help of his brother-in-law. Burrows was also unsure as to whether or not he might face prosecution for having disturbed human remains and sold their grave goods. His critics seldom address this part of the story, insisting that such a cave never existed in the first place, hence no sarcophagus, hence no human skeleton inside it.

Let us assume, for the sake of argument, that the site does indeed exist, and see how far we can follow Burrows into it. His situation would have been extremely complex: He was totally unprepared for such a find (who wouldn't be?), and his own naturally volatile character did not help in a situation where patience was necessarily a virtue. The local *Olney Daily Mail* ran a small article identifying Burrows as the discoverer of a local cave, but provided little more except for this hope: "The university [with which he was allegedly in contact] will probably begin the dig next year. At that time, more information can be given."

Though Burrows did, after all, seek help from the scientific world, he received hostile reactions from its representatives. Soon afterward, one "amateur archaeologist" after another pressed his doorbell. Each one almost immediately demanded to see the cave. His situation was analogous to someone in a leg-cast constantly asked by callous well-wishers whether they can see or sign the plaster. At some point, the answer must certainly be no! These importunate curiosity-seekers had neither basic respect nor regard for his own wishes, often not even bothering to ask about them.

People such as these came away disappointed and hurt because Burrows did not want to play their game, and they consequently voiced scathing opinions.

Some even considered Burrows's presence incidental. One attempt to commercialize the cave occurred in 1994 when Harry Hubbard and Paul Schaffranke claimed the ancient alphabets on the stones were a combination of Latin and Etruscan. The inscriptions revealed, they claimed, that the tomb of Alexander the Great was in Illinois. What made Hubbard stand out from competing theorists was his Jack Russell–type attacks on anyone who disagreed with him. He was described as appearing to spend the majority of his time seeking investors and peddling home-made videotapes. He really did not need Burrows; he was going to find the cave himself. He is a typical example in a long line of interlopers who have tried to use the cave for their own financial benefit, for fame, or to confirm their pet theory—and most often all three mixed into one obnoxious cocktail.

In the "pet theory" category was Joseph P. Mahan, author of a 1983 book called *The Secret*. Eight years later, in a public lecture, he opined that the cave was connected to "sun-related, semi-divine mortals, the descendants of extraterrestrial, immortal progenitors, who had come to Earth in fire-ships, stayed to upgrade the humanoids they found here by modifying the genes of these children of Earth, thus producing a hybrid progeny." Such a conclusion is not based on anything at all that Burrows ever said about the cave, but it is clear that it rubbed off badly on Burrows's image and his find.

In the final analysis, his story is typical of all discoveries. The same, basic stand-off is here, with the scientific experts on one side quick to condemn the artifacts they were shown as "obvious forgeries." By default, these objects could not be genuine, for we all "know" that Columbus was the first to reach America. When the untrained enthusiasts came along, Burrows was unprepared for and unaware of the extent of in-fighting and heated controversy that exists in most amateur organizations—though communities such as those interested in UFOs, Rennes-le-Château, crop circles, and all the rest, have so far easily out-performed anything that the "diffusionists" have done. Burrows had thrown out a giant bone and the dogs were fighting over it. In the process, he was eaten—and so was his story.

Unfortunately, his personal disillusionment led him to dynamite the entrance to the cave six years after its discovery and three years before his co-written book, *The Mystery Cave of Many Faces*, was published with Fred Rydholm. It is an extremely level-headed account of his discovery of the site and the finds inside—and something he regarded as his final word on the subject. Although Burrows often claimed to have lost interest in his discovery (largely due to the difficult people he had to deal with), he was continually drawn back to it, like a moth to a flame. The fact that he could not let go, even though there was nothing in it for him any more, should perhaps be seen as the best evidence that Burrows had indeed made a legitimate discovery. For if it had started as a money-making scheme in 1982, by 1992 he would have long abandoned such hope.

But the story did not die. The next year, diffusionist thinkers had a new magazine to turn to. Throughout the course of the subsequent decade interested parties continued to follow the story of the cave. In 1999, magazine publishing Wayne May got Burrows to sign a contract for disclosure of the cave's location, despite his initial belief that Burrows lied about the place and had actually laid a false trail.

Archaeological Discoveries of Ancient America

I have to say that, from my personal dealings with Burrows in 1992 and 1993, I found him to be a man of honor. If he promised something, he would do it (cue for the critics to laugh at what they will see is my "obvious" gullibility). And that, it seems, is what May felt, as well. So, despite his initial reluctance to believe, Mr. May finally determined the location and persevered with his investigations. His ground-penetrating radar indicated that a cave was indeed there. The problem was how to get in, considering that Burrows's explosion a decade earlier had destroyed the entrance.

Unfortunately, it soon became apparent that the blast had not only blocked the entrance, but had also damaged the interior of the tunnel. During May's various attempts to gain access, each time he stumbled upon huge quantities of water. This seemed to indicate that the gun-powder detonation had diverted the flow of an underground river. As a result, it caused water to gush into the underground complex. It therefore looked as though salvaging anything from the underground complex would be terribly difficult, and largely outside May's current capabilities.

In a nutshell, Burrows Cave represents a nearly 25-year-long quest that has left hardly anyone who looked into it untouched or without an opinion. It is all too easy to label Burrows a hoaxer. People who have known and worked with him have called him many things, but not a fabricator of evidence or a liar. He has a temperamental nature on occasion and has sometimes not been the best judge of character. But his personal flaws are largely incidental to his story. Only his skeptics focus too heavily on them, whereas they should be focusing instead on whether or not he could actually have fabricated any, let alone such huge numbers of, inscribed stones.

If we were placed in the same situation, the end result would be the same, for it is in the nature of such discoveries, and how we react to them, that they tend to produce the same kind of outcomes. Skeptics condemn them as "obvious hoaxes," while proponents speak of "clear evidence." So, the fate of the cave was sealed and doomed, from the moment Burrows slid down into it. Where does that leave us? For nonbelievers to cry foul, they need to come up with better than "obvious" statements. There is, in short, no proof that Burrows faked the stones. More importantly, there is evidence that a cave system does exist just where he said it does. If it is all a hoax, the skeptics will need to provide something more than repeatedly using the word *obvious*. Still, even if the cave system still survives, it may perhaps be lost to us forever. Any operation that could be mounted to provide a conclusive answer would cost an extraordinary amount of money, and such resources are "obviously" not in the hands of the diffusionists. It seems that, once again, the Establishment has won the fight. And that may be the only obvious thing about this entire story.

What sense can we make of all this? Could a golden sarcophagus, allegedly found in an Illinois cave, be proof of pre-Columbian transoceanic travel between the ancient Old World and the Americas, as so many people have claimed? Burrows described the cave's physical characteristics and its contents, and, fortunately, most of the artifacts removed were photographed early on, in part due to the efforts of his coauthor, Fred Rydholm, and University of Wisconsin archaeo-surveyor, Professor Emeritus James Scherz.

Various other researchers have closely studied the Burrows Cave collection, a few specimens of which are pictured here. Unrelenting critics persist in pointing out the confusion of its written languages. But most cultures are a mismatch of influences! London and New York are prime examples of how various cultures create a new one. Things were no different in ancient times, Alexandria probably being the best example. An important clue is that some of the stone slabs displayed a signature that was known in the Old World. It belonged to one Alexander Helios, son of the infamous Cleopatra and Marc Antony, and twin brother of Cleopatra Selene, the future co-ruler of Mauritania (in Africa's western Sahara). This is the angle upon which Hubbard and Schaffranke built.

Amongst Burrows's earliest team of amateur researchers were Jack Ward and Warren Cook, the latter of whom died in 1989. Cook's analysis of the artifacts led him to conclude that creating them would have taken thousands of hours. But, more importantly, he continued Ward's analysis of their possible origin, and argued that they were most likely the remains of a Libyan-Iberian expedition. He identified Mauritania's King Ptolemaeus I (1 BCE to 40 CE), son of Cleopatra Selene and King Juba II (52 or 50 BCE to 23 CE), as the man responsible for this transoceanic voyage. Could it have been possible?

The rulers of Mauritania had fallen afoul of Rome, if only because of the economic power that the kingdom had become. When Emperor Caligula decided to redress the balance, King Juba II and his family had to flee. It is possible that he used the knowledge of the seas his ancestors, the Phoenicians, had gathered: He knew the location of the Azores, whose goods he was able to sell at the highest prices in Rome and elsewhere in the Empire.

If the Burrows Cave artifacts are genuine and the interpretation correct, it is possible that the Phoenician-informed Mauritanian royal family sailed further west, beyond the Azores, to the Americas. If they ended up in Central America, perhaps they entered the Mississippi River and traveled north until reaching Illinois, where they settled, far removed from the squabbles of the Old World. The cave artifacts are not the only evidence of the presence of an enigmatic people during the first century CE.

According to one Native American legend (Yuchi), the region contains the tomb of a king who was not native to America. The tribe once knew its location, but this information is now lost. Could this forgotten place have been Burrows Cave? Furthermore, it is known that Juba II ordered a golden sarcophagus to be prepared for the mausoleum that had been built for him in Tipaza (modern-day Algeria). This was one of the prized possessions the Romans had tried to get their hands on, but never found, despite their conquest of his country. History is silent on the fate of both the man and his treasure. Yet it is clear that King Juba II must have died, and that he and his sarcophagus must have ended up somewhere, perhaps in Illinois. That seems "obvious" logic to me. But logic may be all that we can work with for the foreseeable future.

Cited in Philip Coppens's article as the author of the first full-length book on Burrows Cave, Fred Rydholm is better known as "Mr. Copper." He earned that title as a foremost expert after a lifetime of studying the incredibly extensive mining enterprise undertaken by an unknown people in the Upper Great Lakes Region beginning more than 5,000 years ago. Although archaeologists have known of this immense achievement since the late 19th century, generations of American school children have been taught nothing about it—an academic failure that particularly disappointed Rydholm, himself a public school teacher for more than 30 years.

Three-term mayor and city commissioner, for Marquette, Michigan, Rydholm's contributions to education have garnered numerous awards, from 1941's Louis G. Kaufman Character Award to the Third Annual Marquette Arts Award for "Outstanding Writer/Historian" in 1999. But it is his unique expertise regarding a little-known, though dramatically significant part of American prehistory that merits our consideration and awe.

AN ACHIEVEMENT TO RIVAL THE PYRAMIDS

By Fred C. Rydholm

The half-billion pounds of high-grade copper mined from Upper Michigan in prehistory amounted to the most unique treasure on the face of the Earth. Several theories have been suggested to explain why such huge deposits of native, pure copper could have been naturally deposited and humanly excavated in the Lake Superior region. But before such interpretations might be tackled, we must consider the natural background for prehistoric America's most stupendous drama.

At some early geological period, when our planet was still in a semi-molten state, subterranean plates pushed against each other to produce widespread seismic and volcanic upheavals. Telluric violence forced liquefied copper through cracks in our planet's surface, saturating spongy rock formations and, in some instances, forming great, underground pools.

A more-than-5,000-pound (2,268 kg) copper boulder from Minong, Wisconsin, near the shores of Lake Superior in 1876. How were such enormous specimens extracted and transported by miners 5,000 years ago?

After the molten metal cooled and hardened, the Upper Great Lakes Region possessed unique amounts of copper. These deposits covered several hundred miles, from the south of Lake Superior, beneath what is now Marquette and Alger Counties, extending southwest into Wisconsin to its southern end, and up into Canada on the shore of Lake Superior on its northwestern extremity.

But precisely how so much copper could have come about in its uniquely pure state is an enigma geologists are still trying to understand. They are unable to explain precisely how it was formed and from where it came. For example, how could the copper have hardened in such great masses so relatively close to the surface? Perhaps tremendous global forces about which we may only speculate caused the Earth's crust to buckle. A large area containing the bulk of the copper may have been pushed suddenly downward into a massive fold or syncline extending some 60 or 70 miles (97 or 113 km) from one end to the other.

As the extremities of this fold bent upward, they separated from the rest of the copper formations deep in subterranean regions. Their upper edges (perhaps 60 miles [97 km] long on the northwest end and even longer on the southeast end) formed the land mass known today as Isle Royale. It protrudes from Lake Superior and the Keweenaw Peninsula, barely connecting Michigan's Upper Peninsula. These extruded territories were formed of high mountain ridges, exposing millions of broken pieces of copper.

During the geologic periods that witnessed these dramatic events, the climate began to cool, as successive ice ages throughout several million years sent their glaciers back and forth over the Northern Hemisphere. Some of the glaciers were 7 or more miles (11 km) thick. Throughout the millennia, they crept across upturned mountain ridges, shearing the tops off high ridges as they advanced. Masses of rock were crushed under their relentless pressure. But copper, being malleable, bent and flattened. In some cases, it broke into smaller pieces, but was freed from its stony matrix.

Meanwhile, advancing glaciers tore open great gouges and ravines in the earth, filling others with dirt, rock, and chunks of various minerals. Smaller copper pieces were rolled with gravel, and traveled hundreds of miles. Most of the larger specimens came to rest in the Lake Superior region. They "floated" with the glaciers—hence, "float copper" was and still is found in glacial moraines, as far south as the farthest advances reached during the ice ages: Ohio, Indiana, and Illinois. It is also found in southern Michigan and Wisconsin, but the vast majority was deposited in Upper Michigan and especially the Keweenaw Peninsula.

The earth went through a warming phase known as the Pleistocene, when vast quantities of water were locked in frozen ice sheets—so much so that at one time global sea levels were 300 feet (91 m) below where they are at present. The ice melted rapidly, releasing billions of tons of water in cataclysmic floods.

Perhaps these dramatic natural events formed the geologic background for the numerous "deluge myths" common to virtually all human cultures around the world. Each has its own variation of the same apparent happening. A Pleistocene foundation for such flood legends was detected by John Shaw, a Canadian geographer at Queen's University in Kingston, Ontario. He studied drumlins (elongated or oval-shaped hills of glacial drift formed by currents of melting glaciers) near Livingstone Lake, in northern Saskatchewan. The examples he examined were tall and narrow upstream, and low and broad-tailed at the downstream end. He regarded the drumlin field as the result of a vast, turbulent flood of melt-water that surged beneath the ice sheet late in the last ice age. These formed pits filled with sand and debris carried by the flood. They were molded into hills that remain there today for human investigators to observe and "read" some 10,000 years later.

In the December 1989 issue of *Scientific American*, Tim Appenzeller observed, "Shaw estimated first the amount of ice that must have been removed to the cavities and then the amount of water it would have taken to erode them. He arrived at a figure of 84,000 cubic kilometers, about seven times the capacity of Lake Superior." The resulting flood emptied into the Atlantic and the Gulf of Mexico, supposedly raising worldwide sea levels by less than 10 inches (25 cm).

In fact, however, worldwide sea levels have risen 300 feet (91 m). But one doesn't have to be a geologist or geographer to notice the far-flung effects of floods that once covered the entire Upper Peninsula of Michigan. Where hillsides have been eroded or gravel taken from borrow pits, water-washed gravel layers are 50 feet (15 m). Only by expanding Shaw's findings a hundredfold do we begin to appreciate the full magnitude of the geologic panorama that long ago unfolded across the Upper Great Lakes Region. Massive floods and rains accompanied the end of the last ice age throughout a period of several thousand years, as retreating glaciers scoured the Earth's surface in some areas and left huge deposits of debris in others.

On Isle Royale and the nearby Keweenaw Peninsula of Upper Michigan, the post-glacial floods acted as a giant sluice to separate the gravel from heavier mineral. They washed the light sand and rock away from the copper, which is far heavier than iron. Assorted pieces of copper, from perhaps 100 tons (91 metric tons) to pieces the size of a fingernail, were left sitting exposed on the surface. Most of the small pieces would have been washed along with the gravel to be deposited elsewhere. Those weighing less than a hundred pounds (45 kg) could have been moved over great distances.

In those later years of the great pluvial meltdown, when water was everywhere, the world was transformed by water, but humans could travel anywhere by boat. Ocean-going vessels of one form or another may have sailed from southwest Asia to northern Australia as long ago as 30,000 years before the present. To such seafarers, their home was their ship, and they were known to the Ancient Egyptians (who referred to them as the Meshwesh) and Greeks (to whom they were remembered as the Pelasgians) as an earlier "Sea People."

Climate in the North Atlantic 8,000 years ago was tropical, warm, and balmy. Sea mammals cavorted along the edge of melting glaciers, providing food and clothing for the ancient mariners. These adventurers could travel anywhere on the globe, as proved by remains left by the so-called Red Paint People who voyaged from Britain's Orkney Islands to America's Eastern Seaboard. Visiting the Keweenaw Peninsula (then hardly more than a string of islands), they undoubtedly stumbled upon various-sized chunks of copper scattered about on the surface. What an amazing sight! Undoubtedly some of these early explorers recognized the shiny mineral. Small pieces of copper have been found southwest of the Caspian Sea, where they were used for needles and awls in early prehistoric times. Throughout the next thousand years after discovering the Upper Great Lakes, local inhabitants made sojourns to obtain this curious metal for the wanderers.

They would have been eager to show the foreign traders the greatest source of copper on Earth. Thus encouraged by this easy wealth, the alien visitors continued to return in ever-growing numbers. More explorers would have pioneered new water routes to such a unique source of mineral riches. Several good routes flowed from the south on river systems greater than anything known today. But following the glacial lakes from the west and eventually from the east, other options were likewise available.

Once found, they did their best to conceal all knowledge of these direct water routes from possible competitors. The world had entered the Copper Age, when anything pertaining to the valuable mineral was the ancient equivalent to modern industrial information. Demand for the superior metal grew. Foreign copper was already reaching the Egyptians before the Bronze Age, but they probably wore out more copper tools building the Great Pyramids than could be found in the Nile Valley. By 2800 BCE, India was using bronze (70 to 90 percent copper, 10 to 30 percent tin, with a dash of zinc). Soon, the rest of the civilized world followed.

Organized trade routes were developed, and a systematic large-scale method for handling copper was organized. By the early fourth millennium BCE, waterways across the whole Western Hemisphere were being extensively traveled, but only by the relatively select few who controlled the mining and shipment of North American copper.

Due to needful secrecy employed by the monopolistic enterprisers, word-of-mouth communication superceded all written records, and stories of transatlantic voyages for overseas riches became warped into unbelievable tales with each retelling, especially after all copper commerce came to an abrupt end when the Bronze Age collapsed around 1200 BCE. The so-called Red Paint People (the marine archaic culture) left evidence of their maritime skills on both sides of the Atlantic. The seafaring Celts, from the British Isles and southern Iberian Peninsula, were equally capable of transoceanic voyages. In 1898, a tablet covered with Minoan script from the Eastern Mediterranean island of Crete was found near Newberry, Michigan. At Peterborough, Ontario, not far from Gwinn, Michigan, Ocram and Tifinag inscriptions belonging to Old Irish and pre-Viking Norse were discovered. Any one or all of these peoples, and more, could have sailed to Upper Michigan to mine its prime deposits of the world's highest-grade copper. But from which way did they come, and how could they handle such immense chunks of copper? To begin with, the ancient seafarers possessed a workable knowledge of astronomy, navigation, metallurgy, and ship-building. The same people who transported 300-ton (272 metric tons) obelisks over long distances to raise them perfectly upright, built the bronze Colossus of Rhodes as high as our Statue of Liberty, and constructed the Great Pyramid, likewise moved and cut up 30-ton (27 metric tons) pieces of copper.

The Bronze Age Europeans and Near-Easterners did not skimp on their use of copper. They had 4-, 5-, and 6-ton (3.6, 4.5, and 5.4 metric tons) rams jutting from the prows of their warships. They provided 30 to 50 pounds (14 to 23 kg) of armor for each foot-soldier, and some of their armies were 300,000 strong. They made chariots, furniture, statues, and household decorations with bronze.

Long after the large pieces of copper from Isle Royale and the Keweenaw were gone, the miners kept digging. As they dug for smaller pieces, they excavated larger ones 5 to 10 feet (1.5 to 3 m) underground, and later 15 and 20 feet (4.6 and 6 m) down. They worked them free, then raised them out of the mine on platforms, cut them down to size, and hauled them away. Several such massive copper boulders were found by modern miners in pits 20 and 30 feet (6 and 9 m) deep, still standing on their cribbing, just as they were left there, more than 3,000 years before.

Eventually, techniques for processing iron were developed, and the demand for copper dropped off. When the first Europeans came to the Keweenaw, all they found were holes, large and small. These were pits obviously dug by some industrious, organized people a long, long time ago. There were many of them, everywhere dotting the surface of the land. The evidence was of such a colossal nature that 19th-century scholars knew there had to have been thousands of people involved, throughout centuries, if not millennia.

Theorists have generally settled on the figure of 5,000 ancient mines. But no one seems to have considered the many pits on the north shore of Lake Superior, nor the mines in the hills above the Mulligan Plains, 20 miles (32 km) east of Keweenaw Bay. There are also shafts south into Wisconsin and on Michipicaton Island, and still more on the Meggasy Bluff, near Marquette. Many were completely covered and rendered unobservable after 2,000 years. If all these other, unconsidered pits are factored in to estimates of the ancient mining enterprise, the amount of excavated copper must exceed the half-a-billion pounds usually said to have been removed in prehistory, perhaps by as much as another 50 percent. Modern mining started in the mid-19th century. During the summer of 1844, the first shaft was sunk near Lake Fanny Soo at Copper Harbor on the north end of the Keweenaw Peninsula. Engineers uncovered a vein that proved to be the celebrated black oxide ore that yielded 86 percent pure copper. In their first winter of operations, they removed 26 tons (24 metric tons) of ore. The mine was opened by John Hayes, who discovered the Cliff Mine the following November 18. The cliff was famous for being the first mine in modern times to yield the purest native copper in the world.

A few months later, Hayes found a piece of copper weighing 3,100 pounds (1,406 kg). Later, his men unearthed an 81-ton (73 metric tons) mass of copper. At the time, state-of-the-art furnaces were unable to handle these immense pieces of copper. How, then, were the ancient miners supposed to have used such prodigious specimens? Is it even conceivable that they possessed a technology more advanced than that invented in the Industrial Age? Hayes sailed to England for help.

To demonstrate his dilemma before leading mining engineers, he brought a single copper bolder weighing 3,852 pounds (1747 kg). Before it was sold to King's College on the Strand, the astounded British experts confessed they knew of no methods capable of working his unprecedentedly huge piece of copper. This and similar examples he left in England caused great excitement among scientists, especially geologists, as they had never dreamed such gigantic chucks existed, much less having been excavated by an unknown people in the deeply ancient past.

Returning to Pittsburgh in 1848, Hayes began his own construction of a new, special furnace he and his colleagues invented to handle the incredible tonnage of copper found in his mines. The top of the furnace was removed by a crane, then masses of copper were hoisted in by the same means. His invention proved to be a great success, and the unwieldy boulders were reduced to 10-pound (4.5 kg) ingots. The first batch was sold to Robert Fulton (of later steam-boat fame).

The Cliff Mine grew into a wildly profitable concern, earning $3,858,000 upon an original investment of $108,000 by its owners, the Pittsburgh and Boston Company, throughout a 10-year period, from 1846 to 1856. By 1864, the great Calumet and Hecla Mining Company was formed. Seven years later, it consolidated several other companies to become the most successful enterprise of its kind. Dividends paid every year between 1870 and 1929 amounted to $106 million.

There were more than 80 other mines working the range that collectively produced 90 percent of the world's supply of copper for about 25 years. Much of the copper was freed by huge stamping mills producing millions of tons of "stamp sand." Even today, many beaches of the Keweenaw are gray with finely ground stamp sand. Later, tons of it were reworked to yield 3 percent and sometimes as high as 7 percent or more copper. The last such venture was the White Pine Mine, near Ontonagon. It was yielding 1 percent copper from miles of underground roadways.

But the profit margin eventually became too narrow, and, with more economical surface mines in Utah, Arizona, and Montana, it shut down as recently as 1997. Huge veins of pure copper still remain untouched in the massive syncline beneath Lake Superior from Isle Royale to the Keweenaw Peninsula—too deep and expensive to mine.

In fact, estimates have been made that in all the years of modern mining from the middle of the 19th to the very end of the 20th centuries, only 3 to 7 percent of the native copper has been removed, and more than 90 percent remains unexcavated. Even now, gargantuan masses of pure copper are being located, some of them hundreds of times the weight of the famous Ontonagon boulder.

But nothing compares with the scope, magnitude, or mystery of the mining enterprise undertaken by a great, nameless people in Upper Michigan at the dawn of civilization.

A professional photographer commissioned by directors of the Smithsonian Institution to explore the Grand Canyon returned from his one-man expedition with more than they bargained for. He claimed to have found artificial corridors connecting immense chambers filled with metal, edged weapons and bizarre statues. Fully 100 years later, Smithsonian officials insist they know nothing about his discovery reported in a lengthy, detailed feature article by Arizona's major newspaper. Did the alleged chambers comprise a journalistic hoax, or were they part of a high-level cover-up that persists to this day?

UNDERGROUND CITY OF THE GRAND CANYON

By Frank Joseph

In autumn of 1908, Mr. G.E. Kincaid set out alone with his camera down the entire course of the Colorado River. The long, perilous trip had been successfully completed only once before, and never photographed. In his mid-50s, Kincaid was a native of Lewiston, Idaho, and the first white child born in that state. Although a hunter by profession, he had already

Archæological Discoveries of Ancient America

given 30 years service to Washington, D.C.'s famous Smithsonian Institution as a local explorer and photographer, so he was the right man for the journey.

On an early October morning, he pushed off in his small, covered boat loaded with provisions and tins of film across Wyoming's Green River, a branch of the Colorado. Before his arrival in Yuma, Arizona, late that following winter, he had taken more than 700 images of lofty cliffs, bizarre geologic formations, unfamiliar wildlife, and shoreline not visually documented until then. His personal quest was among the last of the great, one-man expeditions—in the tradition of Joliet or Marquette—through the remaining, little-known territories of North America. But what he found in the Grand Canyon backwaters would ignite a sensation that had nothing to do with conventional exploration.

Kincaid was about 42 miles (68 km) up the Colorado River from El Tovar Crystal Canyon when he noticed unusual stains covering the east wall of a monumental sedimentary formation, about 2,000 feet (610 m) above the river bed. Landing to investigate, he began the difficult climb, eventually reaching a rock-shelf outcropping. Some distance behind it he saw the tall entrance to a cave not visible from the river 1,486 feet (453 m) below. But what astonished him far more than the gaping hole was a flight of stone steps running approximately 30 yards (27 m) to, he assumed, a much higher, former level of the river. The existence of these stairs in this exceedingly remote, unvisited, and unchartered part of the world stunned Kincaid. Almost in a trance of disbelief, he ascended them to the 8-foot-high (2.4 m) mouth of the cave. But he halted there. The darkness inside was impenetrable.

He hastily returned to his boat, then made the arduous ascent again, this time armed with pistol and lantern. Cautiously entering the cave, he progressed several hundred feet through what appeared to be a man-made passageway, until arriving at a large chamber containing the mummified remains of several human corpses. One of these he stood upright in the glare of his lantern for a photograph. Gathering several unspecified relics from the floor of the crypt into his leather knapsack, Kincaid completed the remainder of his trip to Yuma as quickly as possible.

Immediately after his arrival, he dashed off a detailed report of his discovery (together with the mummy photograph and relics) to directors at the Smithsonian Institution. Professor S.A. Jordan was so impressed by these materials that he arranged instant funding for a Grand Canyon expedition headed by himself. He arrived with a dozen fellow professionals in late February, 1909, and Kincaid led them directly to the cave. What they allegedly found there far outstripped their expectations and represented the most important, if not stupendous, discovery in the history of archaeology.

Following Kincaid into the long passageway, the Smithsonian scientists, carrying bright electric lamps, found that it ended in a huge chamber. Numerous corridors, featuring dozens of smaller rooms, spread out at varying lengths in every direction from it like the uneven spokes of a wheel. The main hallway itself was approximately 12 feet (3.7 m) wide, but narrowed to about 9 feet (2.7 m) toward its extremity. Inside, less than 60 feet (18 m) from the cave entrance, corridors opened on both sides to several rooms with dimensions approximately 10 by 12 feet (3 × 3.6 m). Some were larger, however, measuring 40 feet square (3.7 square m). Their peculiar doorways were oval-shaped, and ventilated by perfectly circular holes cut into the 3-foot 6-inch-thick (107 cm) walls. Nothing resembled natural formations, because the passageways and chambers were all uniformly cut into squarish and linear designs laid out with precision in apparently standard forms of measurement.

As some indication of the scope of the engineering enterprise, the central chamber had been hewn out of solid rock 1,480 feet (451 m) under ground, and two passageways measured 634 and 854 feet (193 and 260 m) in length. One particularly long corridor the explorers investigated led to several round chambers, possibly granaries, still containing a variety of seeds. The largest storehouse was 12 feet (3.7 m) high, with copper hooks from which access ladders may once have been hung. But most of the dozens of chambers searched by the Smithsonian investigators were empty, save occasionally for what appeared to be water vessels made of fired clay. However, an immense room, some 40 by 700 feet (12 × 213 m), filled with what looked like cooking utensils, they took to be an important dining hall. Some smaller rooms were filled with a profuse variety of pottery and urns running the full manufactured gauntlet from crude, undecorated clayware to enameled and glazed receptacles, to vases and cups of copper, and even gold.

Copper, in fact, dominated most of the ornaments, weapons, and tools found throughout the subterranean complex. These included at least hundreds of bracelets, headgear, rings, chisels, saws, reamers, hammers, swords, axes, breastplates, shields, arrowheads, and spear-points. The weapons and tools were of hardened copper, a process perfected in the ancient Near East and Europe. This technique became a lost art after the fall of Classical Civilization, 15 centuries ago.

Kincaid led Professor Jordan and his awestruck colleagues back to the so-called crypt, where he had photographed the propped-up mummy a few months earlier. Peculiarly, the walls of this large chamber angled backward by 35 degrees. The interior was surrounded by stone tiers, upon which reposed an unspecified number of mummified human cadavers. All of them were adult males encircled by copper urns and fragments of broken swords. Their mummification process was unusual: All the corpses had been wrapped in fabric made of bark fibers, and clay covered some of them.

Professor Jordan dubbed the majority of artifact-filled chambers "barracks," because they featured mostly military objects and weapon-stores. But the single most dramatic find he and his fellow Smithsonians made was little more than 100 feet (30 m) from the cave opening, in a corridor perhaps three times as long. Here the brilliant beams of their lanterns fell across the life-sized stone statue of a robed man with Asiatic facial features sitting cross-legged on a raised platform, while holding a lotus flower in either hand. He was flanked on both sides by the sculpted representations of a cactus with arms extended. Perhaps a dozen smaller idols encircled the statue and its cacti. These were divided between beautifully wrought god-like and demonic images. Everything had been carved from a lovely, though hard, marble-like stone.

The underground city was awash with hieroglyphs, covering walls, doorways, urns, tools, weapons, ornaments, and, most commonly, stone tablets—perhaps by the thousands. Although some in the Smithsonian party were fundamentally conversant in Egyptian hieroglyphs, they were unable to decipher the cave's numerous inscriptions. During their first attempt at surveying the subterranean site, and to prevent disorientation in the labyrinthine complex, the investigators strung wires from the cave's entrance throughout every corridor leading to the larger rooms.

Returning to Yuma, Professor Jordan announced at a press conference that another, larger expedition, comprising 30 or 40 archaeologists, geologists, surveyors, and photographers, was being prepared for a major scientific assault on the cave and its contents. The site itself, he said, was already protected, because of its remote location on government-restricted land, where unauthorized visitors would not be allowed public access "under penalty of trespass."

And that is all that has been heard of the lost underground city in the Grand Canyon ever since. Kincaid's photo of the mummy (to say nothing of the hundreds of photographs Jordan's crew presumably made inside the caverns) and the relics sent to the Smithsonian have vanished. Everything known about the alleged discovery was published as the front-page story of a prestigious newspaper still in circulation, *The Arizona Gazette*, on April 5, 1909. Its headlines read, "Explorations in the Grand Canyon. Mysteries of Immense Rich Cavern Brought to Light." Photocopies of the original report are available from the Yuma publisher.

Inquiries made to the Smithsonian brought nothing to light regarding Jordan's promised full-fledged investigation of the cave, and not even anything about the professor himself, nor the man who allegedly found the site, G.E. Kincaid. Spokesmen for the venerable institution claim no knowledge of such a discovery. Was the whole story just a hoax concocted by *The Arizona Gazette*? That does not seem likely, if only because it repeatedly cited the Smithsonian as having funded the expedition. No editor would have left him- or herself so vulnerably open to legal prosecution by falsely involving such an influential organization, which, in fact, never took action against the newspaper. Why? Because the report was true?

According to the president of the World Explorers Club, David Hatcher Childress, in his book *Lost Cities and Ancient Civilizations of North America*:

> While it cannot be discounted that the entire story is an elaborate newspaper hoax, the fact that it is on the front page, names the prestigious Smithsonian Institution, and gives a highly detailed story that goes on for several pages, lends a great deal to its credibility. What appears to be going on in this case is that the Smithsonian Institution is covering up an archaeological discovery of great importance, and radically challenges the current view that there was no transoceanic contact in Pre-Columbian times.

Is the idea that ancient Egyptians came to the Arizona area in the ancient past so objectionable and preposterous that it must be covered up? Perhaps the Smithsonian Institution is more interested in maintaining the status quo than rocking the boat with astonishing new discoveries that totally overturn the previously accepted academic teachings. Though the idea of the Smithsonian's covering up a valuable archaeological find is difficult to accept for some, there is, sadly, a great deal of evidence to suggest that the Smithsonian Institution has knowingly covered up and "lost" important relics.

Childress goes on to describe how stone coffins discovered at the end of the 19th century, in Alabama, but suggestive of ancient Near Eastern origins, were sent to the Smithsonian for analysis. Sometime thereafter, the Smithsonian's head curator of the Department of Anthropology, F.M. Setzler, wrote, regarding the coffins, "We have not been able to find the specimens in our collections, though records show that they were received."

During World War II, human cranial remains were accidentally bulldozed to the surface by U.S. Army engineers engaged in building an airstrip on the Alaskan island of Shemya, in the Aleutians. Some of the skulls evidenced artificial head-deformation, as the Mayas performed on their royal infants in far away Yucatán. The remains were carefully packaged and sent to the Smithsonian Institution, where they too were duly received and promptly lost. As the renowned investigator Ivan T. Sanderson asked of its directors, "Is it that these people cannot face rewriting all the textbooks?"

Childress suggests that the Grand Canyon find might represent a double-barreled threat to conventional thinking. He points out that Kincaid:

Archæological Discoveries of Ancient America

...discovered the vaults about 2,000 feet (610 m) above the present level of the river, where steps led some 30 yards (27 m) to the *former* level of the river. That means that the Colorado River, by Kincaid's testimony, has cut some 1,910 feet (582 m) in the canyon since the time of the construction of the vaults. Normal geologic time would place human construction on the canyon walls at this level at easily tens of thousands, if not millions of years ago. Kincaid's testimony actually is evidence that much of the Grand Canyon was cut in a very short time during some cataclysmic Earth change, rather than the slow, steady millions of years claimed by Uniformitarian geologists. It is possible that a huge lake was drained down the Grand Canyon, thus causing the fast erosion.

Childress's "cataclysmic" interpretation is, in fact, not only credible, but absolutely necessary to explain the creation of the underground city 2,000 feet (610 m) up the side of a cliff face!

In an effort to determine the location of the site, he studied a common hiker's map of the Grand Canyon:

I was suddenly shocked to see that much of the area on the north side of the canyon had Egyptian names. The area around 94-Mile Creek and Trinity Creek had areas (rock formations, apparently) with names like Tower of Set, Tower of Ra, Horus Temple, Osiris Temple, and Isis Temple. In the Haunted Canyon area were such names as Cheops Pyramid, the Buddha Cloister, Buddha Temple [both referring to the Buddha-like stone statue Professor Jordan's party saw?], Manu Temple, and Shiva Temple. Was there any relationship between these places and the alleged Egyptian discoveries in the Grand

Canyon? Indeed, this entire area with the Egyptian and Hindu place-names in the Grand Canyon is a forbidden zone; no one is allowed into this large area.

A friend suggested, "That's got to be the place where the vaults are. Why else would it have these Egyptian names?" Childress wondered, "Wouldn't it be interesting if the explorer who gave this part of the Grand Canyon these Egyptian names was named Kincaid?"

But the site, if it really existed, appears to have been less Egyptian than Egyptian-*like*. Jordan and his fellow professionals supposedly found the hieroglyphs not difficult, but impossible to read. Although the site contained mummies, they were not embalmed in the Egyptian style, but wrapped in bark fabric, like the "Beaded Princess" entombed in an earth-mound at Aztalan, the Upper Mississippian ceremonial center of southern Wisconsin, or Guanche mummies found in the Canary Islands, off the coast of Morocco.

It is here that the Grand Canyon find begins to suggest another controversial subterranean location: Burrows Cave, in Illinois, with its Mauretanian or North African themes mixed with neo-Nile motifs and quasi-Egyptian hieroglyphs. Both Burrows Cave and Kincaid's Cave were piled high with similarly inscrutable and inscribed stone tablets. So, too, marble sculpture have been retrieved from Burrows Cave. The Asiatic-featured statue Jordan and company saw in the Grand Canyon was at least "marble-like." Although it suggested a Buddha figure to them, their description of the artwork seems more reminiscent of the Nile Valley deity, Bes. Portrayed in Egyptian temple art as an Asiatic dwarf similarly holding a lotus in each hand, Bes was the divine patron of war—appropriately enough, given the weapons found in profusion at the Colorado River site. The flowers he held signified the saving of life through self-defense. But the Grand Canyon version, featuring a ring of godly and demonic figures with flanking cacti, is not found in Egypt.

Could it be that the two widely separated locations were created by Mauretanian refugees from the Roman conquest of North Africa during the first century CE? Interestingly, a horde of Roman artifacts—including sword blades and Christian crosses—was found not that far away, near Tucson, Arizona, in 1924. In truth, Burrows Cave shares an even more fundamental relationship with the Grand Canyon site: No one knows where either of them are, nor can prove their existence.

Burrows Cave is not North America's only subterranean site for the discovery of ancient inscriptions. Less well known, but even more baffling are plates apparently imprinted with an unknown text resembling electrical circuitry. Are they, in fact, not examples of a written language, but evidence of an inconceivably high technology once possessed by the prehistoric inhabitants of North America?

INSCRUTABLE METALLIC TABLETS OF THE ROCKIES

By Jared G. Barton

In 1887, young George Keller and his Indian playmate, Lone Eagle, were romping through the foothills of the Rocky Mountains above a farm owned by George's father near Manti, Utah. The Kellers were the descendants of freed black slaves, who migrated to the American southwest following the Civil War. Coming to a massive overhang, the Indian boy pointed to a hole in the mountainside, and explained, "This is a special place, the Cave of the Great Spirit. My father says it is the holy place of a people who are dead, and that a great chief protects those who are buried there. My father was shown this place by *his* father when he was a kid. You are the only person other than our people who knows about this place.

You must promise not to tell anyone of our secret! Follow me and I will show you inside."

One of numerous metal plates covered with an unintelligible script from a cave in the Rocky Mountains of Utah.

After they entered the subterranean opening together, George stopped to pick up a few flint arrowheads from the cave floor. The boys then proceeded to cautiously explore the spooky interior.

In the years to come, George kept his promise and never told anyone about the chamber supposedly guarded by the spirit of a great Indian chief. Lone Eagle eventually moved away, and George went to work on the Keller farm, eventually taking up residence in a hillside shed not far away, relatively close to the cave of his boyhood experience in the east. But his subsequent visits to the site were infrequent, and he took no further interest in it, until he met John Brewer, many years later. Brewer lived with his wife in the small town of Moroni, Utah, where he did odd jobs for farmers in the area. For recreation, he collected Indian arrowheads, and, in time, he assembled an impressive collection. In early spring of 1955, his numerous artifacts were displayed at the Sanpete County fair, held annually at Manti. While discussing his finds with friends at a local cafe, he was approached by an elderly black man, who spoke of a secret cave where many more arrowheads were to be found. Approaching the end of his life, George Keller felt it wrong to die without sharing such information.

One of many stone boxes containing inscribed, metal tablets removed from a subterranean location near Manti, Utah.

As Brewer recorded in his personal journal for May 10, "I went and looked for the place but I couldn't find it, so I went and asked him [Keller] again where it was, but all that I could get was a laugh from him. I thought that he was pulling a fast one on me, so I let it go at that." Nine days later, "I went out to the Keller place, and offered him some wine with the promise that he would show me the place he had told me about a while back. He said that he would not only show me the place, but that we would go in! No wonder I couldn't find it; I was on the wrong hill. I went into the cave and found 30 arrowheads right off. I went back to the truck and thanked the man. I then asked how he came to know of the cave, and he said that he and an Indian boy played there as an old hideaway."

Nearly 20 years later, I got to know John Brewer in person. We met at Provo, Utah, in the company of Dr. Paul R. Cheesman, head of Book of Mormon Studies in the Department of Religion at Brigham Young University. Brewer impressed me as a soft-spoken, kindly man, but without much worldly experience. He told us about his encounter with old George Keller, and the difficulties he experienced while locating the secluded cave. In his search for more arrowheads at the site, he was surprised to find a set of stone steps carved into the cave floor. Clearing away some debris, he claimed the steps led to an entrance of a tomb.

Entering this chamber, he saw 10 stone boxes, and opened five of them, each containing small, metal plates inscribed with an unknown script. Nearby lay two large stone coffins. Opening them both, he found mummified human remains. One body allegedly had red hair with skin still attached to its bones, while the other was blond. The mummies were excessively large, he guessed some 9 feet (2.7 m) (!) in length. Brewer made a sketch of the tomb, in which he claimed to have carefully catalogued the position of each plate and box. In removing the coffin lids, he noticed that the mummies were covered with a straw "like cloth." He removed the straw only from the heads of the mummies to reveal their crown and breastplates. Shields and a sword were among other artifacts scattered about the tomb.

To prove his story, he showed us about 60 metal plates of various sizes and shapes. They all featured characters of an inscrutable written language. At least a few of the plates preserved by Brewer under a glass picture frame appeared to be made of gold. Another set, possibly bronze, was encircled by a metal band some 5 inches (13 cm) square. They were bound by a small metal ring opposite the band.

Brewer agreed to take a team from Brigham Young University to the tomb as soon as the snow melted. Spring and summer came and went in the Sanpete Valley, but Brewer made no effort to contact Dr. Cheesman. But word of the inscribed tablets had already become controversial, as gossip about the mysterious discovery spread throughout Manti. Respected BYU professors Dr. Hugh Nibley and Dr. Ray Matheny met Dr. Cheesman and Brewer, but were not favorably impressed with the self-styled discoverer, and condemned his find as a hoax.

Following their unsupportive reaction, an article entitled "John Brewer Has a Cave but He's Not Giving Tours," appeared in Salt Lake City's *Deseret News*. Dr. Jesse Jennings of the University of Utah's archaeology department was quoted as saying that the sandstone tablet obtained from Brewer was a "ridiculous hoax." Jennings referred to Dr. Ray Matheny, who said he "wasted his time exposing the man's works.... It is a clumsy attempt to perpetrate a fraudulent claim of antiquity. Only Dr. Cheesman had mixed feelings: 'They could be real.'"

But Dr. Robert Heinerman, a PhD in anthropology from the University of Indonesia, recalled that he had formerly lived in Manti around 1975, when he learned of the alleged artifacts. He visited Brewer at his home in Moroni, and heard the story of finding the cave with its bizarre contents. Unlike the BYU professors, Heinerman was more favorably impressed, and both men became close friends. Late one night, two years later, Brewer unexpectedly appeared at Heinerman's home and suggested they go off on a midnight hike. They drove to a quarry behind Temple Hill, in Manti, then walked south from the quarry, up the hill to its top, and finally across to the mountain in the east.

Brewer came to a halt, and instructed Dr. Heinerman to remove his shirt and pants, so he could squeeze into the tunnel if he wanted to see Keller's chamber. Dr. Heinerman stripped down to his skivvies, following Brewer into a tunnel that had been dug on a downward track, barely squeezing and squirming like a worm through the narrow passage. After what seemed an eternity, struggling through some 30 feet (9 m) of utter darkness, they came to an opening. Reaching down with his hands, Heinerman felt the edge of stairs. These led into a chamber about 20 feet (6 m) long and 14 feet (4.3 m) wide. The air was stifling, and breathing was difficult.

Several inches of fine dust covered the floor and puffed up with each step. Perhaps three dozen stone boxes were stacked against one wall, with another 20 or so on the other. All of them were wrapped with a cover of Juniper bark with pine pitch smeared all around, so as to make them waterproof. In a smaller antechamber were two entombed mummies. They seemed an incredible 8 or 9 feet (2.4 or 2.7 m) in length. Each had been placed in a cement sepulcher with removable lid. They were a male-female pair. The texture of their skin was almost moist, like tanned leather. Littering the cave was an abundance of weapons, swords, tools, and copper and metal tablets of various sizes. Some of the plates lay shattered like glass into fibrous pieces, not unlike the broken windshield of a car. Brewer stated the steps led into the chamber when he first discovered them. But the overhanging rock had since collapsed over the entrance, so he had to spend some two years digging a tunnel parallel to the stairs, in order to regain entrance into the cavity. This work had been accomplished after nightfall to conceal his activity.

Archaeological Discoveries of Ancient America

Heinerman visited the site several times thereafter with Brewer, always under cover of darkness, save only on one daylight occasion. The chamber, Heinerman remembered, was very warm during this daytime entry. Its interior was cool in winter, suggesting that the cave is not deep underground, with temperatures regulated by outside weather conditions. He claimed that a wall inside the chamber featured an illustration indicating the location of several other caves in the area. Using this map, Brewer discovered another cache, which he also showed to Heinerman.

After an arduous journey west of Wales, Utah, Heinerman stood before the entrance to a natural cave. It lay under an overhanging ledge with a small crawlspace underneath. The interior comprised several tunnels and chambers, where the two men found more stone boxes containing inscribed plates. Some of the boxes featured Mayan-type glyphs or illustrations, and weighed from 60 to 90 pounds (27 to 41 kg) each. In Heinerman's words, as he spoke them to me "the cemented stone boxes were highly decorated with ingenious art work." With great effort, a few of these containers were carried away. Heinerman still has several in his possession. He also owns a large number of the metal plates. He found additional metal weapons and tools similar to examples from the Keller site, but no mummies at the Manti Valley site. Another point of difference was a hunting scene depicted on a wall of the cave.

So far, Heinerman and Brewer are the only persons who claim to have explored both caves. No photographs of either interior, with their giant mummies and metal objects, have been released. Nor are the precise whereabouts of these sites known to anyone, save the two visitors. Until such time as professional investigators are allowed inside his supposed chambers, the authenticity of Brewer's finds cannot be established. But mitigating allegations of his involvement in a hoax are the items he presents on behalf of the cave's legitimacy. The finely made boxes with their inscrutable tablets do, indeed, exist. What are we to make of them? The sheer number and level of craftsmanship of these objects (beyond the abilities of Mr. Brewer to duplicate) should at least give us pause for reconsideration.

But the really troubling aspects of his claims are the alleged artifacts themselves. They appear to be exceptionally well made and very old, but belonging to no known culture—ancient or modern. If archaeologically authentic, they were the remnants of a thoroughly enigmatic people of which modern scholars are absolutely unaware. More unsettling, perhaps, some of the "script" more resembles modern computer schematics than any form of writing. Other red-haired mummies have, in fact, been found in the West, most notably at Nevada's Lovelock Cave.

Some may see in these questionable finds and unaccountable material evidence for Lemurians in ancient America. They were supposed to have been natives of a long-vanished civilization that dominated the Pacific with an advanced technology, until their islands were eventually engulfed by the sea, and a few of their wealth-laden leaders fled to the American West. Whatever the real identity of the Manti items, condemning them out of hand risks losing what may be our continent's most valuable cultural heritage. If ever properly validated and deciphered, they could release a prehistoric legacy far more valuable than the gold plates on which it was inscribed.

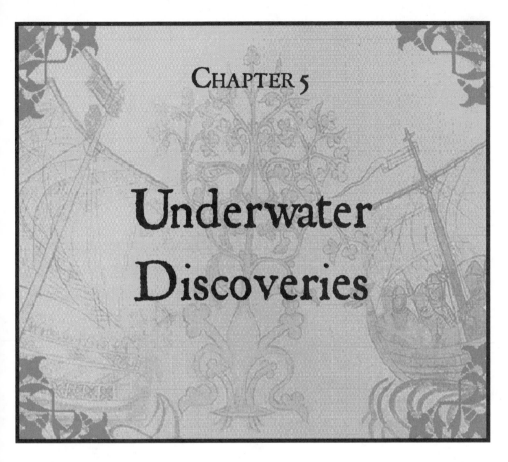

CHAPTER 5

Underwater Discoveries

*S*keptics who argue that no proof exists of visitors to America from the ancient Old World need only search the waters off the coast of New England
for evidence of pre-Columbian seafarers to our continent.

A ROMAN–ERA FIGURINE RECOVERED OFF NEW JERSEY

By Lloyd Hornbostel, Jr.

On April 15, 2004, a scuba diver was hunting shark fossils known to
strew the sandy sea bottom of New Jersey's Redbank River. In fact, it had
been known earlier as Shark River for the abundance of the animal's remains found in the area, some 10 miles (16 km) south of Sandyhook. But
what Nelson Jecas discovered was more than a common fossil.

141

Archaeological Discoveries of Ancient America

At approximately 15 feet (4.6 m) beneath the surface, in limited visibility, the 55-year-old Bernardsville resident fetched a strange, small object from the ocean floor. Returning to dry land, he saw that it was a figurine weighing about 18 ounces (.5 kg), and 4 inches (10 cm) long, carved from a reddish stone of some kind. Although severely eroded through apparently long exposure to underwater conditions, the item still clearly represented a woman atop a man, engaged in sexual intercourse.

Mr. Jecas took it for professional appraisal to New York's Arteprimitivo Auction House, where expert examiners specialize in classifying, buying, and selling ancient artifact collections. Saying nothing about the circumstances concerning its discovery, he showed the figurine to the auction house's gallery curator, Mr. Howard Rose, who, upon examination, easily identified the Shark River find as a common fertility image made in Roman Egypt during the third century CE. Mr. Jecas believes it probably belonged to an Egypto-Roman sailor who reached the New Jersey shore about 1,800 years ago.

The object is important physical evidence for ancient Old World contact in North America, supporting related discoveries along the eastern shores of our continent. South of the figurine found by Mr. Jecas, a man combing the Massachusetts coast with a metal detector near Beverly found eight Roman coins within 1 square yard of the beach. The relatively well-preserved coins were all minted during the fourth century, and identified by numismatologists as belonging to the reigns of emperors Constantius II (337–361 CE), Valentinianus I (364–375), Valens (364–378), and Gratianus (367–383).

According to epigrapher Dr. Barry Fell, in America BC, "As there were 58 emperors of Rome, who issued some 3,000 kinds of coins commonly found in Europe, the chances of a single find-site yielding coins of consecutive rulers spanning only four decades can be estimated as roughly one in one hundred thousand. Thus, the coins are not being found as a result of accidental losses by collectors, but are strongly correlated with some factor linked to a short time-span of 337 to 383 CE, and linked also to a single, very restricted find-site. The only reasonable explanation is that these coins are coming from the money-chest of a merchant-ship carrying current coin in use around 375 CE. Over the past sixteen hundred years, the coins have gradually drifted in-shore on the bottom current, and are now being thrown up by waves in heavy weather."

On March 25, 2001, the chief researcher of a large sunken structure in Japanese waters presented his findings at a special conference sponsored by the Japan Petrograph Society. Masaaki Kimura, PhD, one of Japan's foremost geologists with a world-class reputation, has been investigating the site the last four years. He was one of three speakers at the Fukuoka conference describing recent discoveries in underwater archaeology. As Professor Kimura makes clear, the man-made character of the drowned structure is no longer in question. Precisely who built it, however, is still debated.

A growing number of investigators, both in Japan and elsewhere, nonetheless conclude that the Yonaguni site is at least related to stories of a formerly great kingdom known as Mu or Lemuria, which was engulfed by a natural catastrophe in the ancient past. Lemuria was supposed to have been the homeland of Asian, Polynesian, and pre-Columbian American civilizations. In any case, the underwater find promises to make its effect on our understanding of civilized origins. The following is an interview conducted with Professor Kimura by Ancient American after the 2001 conference.

HAS THE LOST MOTHERLAND OF THE PACIFIC BEEN FOUND?

An Interview with Masaaki Kimura

Ancient American: Where is the sunken structure located?

Professor Kimura: It's in Okinawa Prefecture, near the island of Yonaguni, in the sea about 328 feet (100 meters) off Arakawabana. Yonaguni is an almond-shaped island at the southwest tip of the Ryukyu chain, approximately 6 miles (10 kilometers) long from east to west and 2.5 miles (4 kilometers) from north to south. Some 1,800 persons live there, making a living mainly from farming, fishing, and the tourist business.

AA: When was it discovered, and by whom?

PK: Local fishermen knew of rumors that there was a curious rock structure submerged in the sea for the past half-century or so, but it wasn't recognized as a relic. In 1986, while conducting a diving survey to map diving spots in the Yonaguni area, Kihachiro Aratake started calling it "Iseki Point," based on his impression that somehow it didn't seem to be a natural object. Then, when an underwater survey team of the University of the Ryukyus began to study it, it became widely known.

AA: What makes you believe that this structure is prehistorically man-made?

PK: There are many indications of human involvement. There is something like a road carved around it. In the level rock faces, there are a large number of tool marks. There is a feature that seems to be a drainage canal extending from top to bottom. There are walls angled at a fairly accurate 90 degrees, or right angles, that extend over distances of some tens of meters at several locations. It is surrounded by a stairway-like structure, not just on the south side, but all around. The north side structure shows the strongest indication of having been man-made. Furthermore, one part of it is a stonework stairway.

AA: Why is it under water?

PK: It was built on land, and then, because of global warming, the level of the oceans rose and left it submerged. Another factor to consider is crustal movements, but no concrete evidence of that has been discovered yet.

The man-made construction of Japan's sunken structure off the coast of Yonaguni Island is self-evident.

AA: When was it built?

PK: It was probably built somewhere before 6,000 and 8,000 years ago, possibly even 10,000 or more years ago. At that time, sea level was as much as 131 feet (40 meters) lower than it is now. [Professor Kimura has since revised his date parameters for the Yonaguni "Monument," which, he believes, was more likely submerged by rising sea levels around 3000 BCE, although he states that his much older time frames are still possible. —AA.

AA: What shape is it?

PK: It looks a little like a stepped pyramid with the top part removed; rather like a pedestal. At the base, the dimensions are about 820 feet (250 meters) on an east-west axis, and 492 (150 meters) along the north-south axis. It's a rectangular shape, and the height from the base to the apex is 83 feet (26 meters). The base is submerged 82 feet (25 meters) below sea level, leaving the tip exposed about 1 meter above sea level.

AA: How was it made?

PK: Using tools made from stone that didn't fracture easily, holes could be drilled into the rock, and a wooden or stone wedge, like an arrowhead, could be put in the hole to chip off the rock. This is one idea. We tend to think that people of that era, lacking metal tools, would be unable to cut stone. However, if you know the characteristics of the rock you are working, it can be comparatively easy to cut, or process.

AA: Are there any other submerged archeological relics in the world like the one at Yonaguni?

PK: There aren't any just like it, in the sense of being carved out of an entire knoll or rocky outcropping. However, in bays and lakes throughout the world, there are many submerged archeological artifacts. One good example is found at the Alexandria site, in the Mediterranean Sea. The Alexandria ruins date from a large-scale earthquake that occurred some 1,200 years ago, when a whole city sank below the sea. Such sinking occurs because of either crustal movement or earthquake, as in the Alexandria case, or a rise in sea level. Regarding Yonaguni's relics, it's quite likely that a rise in sea level was the key element.

AA: How about elsewhere on Yonaguni island? Is there anything that might be related to the underwater structure such as legends or records?

PK: Yes, there is. On the northern part of the island in the area fronting the sea there is an oral tradition that "long, long ago an island sank." Also, in the southwest, there is a traditional belief, or cult, known as the *Niraikanai*, and in that tradition, stories are told of an ancient continent sunk beneath the sea.

AA: For what purpose was the Yonaguni structure built?

PK: There is no definitive answer, but there are many theories. There is the fort theory, the place-of-worship theory, the mountain-castle theory (including the Gusuku castle of ancient Ryukyu legend), an underwater-grave theory, an idea that it might have been a quarry, and a pyramid theory, among the many explanations that have been suggested.

AA: Is there anything to indicate that continental sites have sunk in the past? Any proof that submergence can occur?

PK: Yes, there is. In the sea near the Yonaguni site, underwater caves are being discovered one after the other. Stalactites and stalagmites have been found in them. These caves are limestone rock formations that, because of rain water or the flow of rivers or streams, have had the weaker parts dissolved away. This process can only reasonably take place on land. The fact of their existence indicates that first they were on dry land, then they were submerged. On top of that, prehistoric tools have been discovered inside them.

AA: Is there any definitive proof that this structure is man-made?

PK: Conclusive proof is being discovered in rapid succession. By this, I mean things that show human beings were active there. Among the evidence are traces of marks that show that men worked the stone. There are holes made by wedge-like tools still called *kusabi* in many locations throughout the Ryukyu Islands. Around the outside of the loop road there is a row of rocks neatly stacked into a stone wall, each rock about twice the size of a man, in a straight line.

There are traces carved along the roadway that show some form of repairs were undertaken. The structure is continuous from under the water to land, and evidence of the use of fire is present. Stone tools are among the artifacts found underwater and on land. Stone tablets with carvings that appears to be letters or symbols, such as what we know as the "plus-sign" and a V-shape were retrieved from the sunken structure. From the waters nearby, stone tools were found. Two are for known purposes, but not the majority.

At the bottom of the sea, a relief carving of an animal figure was discovered on a huge stone. In two locations, implements that were conceivably used by people who lived there, such as tools struck from stone—very important evidence—have turned up one after the other. And the most convincing evidence is the next piece. Inscribed into San'ninu-dai, there is a large relief carving of a bird.

AA: Are there any other structures on land that might be related to the underwater one?

PK: Yes, the one usually talked about is at Sanninu-dai. From here to the submerged structure off Arakawabana, for a distance of about 1.6 miles (2.5 kilometers), there are what appear to be terraces that are man-made and spaced at sporadic intervals.

AA: What surveys have been conducted since 1986?

PK: After a preliminary investigation in 1992, the University of the Ryukyus has undertaken a consistent, continuous program of research. Studies relying on scuba diving have been conducted underwater, and surveys on land, too, have been carried out, as the main part of the program. In 2000, we made measurements using laser beams, multi-narrow beams, and airplanes. The survey team was put together in 1997. It consists of instructors at the University of the Ryukyus, together with students, and has welcomed the participation of other interested persons: Scholars and specialists from various related fields, journalists, and divers have been among a wide circle of contributors.

Some of them have been skeptical of any man-made hypothesis. From many points of view, energetic arguments are being put forth. Not all of the participants are Japanese. Professor Robert Schoch from Washington

University, and the well-known research-diver, Jacques Mayol, have also lent their varied talents to the survey process.

AA: Suppose that the structure is acknowledged as a submerged artifact. What significance would that recognition have?

PK: Human history, the history of civilization, would probably have to be rewritten to account for the existence of such stone construction on that large a scale in East Asia, so long ago.

William Donato is the world's foremost authority on the so-called Bimini Road, a 1,200-foot-long (366 m) stone structure 19 feet (6 m) beneath the surface of the Atlantic Ocean, 55 miles (89 km) east of Miami, discovered in 1968 off the northern point of the Bahamian island of Bimini. Since 1989, his several dozen on-site expeditions—often with state-of-the art research instruments—consistently debunk mainstream insistence that the formation is nothing more than a natural arrangement of beach rock. More importantly, Donato demonstrates that the sunken ruin belonged to a maritime civilization whose far-ranging seafarers made a lasting impact on human prehistory in the Northern Hemisphere.

BIMINI: THE "ROAD" TO DISCOVERY
By William Donato

The validity of a theory is dependent upon the quality of information supporting it. Conversely, any criticism of such a theory, by its very nature, must have at its foundation undeniable and verifiable facts that render a proposition unlikely. If the hypothesis employs inaccurate, incomplete, or falsified data, then the balance may shift to lend greater weight to an alternate theory. According to such criteria, the "Bimini Road" is unquestionably an archeological site, though neither a "road" nor a "wall," despite its initial, more popular designation when far less was known about it. The "Bimini Breakwater" might be a somewhat more accurate appellation. More than 30 years of sporadic research with varying methodologies have wrung from the controversial site tangible results that cannot simply be dismissed because they challenge the current paradigm about the development of civilization.

At 19 feet (6 m) beneath the surface of the Atlantic Ocean, this cut stone block features a man-made notch as part of monumental construction at the Bimini Road.

In a combined Association for Research and Enlightenment Advanced Planetary Explorations (Virginia Beach, Virginia) research project, a new investigation was undertaken that focused on the Bimini Road, Proctor's Road, and the Andros Platform. Doctors Greg and Lora Little completed initial investigations at the last-mentioned site and at what may be a temple structure on land, also at Andros, largest of the Bahama Islands.

Archaeological Discoveries of Ancient America

The increasing tempo of Bahama discoveries in areas as far separated as Bimini, Andros, Cat Island, and Anguilla Cay seem to describe a widespread cultural phenomenon with clear historical and archeological implications of no small importance. The current official date for man's first arrival in the Bahamas is about 600 CE, a surprisingly recent time frame. Their earliest known inhabitants, the Ciboney, left remarkably little in the way of material culture, whereas the later Arawaks are better represented archeologically.

Several decades ago, maverick investigator Herbert Sawinski photographed a petroglyph in an underwater cave at Andros. Because of its position, Dr. Little and I realized that it must have been made long before 600 CE, even thousands of years ago, when sea levels were low enough to allow for the petroglyph's creation. When he attempted to relocate it, Dr. Little was informed by a local man that the area around the petroglyph had been filled in with sand, a common phenomena there.

Its rediscovery involved considerable labor, and though it would likely prove of greater antiquity than mainstream scholars believe possible, the petroglyph was not probably emblematic of some pre-Ciboney residents possessing a higher material culture needed to produce the massive stone structures underwater off shore. Unlike conventional archaeologists, Bahamian government officials are not opposed to extending the country's history further back in time, and have, in fact, been very supportive of such endeavors.

The first phase of our 2005 investigations entailed a fly-over of the Bimini Road/Proctor's Road area to give us a perspective on its location, extent, and possible anomalies worth investigating. Proctor's Road is about a mile north of the Bimini Road, closer to shore, and consists of lines of stones of differing shapes and sizes crossing several geological zones. Island Air flew us to Bimini, and our plane circled the target area several times, allowing us to get good video coverage and photographs (due to the exceptional clarity of the water), which came in quite handy later on.

Eslie and Krista Brown provided boat and diving services, taking us to Proctor's Road the next day (May 4), where we snorkeled, photographed, and videotaped a large number of stones with holes in them. These included natural formations, coring holes, and at least eight stones that Dr. Little noted resembled Mediterranean anchors. The lines of stone seemed far more haphazard than they had from the air, and appeared to be of generally unmodified shapes, with some exceptionally large boulders interspersed among them. A few stones featured what could have been mortises. Five arrangements of circles of stone resembling Mediterranean mooring elements (as at Coso, Italy), were photographed by Dr. Little and his wife, Lora.

Next, we scuba-dived on the Bimini Road, following up on its inner edge, looking for a wedge-shaped specimen resembling a leveling stone I photographed back in 1977. We failed to relocate it (the road is as long as four football fields laid end to end), though Greg found a stone of similar configuration. Our inability to locate this and the artificial Donnie's Stone (named after its discoverer, diver Donnie Fields) was due in no small part to the amount of sand covering the site. I was able to relocate the stone Rebikoff had discovered, its cut resembling one fashioned by a trenching machine. We were especially fortunate to document several areas with two and three courses of stone, something critics said did not exist.

On the body of the J-shaped terminus there were numerous large blocks supported by smaller stones, generally in the center. One of these was almost square, with another supported by a rectangular slab. Especially noteworthy was an arrangement of three similarly sized rectangular slabs leaning against each other at a diagonal angle on the northern side of one of those larger stones supported by a smaller one. Dr. Little photographed another example with a U-shaped (semicircular) hole cut through the bottom that could have served a conduit function of some kind. Other areas also appeared to exhibit a sort of inverse corbelling—overlapping stones extending out almost like steps.

May 5 was to be the most archeologically significant day in the history of the Bimini Road, as more artifacts were discovered in less than one hour than all previous searches in their entire expeditions. At the curve of the J, I observed that the outer periphery was defined by large, similarly sized rectangular blocks clearly placed in an actual arc, for which no geological argument can account. If these were several courses higher they would clearly serve the purpose of a breakwater. Heading up the inside curve of the J, I discovered a generally square 3-foot 5-inch (104 cm) stone with a U-shaped mortise. There is no doubt as to its archeological identity.

Several feet away, the Littles documented a stone resembling a Mediterranean anchor.

We followed the body of the J north, kicking across it to the outer edge. I noticed a beige/tan siltstone shaped like the broken segment of an arch with a 7-inch (18 cm) cut straight across it varying from 3/4-inch (2 cm) to 1 1/8-inch (3 cm) in depth, with an edge that was clearly intentionally smoothed. Swimming to the J's edge, I saw a flat, slightly curved stone partially under another, and signaled to my colleagues. Dr. Little began cleaning off the outside, and we both pulled out stones in the sand. Most were black and of a composition I never before encountered at the road. I then noticed similar stones on the opposite side and behind me, and wrote to Dr. Little on the dive slate: "These are all artifacts!"

He surfaced with our collection, and asked me, back on deck, what I thought they might be. I said they appeared to be related to granite. Similar stones found by Ron Smith at nearby Cat Island the previous year were identified as black granite by a geologist at the University of California-Davis. A retrieved sample Dr. Little later had analyzed back in the States turned out to be a hard "contact metamorphic" stone (gray marble) designated *biosparite* and native to the Bahamas, but not the Bimini area. It implies that whoever built the road most likely belonged to a native population and knew where various types of stone may be found. Another specimen was similar to either volcanic stone or a geode, according to the head of a college geology group staying on South Bimini. The black stones had been artificially shaped, and some showed small, fine cuts. One resembled a fireplace brick, several others were like pieces of broken, rectangular slabs, and another could have passed for a large, irregular doorstop!

Following our expedition to Bimini, we sailed for Andros on May 6 in water rarely more than 20 feet (6 m) deep. Two days later, we dove on the Andros Platform. It covers a far greater expanse and shows much less disturbance than the Bimini Road, and appears to rise in low tiers the farther one goes out. The stones are fitted close together—barely an inch apart in some places—and there is a definite terminus about 100 feet (30 m) from shore at the southern end. The harbor inside has silted in to a great extent. I had difficulty determining where it ended to the north, as the stones seemed to fade under the seabed. When I probed with a rod, it would barely go down a few inches before hitting stone over most of the feature—significantly different from Bimini. Some of the smaller stones filling in the spaces between the larger ones were slightly deeper, as if to form small drainage rivulets.

On May 9, we met with a group of geologists staying on South Bimini. They offered their opinions of our retrieved samples. Atypically, the head of the group thought that the Bimini Road was artificial! We headed back to Proctor's Road and then to the J for more dives. On the third dive, we began at Rebikoff's Pier, an underwater formation named after Dimitri Rebikoff, the late pioneer scientist at the Bimini Road. I recognized a coring hole that had been drilled by Joan Hanley, another independent researcher, in 1993. A marine geologist subsequently determined that the stone was not natural beach rock.

The following Tuesday, we descended twice more on the J to document a pair of coring holes on adjacent blocks at the western side. We also saw what appeared to be a sort of pavement pattern of small, flat, irregularly shaped stones, which I indicated to Lora, who videotaped while I photographed. She and Dr. Little concluded our activity with a final overview of the site from the surface vantage-point of being towed behind our expedition boat.

Skeptics of the Bimini Road's man-made identity have primarily restated the positions of two alleged authorities (with no background in archaeology at the time) without evaluating their work with a critical eye, apparently because they supported their ideology. But ideology is not science. It is opinion. Critics state that the Bimini Road is a single-layered Pleistocene beach rock feature of local and recent formation parallel to the beach without any evidence of man-made influences. None of that is true. When a coring was extracted in 1993, I asked the marine geologist in charge of the drilling if it was beach rock, to which he simply replied no, and none of our samples have ever been found to be beach rock.

Also, the feature is not parallel to the beach. Rebikoff's Pier (the two parallel, inward lines) are 7 degrees out of alignment with the ancient beach line, and the J is another 7 degrees (a total of 14) off—an astronomically remote statistical possibility for a "natural feature," but likely if placed there by man.

Micrite was found by both Dimitri Rebikoff and author Dr. David Zink. Micrite requires the presence of rainwater to have come about, and clearly cannot form in a tidal zone, like beach rock. Neutron activation analysis, which showed significantly less trace elements than the sea bottom or beach rock (as would be expected if it was on the surface without seawater percolating slowly through it), is dismissed—with no valid explanation. Adjacent stones with differing forms of crystalline calcium carbonate (aragonite and sparry calcite) show formation in different environments.

The area of the road is flat, and not on a slope, which would be a prerequisite for beach rock formation. Furrow spacing between road stories is of two patterns—27 inches to 31 inches (69 to 79 cm), and 4 inches to 6 inches (10 to 15 cm), while the beach rock is 11 inches (28 cm). Road stones above a fracture in the ocean floor are diagonal to instead of coinciding with it. The curve of the J is composed of similarly sized stones set in an arc—hard to justify by a geological argument.

The most flagrantly false statement about the road is that it is made of only a single layer of stones. This assertion is easily disproved by simply swimming at the bottom along the inside of the J, where numerous examples of two and three (and more) layers are readily apparent. In 1998, Donnie Fields discovered the Trinity Stones near the curve of the J. These are three stones sitting directly atop one another with the middle stone showing clear modifications. Beach rock is a single-layer phenomenon. The critics' cursory and limited observations are obvious. Dimitri Rebikoff, who had extensive familiarity with Mediterranean harbor works, noted that the road used the same live rock foundation engineering system.

Dr. Little's research has shown that the peculiar "reverse J" shape is also found at Atlit and Dor in the Eastern Mediterranean. A minimum of five stone circles at Proctor's Road likewise correspond to mooring facilities in the Mediterranean. Dr. Little's observation of stone anchors identical to Mediterranean (even Minoan) anchors can hardly be coincidental.

Archæological Discoveries of Ancient America

In the 1970s, Dr. Zink's expeditions discovered a "tongue and groove" stone, the keystone, a drilled stone, a piece of modified marble, and a metate cemented into the ocean floor (suggesting Native American associations). In the early 1990s, Donnie Fields discovered a stone with a projecting tenon, rounded corners, and an indentation analogous to Zink's keystone. I examined it *in situ* and noted extensive tool marks, that it was setting on another stone, and was next to a line of larger stones.

In 1995, dive master Bill Keefe retrieved a rectangular stone with tool marks and a unique triangular paraboloid mortise from Rebikoff's Pier. Researchers at the University of Colorado, in Denver, analyzed a piece, determined that it did indeed feature tool marks, and had apparently been walked on for a long time, like a step.

I have personally documented several mortised and tenoned stones that show extreme erosion. These items are of a unique style that often have rounded and angled mortises and tenons, demonstrating a superior knowledge of stress factors. All of them were found either on or near the Bimini Road. The items we found on May 5, 2005, were actually in the road, apparently broken items used as a sort of fill. This find directly associates artifacts with the Bimini Road.

Absence of any professional archaeological background on the part of the critics, as well as the limited scope of their investigations and flawed observations, throw their analysis into serious question. Our analyzed samples have never shown any obvious bedding planes, yet skeptic Eugene Shinn's major argument was of bedding planes from his 4-inch (10 cm) corings, which he now says one can't determine from 4-inch corings! He initially stated that, of 19 corings (two carried out on the shore), in two locations, less than 25 percent showed bedding planes in 1978. But in a 1980 *Nature* article, he stated that *all* of the corings showed bedding planes, which they didn't. The bulk radiocarbon dates, which he placed under the direction of a student, he now admits aren't reliable.

Although most of the road stones are variations of limestone, the presence of "intrusives" (granite, marble, micrite, metamorphic stones, and so on) strongly indicates importation, and thus a human hand in its formation. Geological and archeological data clearly show that the Bimini Road is man-made, probably the remnant of some port facilities, and similar in structure to analogous Mediterranean constructions. There is one difference: The Bimini harbor works are likely older. Uninformed critics who do not take our investigations seriously often possess their own, extra-scientific agendas. They have succeeded in doing something no credible or ethical scientist would ever do: slanting the data to fit their preconceptions. And they did worse: They hindered proper scientific investigation, and used character assassination against anyone who opposed their position.

Questionable ideologies, poor observations, biased positions, sloppy research, a lack of serious scientific rigor, fallacious statements, and the reporting of false results do not make for good science. It makes for *no* science. For the last 30 years, the skeptics have tried to pass off their flawed opinions as facts. All we ask is that fair-minded observers examine the data. By that criteria, the independent investigators who endured decades of academic scorn for their efforts to establish the Bimini Road's archaeological validity are assured vindication.

><ᐧᐧ◆ᐧ◯ᐧ◆ᐧᐧ≺

Wisconsin Indians residing in the vicinity of their most sacred lake between Milwaukee and the state capitol at Madison told early-19th-century pioneers of a "city of the dead" hidden beneath its murky depths. Since then, divers have searched for the elusive necropolis with varying degrees of success. By way of introducing readers to this uniquely compelling site, a chronological outline highlights its origins, ruins, and the human effort to find them.

A Rock Lake Time Line

By Frank Joseph

12,000 to 10,000 BCE—A retreating glacier carves out a small valley, depositing an oval-shaped lake (hardly more than a pond) 30 feet (9 m) deep, approximately 100 feet (30 m) long from north to south, and perhaps 75 feet (23 m) wide. Some time thereafter, a powerful river runs from west to east no more than half a mile due north of the lake. As the glacial mass continues its retreat, southern Wisconsin rebounds, dropping 1 foot (30 cm) per century. This subsidence gradually spills waters from the northern river into the glacially created valley and its little lake, deepening and widening it in time.

3000 to 1200 BCE—The original volume of the lake increases by another 30 feet (9 m), maintaining its new level for at least several centuries. Around its expanded shoreline, the earliest known man-made stone structures appear in the configuration of tent-like burial mounds averaging 100 feet (30 m) in length.

1200 to 200 BCE—Lake levels increase again and hold steady at 40 feet (15 m). Additional stone structures appear: conical mounds, at least one ridge-top mound, and walled village sites.

200 BCE to 1000 CE—Lake levels rise another 10 feet (3 m). New structures appear around the expanded shoreline: effigy mounds, sundials, stone circles, and a 900-foot (274 m) delta-mound.

After 1000 CE—Mostly unwalled village sites appear, as well as one known walled precinct of circular foundations, garden beds, effigies, and some stone cairns.

1820s—Modern Europeans artificially raise lake levels by about another 10 feet (3 m), submerging all sites still remaining above water. Resident Winnebago Indians tell white newcomers of sunken "rock tepees"—hence, "Rock Lake."

1890—A 40-foot (12 m) mound at the south shore of Rock Lake is demolished to make way for a train trestle. During the course of the earthwork's destruction, unknown thousands of human bones are found and discarded.

Summer 1901—Claude and Lee Wilson discover an underwater "pyramid" while boating during a severe drought. Their find is verified by numerous residents of Lake Mills, the town bordering Rock Lake.

1915—State archaeologist Charles Brown surveys and excavates the last of thousands of burial mounds that surrounded the perimeter of Rock Lake before housing construction destroys them. He uncovers the grave of a man buried with mining tools from Michigan's Upper Peninsula.

Winter 1930—A German nanny crossing on foot to her employer at the opposite shore of Rock Lake peers through the clear ice to see "an amphitheater" deep in the water.

1933 to 1935—The first scientific investigation of Rock Lake is undertaken by schoolteacher Victor Taylor, and funded by the State of Wisconsin.

1937—Max Gene Knohls tries out his newly invented subsurface camera and Aqua-Lung in Rock Lake specifically to search for its "pyramids." He photographs what he claimed was a tall, stone structure shaped like an inverted ice-cream cone.

1941 to 1945—U.S.A.F. student bombardiers aboard training aircraft operating between Madison and Milwaukee claim to have seen pyramids in Rock Lake.

1967—Diving instructor John Kennedy runs into a ridge-top stone mound at 40 feet (12 m) below the surface of Rock Lake.

Late 1960s through late 1970s—Various diving teams from across the United States search in vain for any subsurface structures at Rock Lake.

1982—James Scherz, professor of civil engineering at the University of Wisconsin (Madison), working with local scuba divers in Rock Lake, discovers and surveys an apparent effigy mound with a distinctly triangular terminus.

1987—A man-made stone brick with ancient-style tool-marks is found in Rock Lake.

1989—Side-scan sonar equipment is deployed in Rock Lake. The first ridge-top mounds are found at 60 feet (18 m) below.

1990—Master diver Douglas Gossage finds a 40-foot-long (12 m), linear mound under 30 feet (9 m) of water in the southeast quadrant of the lake.

1991 to 1995—Numerous subsurface investigations of Rock Lake reveal approximately 11 different structures until deteriorating water clarity due to pollution makes further attempts at visual research impractical.

Archaeological Discoveries of Ancient America

1996–A team of scuba divers completing a documentary for NBC Television's *Unsolved Mysteries* series accidentally discovers and photographs the largest conical mound—protruding about 18 feet (5 m) above the silt bottom—thus far found in Rock Lake.

1998–Archie Eschborn, founder of Illinois's Rock Lake Research Society (RLRS), undertakes the first mapping of the lake floor with high-resolution sonar, revealing subsurface village sites, effigy mounds, and measurement of the delta formation.

1999–Near the south end of the lake, in shallow water, RLRS sonar operators discover a stone effigy resembling some fabulous creature not unlike a dragon.

2000–Professor Scherz finds another dragon effigy, this one on land, very near shore, and virtually identical to but much smaller than its underwater counterpart. Both effigies appear to memorialize local Native American belief that Rock Lake is inhabited by a monstrous "spirit guardian."

2001–Divers find two oval stone mounds, each about 8 feet (2.4 m) long, 7 feet (2.1 m) across, and 6 feet (1.8 m) high, in shallow water (about 10 feet [3 m]) off the northeast shore. Both structures had been observed and even photographed from spotter aircraft since at least the late 1980s.

2002–Aerial reconnaissance undertaken by RLRS cameramen over Aztalan, a nearby ceremonial city dated to the 13th century CE, reveals the outline of a triangular formation similar to the delta platform at the south end of Rock Lake.

2008–Water clarity vastly improves after years of agricultural runoff and housing construction pollution are finally brought under the control of civic-minded Lake Mills city officials, thereby improving subsurface conditions for divers in search of archaeological evidence.

Was a Viking "sunstone" found by a local boy diving beneath the surface of Rock Lake? The possibilities are intriguing!

THE CRYSTAL PYRAMID OF WISCONSIN'S ROCK LAKE

By Frank Joseph

Located in southern Wisconsin between Milwaukee in the east and the state capitol at Madison in the west, the figure-8-shaped body of water seems no different at first sight than any other recreational lake—on the surface, at any rate. But sitting in its depths is allegedly an ancient necropolis, a city of the dead, complete with circular family crypts, sundial-like pyramids, statues of turtles and headless men, and immense, stone mounds memorializing the long-deceased movers and shakers of a lost civilization. For the last 20 years, I have conducted well more than 100 dives into the lake, written several magazine articles and two books about it, and presented my findings in a number of public lectures.

Early endeavors undertaken by colleagues and me to document the elusive necropolis attracted local attention by 1989, when I was approached by a woman in her 70s who resided near the western shore of Rock Lake all her life, along with her husband, who had recently passed away. Since he was a boy, he saved all manner of curiosities picked up around and in the lake, until he owned a sizeable collection of knick-knacks at the time of his death. His widow was kind enough to share them with me as possible artifacts belonging to the sunken structures we hunted. But there was no such evidence among the mollusk shells, rusted iron fragments, or vintage automobile license plates he left behind.

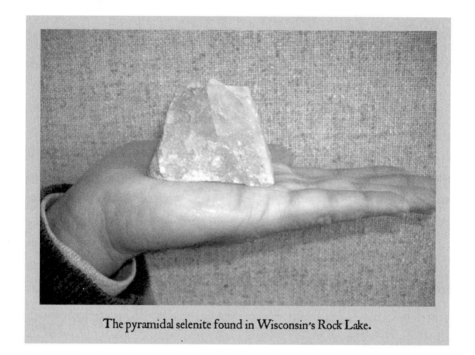

The pyramidal selenite found in Wisconsin's Rock Lake.

I was, however, sufficiently taken with an unusual, crystal-like rock the widow gave me, though it appeared to have absolutely no connection with or bearing on our research. The object weighs 9.4 ounces (266 grams) and is 1.9 inches (5 cm) in height. My fanciful imagination saw in its almost uniform measurements the man-made model of a Meso-american monument, even to the squarish knob at its summit, like an altar. Indeed, its undoubtedly circumstantial if uncanny resemblance to an actual Maya ruin—the El Puente Pyramid at Copan, in Hondu-ras—seemed remarkable.

I guessed the rock itself was a kind of common calcite, although its actual mineral composition eluded me. Unlike ordinary crystal, however, it did strange things with light. As an experiment, in an otherwise pitch-dark room, I photographed the presumed calcite while shooting it with a beam from my laser-pointer. Surprisingly, all the interior spaces of the stone went entirely aglow with amber light.

The widow told me her husband found the object during the summer of his 14th year while skin-diving further out in Rock Lake than he should have been. The squarish crystal, its top barely poking above the silt some 12 feet (3.7 m) beneath the surface, had glinted in the bright afternoon sunbeams that probed the clear depths, attracting his attention.

For the next 18 years after I received the gift, because of its roughly pyramidal form, I used the specimen as a paperweight keepsake of our underwater expeditions in search of much larger, if similarly configured, monuments, but rarely gave the souvenir another thought. Only in late summer 2007, on holiday in the Rocky Mountains of Colorado, was I made to notice it as never before. While casually browsing among the showcases and bins of local minerals displayed at an Estes Park rock shop, I chanced upon a large barrel filled with dozens of fragments identical to the crystal retrieved during the early 20th century from the bottom of Rock Lake. I asked the shopkeeper to tell me everything she knew about her abundant samples.

"That's selenite," she explained, "after the Latin name for the moon—Selene—because of its of pale, lunar appearance. Comes only from Kentucky."

"What about Wisconsin?" I asked.

"Not a chance."

Back home, I looked up "selenite" on the Internet to learn some peculiar things about it. Not only is this crystalline mineral found in Kentucky, but in a very special place—Mammoth Cave, the longest cave system known on Earth. It has more than 367 miles (591 km) of passageways, with new discoveries and connections adding several miles to this figure every few years. According to the National Park's official Website, the subterranean labyrinth has been visited since Paleo-Indian times.

But something extraordinary occurred there about 3,000 years ago. A people unrelated to the native populations who had tentatively poked inside the entrance for the previous 30 or so centuries penetrated the cave to more than a mile deep. They were not a handful of brave explorers, but a large numbers of miners, who excavated *tons* of selenite throughout the next 200 to 300 years. The identity of these hardy souls and why they ventured more than a mile into a dangerous network of underground passageways to perform strenuous labor are utterly unknown.

Could the selenite found in Rock Lake have been a trade good that made its way north into prehistoric Wisconsin from Kentucky's Mammoth Cave? More curiously, why would second-millennium BCE Americans have gone to the dangerous trouble of mining selenite by the ton? It does not appear among the ritual materials of historic tribal peoples, who preferred quartz crystal.

Returning to the Internet for answers, I learned that selenite is valued today, as it was in the past, as the essential component in optical instruments for both naval and aerial navigation, due to its special ability to refract and polarize light. Some historians speculate that pre-Christian Scandinavia's legendary "sun stones" that enabled the Vikings to cross vast stretches of open water were selenite rocks, which do, in fact, polarize daylight sufficiently to determine the position of the sun, thereby allowing mariners a rough determination of their position at sea. Scholars know the Norse inherited much of their maritime technology, including the *labstraeked*, or "klinker-built" hulls of their longships from earlier peoples with roots in pre-Classical times.

Could the Kentuckians of 3,000 years ago have likewise understood the refraction capability of selenite for navigational purposes? If so, then contemporary Bronze Age influences from the ancient Old World are implied. Such a conclusion is underscored by another mineral the prehistoric miners at Mammoth Cave simultaneously excavated by the ton: magnesium sulfate, better known as Epsom salt. In bath solutions, Epsom salts are first aid for barium poisoning, while in paste form magnesium sulfate acts as an agent for dehydrating, or "drawing," boils and carbuncles. When absorbed into the skin, it reduces inflammation, curing cuts and bruises. Epsom salt is also important in treating severe exacerbations of asthma. In fact, a 2005 study demonstrated that magnesium sulfate reduces the symptoms of acute asthma. It is also used to treat pre-eclampsia in laboring women, slowing labor to delay pre-term birth.

In addition to its broad, medicinal use, magnesium sulfate is important for agriculturalists, and indeed any population depending for its sustenance on regular harvests. The chemical compound is highly valued by farmers and gardeners to correct magnesium deficiency in soils, and is most commonly applied to potted plants or magnesium-hungry crops, such as peppers, potatoes, roses, or tomatoes. It was possibly the agricultural utility of Epsom salt that meant most to the miners who removed such prodigious quantities of the mineral in 1000 BCE.

But therein lies a perplexing dilemma, because the beneficial qualities of magnesium sulfate were not known until 1618, when a farmer at Epsom, England, accidentally noticed that water mixed with the salt on his property healed scratches and rashes. It would appear that ancient Americans at Mammoth Cave understood and applied magnesium sulfate more than 26 centuries before its beneficent qualities were discovered in England. Perhaps they were far ahead of their time in other things we cannot guess at in our wildest imaginings, as suggested by the vast quantities of optical selenite they went at such lengths to possess.

Archaeological Discoveries of Ancient America

According to James P. Scherz (professor emeritus, University of Wisconsin, Madison), who spent many years professionally surveying the Rock Lake area for its archaeo-astronomical significance, the last Native American ceremony undertaken at its shores was conducted more than 70 years ago by Indian elders, members of the Midewiwin lodge, an old secret society pledged to preserving the spiritual wisdom of the past. In 1930, they quietly returned a highly valued, if arcane ritual item to its depths, known to them as the *Megis*, or "Shining Shell."

As stated on an authoritative Native American Website, "For the Anishinabek, Ojibway, Pottawatomie and Odawa, the Megis Shell played an important part in their migration from the St. Lawrence Seaway area west to what is today northern Michigan, northern Wisconsin, northern Minnesota, southern Ontario, and as far west as Manitoba, and northern Montana. According to Ojibway oral history, each major stopping-point during the Anishinabeg's migration would be marked by the appearance of the sacred Megis Shell. According to Anishinabeg prophecies, the Ojibway people were to follow the direction of the Megis Shell, and by doing so would find their final destination; a place identifiable because it was where "food grows on water." After centuries of following the sacred Megis Shell's appearance, the Anishinabeg were eventually led to northern Minnesota, where they found *manomin* (wild rice) growing on water. This marked the end of the last great migration of Ojibway people."

Now, these Megis are white, commonplace cowrie shells, quite incapable of indicating the least direction in any form. Could they instead merely signify, in the secret symbolism of the Midewiwin lodge, a pale rock that actually assisted them in their long migrations from the St. Lawrence Seaway to the Upper Midwest and southern Canada?

Interestingly, the surreptitious arrival of the Indian medicine men to drop their Megis Shell in Rock Lake coincided with the teenage skin-diver's find under 12 feet (3.7 m) of water there. Could it be that their Megis is a "Shining Shell" metaphor for the light-refracting selenite crystal pyramid that now sits on my desk?

Aztalan, "the Place near Water," was a 45-square-acre (182,109 square m) city straddling both banks of the Crawfish River in southern Wisconsin beginning abruptly in 1100 CE. Three immense stockades regularly interspersed with square watch-towers surrounded the impressive population center of astronomically aligned pyramids, an urban precinct, an agricultural area, and a ceremonial arena. For more than two centuries, trade goods flowed into Aztalan from as far as the Upper Great Lakes, the Gulf of Mexico, and the Virgin Islands. Then, just as suddenly as the city sprang into existence, its walls, crops, and well-built houses burst into flame.

Investigators have long suspected an important link between Aztalan and Rock Lake, just 3 miles (5 km) away. But a connection could never be established—until now.

The Great Triangles of Rock Lake and Aztalan

By Frank Joseph

Early investigators of Aztalan were struck by an obvious repetition of the numeral 3 throughout its construction. The ceremonial center's three walls enclosed a trio of pyramids and a triangular pool, among other instances of what seemed to be a sacred number underscored by a delta-shaped stone buried dead-center inside the archaeological zone. Although its significance to the original inhabitants has not come down to us, triune symbolism among many even apparently unrelated cultures is remarkably similar, and worth knowing about, because it

A closer view of the triangular structure beneath the surface of Rock Lake.

may illuminate the otherwise murky prehistory of this important site.

To the Indus Valley civilizers of the early third millennium BCE, Bronze Age Greeks, Gnostics, and Buddhists, 3 signified godhood. Before the Christian trinity, a trident scepter was wielded by Vishnu and Poseidon. Buddha's *mudra* of three fingers of the right hand touching the ground was his holiest oath: "I swear by the Earth, the Mother of us all, that what I have spoken is true."

More specifically, the ancient Aztalaners may have chosen 3 as a sacred number for their ceremonial center to metaphysically connect themselves with the powers of heaven. After all, the site's many celestial orientations identify it in part as an astronomical observatory. Professor James Scherz ascertained through his standard surveying techniques that Aztalan's largest temple platform, the Pyramid of the Sun, was aligned with dawn of the Winter Solstice. Ten burials of both men and women in the opposite Pyramid of Venus were oriented to the appearance of the Morning Star.

An aerial view (3,500 feet [1,067 m]) reveals a sunken delta platform in the south end of Rock Lake.

A third earthwork (plowed out of existence by late-19th-century farmers) in the precinct's southeastern quadrant was aligned with the rising of the moon at its most northerly point, when it appears largest in the heavens—an orientation that may have had something to do with Aztalan, as the most northerly outpost of Upper Mississippian culture. The so-called Greenwood Group of five earthworks outside Aztalan's walls, together with Pipestone Hill facing directly west, all originally featured tall, red-painted cedar posts at their summits. They stood as observational gun-sights against the sky for astronomer-priests making their celestial calculations from atop the ceremonial center's three platform-mounds.

Archaeological Discoveries of Ancient America

The amount of data thus furnished must have amounted to a constant flood of cosmic information used for spiritual as well as agricultural purposes. Through the observatory told farmers when to plant their crops, it also put its operators in accord with natural cycles evident in the sky. Society was made to conform to the will of the gods, as expressed in the movements of the sun, moon, and stars. The same concept appears to have been intended at another prehistoric site about 250 miles (402 km) to the northwest.

The Saint Paul Mounds, atop a high bluff overlooking the Minnesota capitol, were originally seven mounds aligned with the Pleiades when the stars were directly overhead 2,000 years ago. Clearly, the Saint Paul Mounds' unknown builders meant to establish a connection between themselves and this special constellation. If a similar purpose was incorporated by the Aztalaners into their 50-acre (202,343 square m) metropolis, then they may have similarly chosen a particular celestial phenomenon from which they derived 3 as their sacred numerical link to heaven.

To dismiss as merely coincidental the recurrence of this almost universally sacred numeral in Aztalan would be to overlook an important theme of the site's religious significance. In our consideration of the number 3 coursing through its design, we may even find revealing contacts in prehistory to cultures beyond the "Old City," as the resident Winnebago or Ho Chunk Indians referred to its charred ruins on the banks of the Crawfish River. For example, Aztalan's three-to-one ratios find their only pre-Columbian correspondent at a site north of Mexico City, in the great archaeological zone of Teotihuacán. This is the same ancient urban center connected by geographical units of measurement (STU, or Standard Terrestrial Units) to Aztalan itself, according to mathematician Hugh Harleston.

A more obvious connection lies only 3 miles (5 km) west of Aztalan. It was here that pilot Armand Vandre and his observer, Elmer Wollin, made a startling discovery at Rock Lake. During March 1940, they were circling about 500 feet (152 m) over the surface, specifically in search of Wisconsin's legendary sunken pyramids. The winter icecap had recently melted, resulting in exceptionally clear conditions. Banking over the south end of the lake, the Lake Mills aviators looked down to behold an enormous, uniformly triangular platform lying beneath the water. They estimated that each one of its sides was 400 feet (122 m) long. Near its apex was a pair of black circles—perhaps circular, stone structures that seemed to stare up at the flyers like the eyes of this ghostly formation.

Since their discovery some 60 years ago, the great triangle has been spotted infrequently by both military and civilian pilots. Boeing B-17 Flying Fortress crewmen on training missions from Madison to Milwaukee over Rock Lake throughout World War II actually photographed it through their Norton bomb sights during several practice runs, although prints and negatives have since been lost somewhere in the Air Force bureaucracy. Then, 20 years later, a high-altitude state government survey of Rock Lake revealed the sunken triangle. In spring 1987, Steve Dempsey, an award-winning photographer and photojournalist for *The Chicago Sun-Times*, chartered a flight out of neighboring Watertown to shoot the lake. He knew nothing of the underwater figure and, surprised at seeing it for the first time, imagined that no one else before him had captured it on film.

When the Rock Lake Research Society got underway more than 10 years later, clear photographs taken by one of its founders, Jack LeTourneau, enabled investigators to locate the structure. It was far too large to be distinguished by divers in the turbid water, so, acting on instruments, they determined that its length on each side was more than twice that speculated by Vandre and Wollin in 1940. It appears to have been a natural mound terraformed by human engineers into a triangular shape by sloping walls of undressed rock 900 feet (274 m) long. Although the depth of its base is unknown, its uppermost section lies less than 20 feet (6 m) beneath the surface. Although researchers are not sure of the formation's specific purpose, it probably served as a dock for the far-ranging sailors who flourished at Rock Lake before rising water levels drowned the facility.

Whatever its actual utility, the great triangle connects with nearby Aztalan. There, the prehistoric builders excavated a large, three-sided pool, likewise at the south end of the triple-walled precinct in a correlation that seems more than coincidental. Indeed, sharing a common design at either location appears to have been an obvious attempt by its users to symbolically and spiritually link both sites. Interestingly, the Rock Lake triangular formation is a *raised* feature, whereas Aztalan's triple-sided figure is *indented*, an intaglio. It was discovered by a renowned surveyor of the early 19th century, Increase Lapham. He was surprised to observe that it had been engineered as a pool perhaps originally lined with some means (tiles?) to contain water. Nothing remotely like it has ever been found anywhere in the Americas before or since.

Curiously, the Aztalan triangle was intended to *hold* water, whereas its Rock Lake counterpart was meant to *displace* water. This comparison implies an intimate relationship between the two sites acting on a shared, metaphysical principle similar to the Chinese concept of yin and yang, or the Pythagoreans' "Sacred Duality," wherein harmony is achieved through the balance of opposites. Perhaps the ancient Wisconsonites wanted to maintain social stability by striving for symbolic equilibrium throughout their building projects, in which mutually supporting energies were exchanged between Aztalan and Rock Lake; the former held the sacred essence of the latter in its pool with the triune symbolism for godliness, while Rock Lake possessed the holy ground of the Crawfish River's ceremonial center at its dry-land platform.

Not long after Aztalan was surveyed in the 1830s, the site was purchased by a private farmer, who filled in the pool and planted over it. Lapham was the only professionally trained observer to have actually seen it, and the feature was deemed irretrievably lost. Consequently, even some archaeologists doubted the accuracy or even the veracity of his report, until official neglect forced it into obscurity. With the post–World War II advent of aerial archaeology, however, possibilities arose for the Aztalan pool's rediscovery. An early success was locating lost Etruscan cities in western Italy. These and other surveys at altitude revealed that even centuries of natural ground erosion and human development could not completely erase the telltale traces, however faint, of outlines left in the soil by former habitation sites.

The same technique had been applied, as mentioned, at Rock Lake, where it was the sole means whereby the underwater triangular structure could have been found. In hopes of making similar progress over Aztalan, Rock Lake Research Society President Archie Eschborn mounted an aerial survey of the ceremonial center in the spring of 1999. He was not disappointed. His cameras photographed the distinct outlines of a large triangle, just as Lapham had described. It had not been seen for nearly 170 years. Establishing the pool's existence not only validated Increase Lapham's on-site observations, but also tended to establish its link with Rock Lake.

Throughout the 20th century, unconventional investigators concluded that the ancient Aztalaners used its shores to inter their dead, thereby rendering the lake a necropolis. Such interpretations were condemned out of hand as unsubstantiated fantasy by salaried academics, who insisted that no evidence existed for connections of any kind between the two locations. Prevailing expert opinion was nevertheless unable to explain the absence of any cemeteries at Aztalan, where a population of some 10,000 residents flourished between 1100 and 1325 CE. A 3-mile (5 km) leap westward to consider Rock Lake's prehistoric mounds formerly scattered around its perimeter but still under its waves could not be contemplated.

But a connection between Rock Lake and Aztalan may manifest itself in an earth-sky relationship not unlike the Saint Paul Mounds' deliberate configuration after the Pleiades. Each September, approaching the autumnal equinox, a constellation known as the Summer Triangle appears directly over southern Wisconsin, toward the south. Its uppermost corner is lit by a star (Deneb) almost precisely in the middle of the sky. The Summer Triangle is still almost directly overhead just after nightfall. Due to precession, Deneb is not as perfectly fitted in the center of the sky today as it was in the ancient past, but even so, *three* bright stars from *three* separate constellations still converge to make up the *three*-pointed formation: Deneb in the constellation Cygnus, the Swan, at the top; Vega in Lyra, the Harp, to the west; and Altair in the constellation Aquila, the Eagle, at the bottom.

This unique triplication of the number 3 in the heavens may have been perceived as the sacred numeral on which Aztalan was designed and built for the spiritual harmony of its residents. Perhaps the occult notion of "as above, so below" was no less understood and employed in prehistoric Wisconsin than in the ancient Old World. In other words, the large, triangular formations at the southern ends of both Aztalan and Rock Lake were meant to be earthly counterparts of the Summer Triangle in the southern part of the night sky. The Aztalan excavation was almost certainly a reflection pool, in which astronomer-priests observed important celestial phenomena, perhaps even the Summer Triangle itself. At that instant, Aztalan and heaven would have been in perfect accord, an opportune moment for special rituals aimed at pulling down the powers of the cosmos.

Triangular correspondences between earthly sacred sites and the heavens were not confined to the Upper Midwest during pre-Columbian times. Ancient Greeks saw a metaphysical relationship between the three-pointed Mediterranean island of Sicily and the constellation Triangulum. Similar to the Summer Triangle, it appears in fall, only later, culminating on midnight of October 23. The five stars that compose its formation are located between

Andromeda and Aries. According to Greek myth, Sicily was shaped to resemble Triangulum at the behest of Demeter, the Earth-Mother goddess, who asked Zeus, the Sky-Father, for rain and sunlight to successfully grow her crops. A similarly reciprocal arrangement between heaven and earth is implied by the triangular structures at Rock Lake and Aztalan.

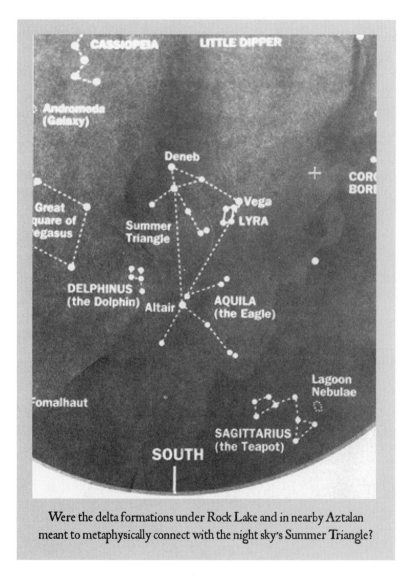

Were the delta formations under Rock Lake and in nearby Aztalan meant to metaphysically connect with the night sky's Summer Triangle?

Archaeological Discoveries of Ancient America

Contrary to official intransigence regarding such interpretations, man-made, otherwise-unique triangular formations do indeed sit at the south ends of both Aztalan and Rock Lake. Their presence has been undeniably confirmed, respectively, by aerial photography and sonar read-outs from the Rock Lake Research Society. Insisting that this shared imagery formed no relationship between the two sites is to ignore the metaphysical ground upon which flourished an ancient, enlightened, though little-understood civilization.

CHAPTER 6

Enigmatic Effigies

W ho could have fashioned the world's ugliest (though extraordinarily well-made) pipe, and for what purpose? In an Ancient American exclusive, the secrets of this uniquely grotesque artifact are probed by the publisher.

THE HIDEOUS SPIDER PIPE OF PREHISTORIC TENNESSEE

By Wayne May

One of the most dramatic artifacts ever associated with Native America was excavated unknown years ago from a prehistoric burial mound in Tennessee, and presently belongs to a private collector. Weighing little more than 2 pounds (.9 kg), the object is about 6 inches (15 cm) long and 4.5 inches (11 cm) high. Although this particular specimen appears to be unique, many thousands of ceremonial smoking pipes were made throughout our continent in pre-Columbian times.

Side view of the spider pipe.

According to British scholar Alfred Dunhill in *The Pipe Book*, they originally "led many investigators to doubt their Indian authorship. Certainly, they are far superior to the work of the same character executed by Indians since the Discovery, but in the history of every nation, we may observe such cycles of growth and decay in the sphere of the plastic arts, as a study of Egyptian and Greek sculptures and of European paintings will immediately reveal. The mound-builders were the 'Old Masters' of the Indian tribes."

Their ritual smoking instruments have been found across the American Midwest, especially in the Ohio Valley. Dunhill writes that one site in particular, Mound City, outside Chillicothe, Ohio, contained the greatest known concentration of ritual pipes. Investigators believe the ceremonial center was built and occupied between 200 BCE and 400 CE by a people belonging to the so-called Hopewell Culture. This is a modern name used by archaeologists to identify a sophisticated society of mound-builders and coppersmiths who dominated the region for about eight centuries. Among the numerous masterpieces they crafted were stone effigy pipes. At Mound City, one earthwork alone yielded more than 300 such items.

They were commonly configured into the shapes of familiar animals: frogs, birds, snakes, grasshoppers, lizards, and so forth. Dunhill believed such figures were examples of "totem worship"; that is to say, each clan or subdivision of a tribe held some particular animal to be sacred to it, and in some way to represent the clan. Many legends associated totems with clan ancestors, and as tribal emblems.

Front view of the spider pipe.

"An Indian craftsman lavished utmost care on the carving of his totem animal," according to Dunhill, "and it is because such figures, beautifully sculptured in stone, are characteristic of many mound pipes, that these possess so great an interest and value."

This interpretation may hold true for some of the effigy pipes, but it does not explain them all. For example, they had nothing to do with smoking as it is understood today, but were used only by shamans, or medicine men assigned to look after the physical and spiritual health of the tribe. The herbs they used were hallucinogenic, distilled from relatively mild narcotics in wild tobacco to powerful, mind-altering substances. All of them were used to assist the shaman in extending his vision beyond mundane reality into the spirit world for the purposes of healing and guidance.

But what could the artist have had in mind when he created the spider pipe? It appears to be absolutely unique, not only for its arachnid imagery, but more especially because animal and human elements are combined in the addition of a skull.

Dunhill quotes an eyewitness to the smoking practices of a California Indian in the early 19th century:

> One mode [of healing disease] was very remarkable, and the good effect it sometimes produced heightened the reputation of the medicine man advising it. They applied to the suffering part of the patient's body the *chacuaco*, a tube formed of very hard, black stone; and through this they sometimes sucked and sometimes blew, but both as hard as they were able, supposing that the disease was either exhaled or dispersed. Sometimes the tube was filled with *cinaram*, or wild tobacco lighted, and here they either sucked in or blew down the smoke, according to the medicine man's directions; and this powerful caustic sometimes, without any other remedy, has been known entirely to remove the disorder.

We may infer, then, that the Tennessee pipe was designed specifically for use by a medicine man in his treatment of deadly illness—perhaps specifically to treat spider bites. It was probably interred with the shaman at the time of his burial in a funeral mound. We will probably never know the full purpose or meaning of this bizarre artifact, which is nonetheless part of a wider mystery concerning many other pre-Columbian pipes, portraying as they do creatures, such as tarantulas, not native to the Ohio Valley.

Iowa's once-famous Elephant Pipe clearly shows an animal with a long proboscis, yet the last pachyderm to roam North America died before the end of the last ice age, 12,000 years ago. Skeptics believe the Elephant Pipe actually represents a long-snouted tapir. But even if the effigy does depict such a beast, tapirs are found in Central or South America, thousands of miles away from Ohio. Still other pipes are fashioned in the unmistakable likeness of a manatee (or sea cow), which haunts the South's tropical rivers and shores, but is never found further north than Florida. Some investigators conclude that such effigies date back to a time when our continent's climate and animals differed substantially from today's creatures and ecology, but evidence is lacking to show that the mounds in which the pipes are found belong to such remote periods. More likely, the prehistoric artist personally visited distant regions, or learned about the unfamiliar animals from some traveler acquainted with them.

Whatever the thoughts that went into their creation so long ago, the finely crafted effigy pipes are among prehistoric America's most intriguing treasures.

Dr. John White is president of the Midwest Epigraphic Society (Columbus, Ohio), and the editor of its journal since 1988. As such, he has publicized

numerous discoveries revealing overseas effect on ancient America, of which the Menorah petroglyph is among the most compelling.

PRE–COLUMBIAN HEBREWS IN MICHIGAN
By Dr. John White

The word *discoveries* is used here to signify subjects that catch the eye, and suggests the possibility that if the objects are what they may be, then progress with some particularly interesting model of history may be advanced. Ways that advancement may be achieved in ancient culture include visiting great museums and scanning great books. Occasionally, an image appears in the course of such research that is out of place. In other words, the context of an anomalous find is not consistent with conventional knowledge of history as generally understood. Such encounters may be exciting, but we must remember that alleged discoveries are often explained by unforeseen realities.

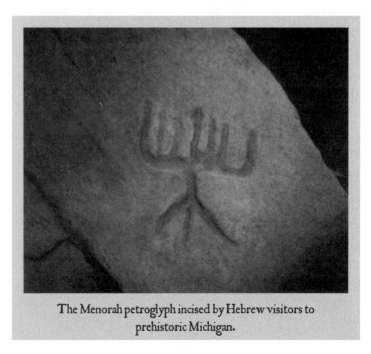

The Menorah petroglyph incised by Hebrew visitors to prehistoric Michigan.

Thus cautioned, readers are asked to examine the Indian rock carving presented here. The petroglyph may be seen at the Ziibiwing Center, near Mt. Pleasant, Michigan, a new Native American museum dedicated to showcasing the Anishinabe culture. Although the Anishinabe created a number of significant rock-art drawings, our image is not one of them. It might be Ogham writing, or possibly a stylized depiction of the legendary Thunderbird. But, far more likely, it portrays a menorah sitting on a three-legged stand.

The Michigan rock art serves to emphasize the notion that ancient Mediterranean mariners (Phoenicians, Carthaginians, Hebrews, and so on) explored new territory extensively in search of raw materials to harvest and trade. Mainstream skeptics may scoff, but they are hard-pressed to explain why Columbus found Indians throughout the Caribbean in possession of iron hatchets. These implements may have come from Brazil or Africa, but their technology was likely Carthaginian.

In contrast to Michigan's small Menorah petroglyph, the landscaped image of a monstrous snake writhing through the Ohio Valley poses an entirely different mystery. But now fresh evidence reveals the extraterrestrial origins of this colossal effigy mound.

THE SERPENT AND THE METEOR
By Frank Joseph

Scientists have determined that an ancient structure about 200 miles (322 km) southwest of Cleveland, in the Appalachian countryside, was terraformed atop the rim of a monstrous crater created by a fallen meteor or asteroid that struck the Earth with the force of a major nuclear event. The effigy mound lies on a steep hill near Locust Grove, in the Ohio Valley, where it is preserved in its own public park. Visitors enter the site off the main road via an ascending driveway that terminates in a parking lot before a small museum.

An overlook of the 1/4-mile-long (.4 km) terraglyph is afforded by climbing to the top of a 40-foot-high (12 m) observation tower nearby. From this elevated perspective, the snake image appears to writhe across the ridge in seven humps, its huge jaws agape before an egg-shaped mound, its tail ending in a perfect spiral. With an average width of 20 feet (6 m), and 5 feet (1.5 m) of height, the earthwork's overall length is 1,254 feet (382 m). Although the Great Serpent Mound, as it is known, is clearly discernable at ground level, and more so from its observation tower, it may only be fully appreciated from the vantage point of an airplane circling overhead at 500 feet (152 m) or more. From any point of view, however, its graceful proportions testify to the technical and artistic sophistication of its creators.

Whoever they were, they thoroughly cleaned up after themselves: Not a trace of their tools, implements, or weapons of any kind have ever been excavated in the mound's immediate vicinity. Archaeologists nonetheless know that construction demanded careful planning, in which flat stones were selected for size and uniformity, while lumps of clay were laid along the ground in a predesignated pattern to form a serpentine configuration. Then baskets full of soil were piled over the pattern, and finally sculpted into shape. Crude as this construction technique may seem, it has nevertheless maintained its appearance in spite of wind and rain erosion throughout the course of millennia at the crest of a gusty hill. In truth, nothing about the Great Serpent Mound suggests the primitive. Not only does it imply the cooperation of an organized labor force and both artistic and engineering genius, but also the application of a standard system of measurement and orientation.

Ohio's Great Serpent Mound as it appears from the top of a
40-foot (12 m) tower nearby.

The vicinity of the effigy was never inhabited, serving instead as a ceremonial center, and rests on the rim of a curious depression 5 miles (8 km) across, with local layers of bedrock broken into enormous cracks. Some of these blocks were forced steeply downward, and others sharply upward. Early investigators of this feature concluded it was created by rising pressures generated by volcanic forces from below that never quite reached the surface—hence its description as "crypto-volcanic."

In my 1992 book, *Sacred Sites* (Llewellyn Publications), I speculated that this wide depression was not caused by the questionable agency of some "crypto-volcanic" phenomenon, but by a meteor's collision with the Earth. Then, 10 years later, in *The Destruction of Atlantis* (Bear & Company), I wrote that "only the impact of an object approximately 200 feet (61 m) in diameter, traveling at some 45,000 miles (72,421 km) per hour, could have produced the same kind of features found at Arizona's meteor crater."

In April 2004, an international team of earth scientists headed by geologists from the Ohio Department of Natural Resources announced their discovery of quartz crystals beneath the Great Serpent Mound fractured like those typically deformed by a massive energy burst on the scale of a hydrogen-bomb blast. Known as shatter cones, they were found in geological formations more than 1,000 feet (305 m) beneath the effigy. Their suggestion of a nuclear-like detonation was underscored by the retrieval of higher-than-normal concentrations of iridium—a rare, extremely heavy metal occurring only at the molten core of our planet, due to its heavy weight. The silver-gray metal could be extruded or brought up to the Earth's surface by volcanic activity, but lava flows are absent from Ohio.

More certainly, the thick iridium deposits beneath the Great Serpent Mound were laid down by the impact of a meteor or asteroid, which is commonly composed of iridium. Moreover, the cracked crystals speak eloquently of a cataclysmic collision, not a volcanic eruption, at the site of the geoglyph, where iridium deposits are 10 times beyond what is usually present in the Earth's crust. As state geologist Mark T. Baranowski observed, in a 1997 GSA *Today* article, "I think we can say with authority today that this is an impact from a meteorite. It affected the region in a spectacular way. The site's significant enrichment of iridium is good evidence for an impact origin."

The crater instantly excavated by the celestial object is so large it encompasses portions of Adams, Pike, and Highland counties. Its creation needed something much larger than the trailer truck–sized meteor I envisioned in *The Destruction of Atlantis*. Instead, astronomers now believe the object was perhaps three times larger than the Cleveland Browns' Stadium, and traveled faster than a speeding bullet. Its collision carved a 1,000-foot-deep (305 m) hole in seconds, pulverizing rocks at the 1,500-foot (457 m) depths from which the scientists' bore-holes retrieved fine grains of sand. Microscopic examination revealed that the tiny crystals had been deformed by the ancient impact, and were even accompanied by soot particles from limestone disintegrated and scorched by the exploding asteroid's intense heat.

The object itself vaporized on impact. "I don't think we'll ever find it," Baranowski stated. "It would have gone up in smoke. If anything was left near the surface, it would have been eroded away."

To one of his colleagues who studied the Ohio Valley core samples, the impact theory makes sense of the complex terrain around the Great Serpent Mound, which seems otherwise inexplicably jumbled. According to geophysicist Doyle Watts at Wright State University in Dayton, in the same article, although some rock formations stand 1,000 feet (305 m) above the ground, others appear to have slid straight down. "But why would Native Americans lug tons of soil and shape it into a slithering serpent?" he asked. "Why would they choose to do so on the scar of an ancient impact when they had all of Ohio and the Midwest? My guess is that they could have noticed something strange about the rocks. It has to be more than coincidence."

It undoubtedly was, but the mound-builders noticed something more than "strange" about the rocks. Considering the Great Serpent Mound's location atop the ridge of a major astrobleme, or impact crater, this effigy must reflect the grand cosmic event responsible for its immense crater. In other words, the mound-builders must have been personal witnesses to the nuclear-like impact of the asteroid that once decimated the Ohio Valley.

Archaeological Discoveries of Ancient America

Most astronomers believe that it occurred some 275 million years ago, long before man evolved. But perhaps it took place during the far-more-recent past, as suggested by Native American oral tradition. The Hopi Indians of the American Southwest, far from Ohio, know of the Serpent Mound, and claim it was raised by a related tribe, the Snake Clan, whose members escaped the destruction of their island homeland far out into the Eastern Ocean.

Remembered as "the Third Emergence," their mass migration was made possible through the leadership of Pahána, the "White Brother." He piled people and animals into fleets of large reed boats, which floated them to a new life in America. Soon after landing, they set up a shrine to their serpent-god on the east coast in gratitude for surviving the catastrophe. He was, after all, the spirit of regeneration, and they had escaped the violent destruction of their homeland. Migrating westward, they passed into the Ohio Valley, where they raised the Great Serpent Mound, naming it *Tokchii*, the "Guardian of the East," to commemorate the direction from which they fled the Deluge. Descendants of the Snake Clan still wear seashells to memorialize their oceanic origins.

It is remarkable that the Hopi should claim descent from the Snake Clan, survivors from a lost island in the Atlantic Ocean, and the designers of the mound representing a serpent disgorging an egg, while the Greeks, separated from the Hopi by half a world and thousands of years, recorded that their ancestors were a "Serpent People," the Ophites, from the Western Sea, and whose emblem was a snake with an egg at its mouth!

The Mandan Indians, who were the earliest people known to have resided in the vicinity of the mound, said it was built by a race that preceded them. They were powerful, even fearsome men, the descendants of survivors from a terrible flood in the Gulf of Mexico. Supposedly, the Mandan were not only forbidden to visit the Great Serpent Mound, but they were also not even allowed to look in its direction. Eventually, the Indians, finding conditions unbearable under the domineering mound builders, migrated westward to the Missouri River.

Particularly remarkable about their scant memories of the serpent mound is the fact that the Mandan, of all the plains tribes, preserved the most elaborate ceremony commemorating the Great Flood. Known as the *Okipa*, or "Bull Dance," it was personally witnessed by a famous portrait artist and explorer of the early American west, George Catlin. Documenting the Okipa in words and paint, he described how an entire Mandan village reenacted the drama of the Deluge, wherein Indians daubed themselves with dyes from plant fibers to impersonate the red-headed, white-faced survivors who arrived in a large, wooden vessel. Even this element of the myth was reconstructed and placed at the center of the village.

Comets are commonly represented worldwide as dragons or serpents, from the bible to Aztec myth. Their sinuous progress across the sky finds an obvious symbol in the snake. The Ohio mound's prodigious size, together with the "egg" being spat from its mouth, suggests the builders saw the event that excavated the same crater at which the effigy is located. In other words, the builders of the Great Serpent Mound must have witnessed the meteor-fall.

The geoglyph was originally thought, soon after its discovery by noted archaeological surveyors Squire and Davis in the first half of the 19th century, to date back only a few generations, despite testimony of resident Indians to the contrary. Radiocarbon studies during the later decades of the last century determined that the bioglyph was less than a thousand years old. Even though the tested materials could not be connected with the mound-builders, mainstream archaeologists uncritically accepted a circa 1200 CE date as an official time line for the effigy. Almost needless to add, no meteor struck Ohio within the last 800 years, so the men who created the serpent mound in obvious reference to such an event must have witnessed it in a period far more remote than the 12th or 13th century.

Indeed, archaeo-astronomers have long known that the Great Serpent Mound was built during the last century of the late fourth millennium BCE, because its first hoop was at that time perfectly aligned with the Pole Star. This period coincides remarkably well with a series of asteroid collisions the Earth underwent more than 5,000 years ago, according to 1997's international symposium of world-class astrophysicists and related scientists from the Society for Interdisciplinary Studies in Cambridge, England. They concurred that a comet made a close pass to our planet circa 3100 BCE, when it fired off a barrage of meteoric debris in a swath of fiery destruction across the Northern Hemisphere. This appears to have been the heavenly cataclysm observed by the Ohio mound-builders and commemorated in their Great Serpent earthwork.

The sky-snake spitting a meteoritic oval as an obvious metaphor of the catastrophe was also found beyond the Ohio Valley: Greeks of the Classical Age told of their prehistoric predecessors, remembered by them as the Pelasgians, or "Sea Peoples." They were said to have emerged from the Cosmic Egg disgorged "from the fangs of Ophion." This oldest creation myth in Greece held that Ophion ("Serpent") was swimming alone in the primeval sea before the beginning of time, when Boreas, god of the north wind, accidentally dropped a seed into the waters. Ophion swallowed it, and soon after the Cosmic Egg sprang from his mouth. It seems clear that the pre-Greek story of Pelasgian origins is the same idea implicit in the Great Serpent Mound perched on the western rim of an astrobleme. The "seed" accidentally dropped by Boreas, personification of tumult in the sky, was the meteor that fell into the ocean, triggering the geologic upheavals from which the Sea Peoples emerged as survivors and culture-bearers.

These interpretations are supported by the latest finds far beneath the Great Serpent Mound, and associate its relationship with the natural catastrophe its builders meant to memorialize.

Conventional scholars were surprised to learn that the images of men and animals drawn in the sands between Los Angeles and the Hoover Dam were far older than suspected. But if historic Indians were not the artists, who could have laid out such immense figures so long ago? And to what purpose?

GIANTS OF THE CALIFORNIA DESERT
By Lloyd Hornbostel, Jr.

The colossal images of giant animals, plants, geometric figures, and apparently interminably straight lines spread out across the Nazca Desert of Peru are world-famous. They are so huge that they may only be properly appreciated from the vantage point of an airplane circling high overhead, and archaeologists are not sure who made them, when, or why. The creation of master surveyors, the patterns are complex, but simply constructed by moving aside a grayish top level of earth to expose yellowish-white sand beneath.

The Nazca Lines are intaglios, or incised designs, as it were, below the surface. The pre-Inca Peruvians were not the only artists to employ this method on a grand scale. On the other side of the Atlantic Ocean, Bronze Age Britons etched the vibrant image of a galloping steed onto the side of a high hill outside Oxford. Known as the White Horse of Uffington, its creation has been recently dated to circa 1200 BCE. In Dorset, about 8 miles outside Dorchester, a hill figure known as the Cerne-Abbas Giant still wields his 30-foot-long (9 m) club after unguessed centuries. Sub-soil tests in the 1970s identified him as a representation of the demi-god Hercules. To the south, toward Bristol, is another giant, the Long Man of Wilmington, a faceless man apparently walking through his 300-foot-high (91 m) doorway.

Similar to their South American counterparts, these British hill figures are monumental intaglios. Such outsized artwork appears in only one other location on Earth: in the desert of southeastern California. Far-less-well-known than either European or Peruvian examples, their most impressive specimen is likewise the depiction of a giant. The 167-foot (51 m) figure was discovered accidentally by a U.S. Army Air Corps pilot flying over the town of Blythe from Hoover Dam to Los Angeles in 1932. Other massive intaglios were spotted, including serpents and unidentifiable quadrupeds, but these have been mostly lost in the last decades.

Aerial view of colossal images representing a man and a horse in the desert near Blythe.

During World War II, General George S. Patton used the Blythe area as his "Desert Training Area." His tanks and other motorized vehicles obliterated an unknown number of geoglyphs, leaving still-visible scars. Today, the Bureau of Land Management oversees the remaining images and has raised fences around them. Arthur Woodward, an ethnologist from the Natural History Museum of Los Angeles, in a *Literary Digest* article entitled "Giant Etchings on California Desert Sands," was said to have made "efforts to find out who made the figures, but to no avail. The Mojave and Chemehuevi Indians who once frequented this area said they had no knowledge of them."

Later, Richard Pourade, at the San Diego Museum of Man, tried to establish a date for the construction of the California intaglios. As he wrote in *Prehistoric Images*, "One of them is a crude representation of a man; the other of a horse. The horse clearly places these gravel arrangements in the historic Indian period, as the Western horse vanished from the continent many thousands of years ago and only was reintroduced by the Spaniards arriving from Europe."

That seemed a logical deduction in 1966, when the Blythe geoglyphs were officially attributed to the Mojave Indians, and confidently dated to post-Columbian times from 1540 to as late as 1800. But the archaeologists were in for a shock 30 years later. Advanced dating methods, which accurately measured the number of years from the present to when the gravel was moved aside to create the desert drawings, were brought to bear at the Blythe Giant and Horse by geologists from the University of California (Berkeley). Repeated testing revealed a consistent date of 900 CE (give or take 100 years). This meant that someone in California knew enough about the horse to represent it on the desert floor seven centuries before the Spaniards reintroduced the animal to North America.

Archaeological Discoveries of Ancient America

What was going on in the rest of the world about 1,100 years ago? During that time, the civilization of the Mayas abruptly shut down for reasons still not understood. They simultaneously abandoned their ceremonial cities across Yucatán, just as the Toltecs began their rise to prominence. At the same moment, the Mississippian culture flowered above the Rio Grande River. The megalopolis at Cahokia was built in western Illinois, opposite the location of modern-day St. Louis, Missouri. But the Mayas, Toltecs, and Mississippians did not construct earth intaglios. Nor did they know of the horse.

Some investigators believe the Nazca Lines could date as late as the fourth or fifth century, but that is still too early for any direct connections with the late-ninth-/early-10th-century figures in California. Moreover, the Peruvian geoglyphs are superbly wrought, whereas the Blythe figures are crudely laid out. Their single point of comparison is South America's only anthropomorphic giant at Serro Unitas in coastal Chile. Even here, however, the Chilean specimen is far superior. There are, as mentioned, two hill figures representing giants in Britain. But these too are stylistically worlds apart from California's desert drawings, and pre-date them not by centuries, but millennia.

The only North American parallel to the Blythe giant is the intaglio of a life-size human figure in British Columbia. As Frank Joseph described it in his book *Sacred Sites of the West*:

> The old story was told by Coast Tsimshian Indians of the man who fell from heaven, and left proof of his fall at an unusual rock. They said he was a great chief who was an even greater Shaman, because he conjured unseen forces at his command. As an example of his powers, he once went into a deep trance, then slowly levitated his body from the ground. He continued to gradually ascend until he was entirely lost to

view above the clouds. Several days later, the Shaman was seen falling from the sky, and he landed flat on his back onto a slab of rock. He survived the experience without a scratch, and, when he arose from his landing spot, observers were amazed to see the outline of their chief pressed into the face of the rock.

Native America's flying hero was known as Metlakatla, which in the coastal Tsimshian dialect means, "Him from Across the Water." The name may signify his overseas origins, perhaps among the Pacific Northwest islands, some of which are still revered as sacred. Today, as though in confirmation of the Native American legend, visitors to the Tsimshian Reservation may see the man-sized carving of the Metlakatla figure, an anthropomorphic image cut into the almost smooth surface of a roughly rectangular rock outcropping.

Perhaps the British Columbian intaglio compares with California's much-larger geoglyph, which might also have been dedicated to a shaman, its gigantic size stressing his importance. Both sites are oriented to the sky, and traditions around the world, from Peru, with its desert drawing of an owl-headed figure, to the Lapplanders of the Arctic Circle, speak of shamans exercising the power of flight. The studies of pharmacological anthropologists such as R. Gordon Wasson have demonstrated that "the flight of the shaman" these medicine men and women experienced was their drug-induced trance. Only in such a deep state of altered consciousness were they able to fly their souls to the spirit world, from whence they returned, like Metlakatla, with high guidance for their people. Dr. Jordan Detzer, a University of California (Berkeley) archaeologist who investigated the ground-drawings for more than 20 years, concluded, in his book *California Archaeology: 1940 to 1960*, that "These intaglios were shown great reverence, as the natives used them for the performance of dances and mysterious, shamanist rites, always beseeching heavenly deities for help."

Archaeological Discoveries of Ancient America

Metlakatla's name, "Him from Across the Water," does indeed suggest an outside influence. Perhaps itinerant shamans once roamed the world, practicing their spiritual powers from one people to another, from deeply prehistoric times until at least the 10th century. If so, then the Blythe Desert drawings may have been made by the Mojave's ancestors as memorials to some visiting medicine man who rode into Southern California on his horse more than a thousand years ago, centuries before the animal's introduction into the Americas by modern Europeans. But from where he might have come is still anybody's guess.

CHAPTER 7

Lost Kingdoms

Earl Koenig is resident professor of anthropology at the Colegio de Arqueologica in Trujillo, Peru, where he additionally serves as curator of the city's science museum, a position he has held since 1992. Regarded as the leading expert in Peru's earliest cultures, the Austrian-born authority affirms that the new discovery of a long-lost city is making terrific impact on our understanding of America's civilized roots.

FOUND: THE PRE-INCA CITY OF GRAN SAPOSOA

By Earl Koenig

On August 15, 2007, after hacking their way through the rainforests of northern Peru for more than a month, a joint team of U.S. and Peruvian explorers finally stood before the mighty ramparts of their quest. All they had to go on were years of preliminary research into legends and rumors of an otherwise forgotten metropolis deep in the Amazon jungle.

"It's a tremendous city," exclaimed Sean Savoy, the team leader, "containing areas with etchings and 10-meter-high (33-foot) walls." Sean is the son of Gene Savoy, who accompanied the expedition, and whose earlier discoveries, such as the sacred city of Peru's Gran Pajaten, have been featured in past issues of *Ancient American*. He christened their new find *Gran Saposoa*, after the nearby village of Saposoa.

Although the area had been mapped out with preliminary drawings, the explorers were surprised by the vast extent of the ruined city, located 9,186 feet (2,800 m) above sea level. Its 39 square acres (157,827 square m) enfold five citadels standing among waterfalls and lakes, all surrounded by massive walls hung with thick vegetation. Matted jungle growth covers their numerous carvings and figure paintings, Sean Savoy reported. He went on to say that his team also found well-preserved cemeteries containing the mummified bodies of Gran Saposoa's original inhabitants "in almost perfect condition."

Study of the remains may help to confirm 16th-century accounts of the Chachapoyas, a fair-complected people encountered by early Spanish explorers, renowned for their prowess as outstanding warriors. The Chachapoyas were already virtually extinct when Francisco Pizarro and his Conquistadors overthrew the Inca Empire, which had absorbed the earlier civilization, and established its own settlement (perhaps a garrison) within the walls of Gran Saposoa.

Until its discovery, little of the Chachapoyas was known, save for a number of oversized burial caskets attesting to their reputed tall stature found in Peru's northern jungle region. Similar to Egyptian sarcophagi, the coffin lids had been sculpted into representations of the deceased. The Chachapoyas appear to have been the white-skinned "giants" described throughout Andean legend allegedly responsible for building the pre-Inca city of Tiahuanaco in remote antiquity.

Around 700 CE, 10,000 of them flourished in Gran Saposoa, when its farming terraces were watered by an ingenious system of stone canals. Their application during the eighth century proves the Incas, who rose some 600 years later, inherited rather than invented, as historians assumed, these sophisticated agricultural and irrigation techniques.

Discovery of the lost city is an important achievement in Peruvian archaeology, because it promises to shed new light on the development of Andean Civilization.

A resident of northern Wisconsin near the Michigan border, David Hoffman is a frequent speaker at Ancient American *conferences and a longtime contributor to its magazine. During his circumnavigation of the world some years ago, he was made profoundly aware of the interrelationship experienced by ancient cultures, contrary to their alleged development in strict isolation, as proposed by Establishment anthropologists. Here, David Hoffman summarizes the conclusions of his truly global observations to show the prehistory of our continent as it is not taught in the classroom or presented on television.*

THE RISE AND FALL OF PREHISTORIC AMERICA

By David Hoffman

More than 2,000 years ago, what much later became the nation of Brazil was covered with at least 30,000 square miles (77,700 square km) of man-made earthworks surrounded by raised fields and linked by causeways. An unknown people had transformed the entire Amazon River Basin into a prehistoric garden. Even conservative estimates place about 12 percent of the non-flooded Amazon forest as anthropogenic. But a soil geographer in the late 1990s discovered swaths of *terra preta*—rich, fertile "black earth" that anthropologists increasingly believe was created by the human element on a far vaster scale. Terra preta perpetuates, regenerates itself, like fusing a microorganism-rich starter into plain dough for the baking of sourdough bread.

Other feats of ancient American grandeur were raised on a similarly impressive scope. The Aztec capital of Tenochtitlan, first visited by Hernando Cortes in 1519, was larger than contemporary Paris, with ornately carved buildings and market goods from hundreds of miles away. He remarked on the degree of civilization upon seeing botanical gardens and hundreds of men maintaining and cleaning the crowded streets, while his fellow Conquistadors compared Tenochtitlan favorably with Seville, Spain's loveliest city.

In the American Southeast, a Caddoan-speaking civilization developed monumental architecture: public plazas, ceremonial platforms, and mausoleums, and boasted a population of 200,000. Near the confluence of the Mississippi and Missouri Rivers, on the Illinois side opposite St. Louis, Missouri, some 30,000 residents occupied the ceremonial city of Cahokia in 900 CE, making it larger than London at the time. The completion of Cahokia's earthworks, the largest structures north of Mexico, would have required 100 men working nonstop for 50 years.

Henry Brackenridge wrote of the ruins in 1814: "If the human species had at any time been permitted in this country [America] to have increased fully, and there is every probability of the fact, it must, as in Mexico, have been astonishingly numerous."

His astonishment was actually eclipsed by an even greater material achievement spread across the Upper Great Lakes Region, when prehistoric miners excavated truly prodigious quantities of the world's highest-grade copper. Found at many of their surviving pits were discarded hammer stones, the byproducts of mining. At one Upper Michigan site alone, enough broken mauls were collected to have filled 10 wagons weighing 1,000 tons (907 metric tons). Grooves, where the hammer stones would have been tethered to a handle, were nearly obliterated on the upper side, but the bottom side of the stones had a fairly fresh appearance, because of less exposure to atmospheric conditions throughout a very long period.

The ancient mining was accomplished with hot fire doused with cold water, thereby *spalling*, or cracking open the copper mineral from the rock. Charcoal found at the bottom of several pits registered a carbon-14 dating to 3,800 years before the present. When confronted by just a fraction of the 5,000 prehistoric mines pockmarking the Upper Peninsula, a modern engineer was asked how many men would have been required to work them. Given the daily demands for feeding, housing, and transporting the miners, he estimated that 10,000 men could not have exhausted the mines in less than a thousand years.

But what became of the powerful societies responsible for these immense agricultural, urban, and industrial accomplishments centuries and even millennia before the arrival of modern Europeans? The answer may lie in history's worst demographic calamity. Disease preceded full colonization, slowly making room for the influx of colonists. Immunity was localized and not sufficient to protect humans from foreign infection. Typhoid, bubonic plague, influenza, mumps, measles, whooping cough—all rained down on the Americas beginning in the early 1500s. Smallpox alone eliminated more than half of the Inca empire. Viral hepatitis may have killed 90 percent of the native population in coastal New England. At Plymouth Colony in 1620, an English trader, Thomas Morton, noted that the Indians "died on heaps, as they lay in their houses."

The aforementioned Caddoan-speaking people in the Southeast experienced a precipitous population decline during a 150-year period spanning the arrival of DeSoto to LaSalle's visit. From an initial estimate of 200,000 persons to about 8,500, substantiates a drop of nearly 96 percent. By the 18th century, the population had further declined to 1,400 indigenes. Spanish, Portuguese, and British colonizers were alarmed by this increasing death rate among the Indians, not for any humanitarian considerations, but because of a perceived worker shortage such inadvertent genocide entailed. Faced with a dearth of cheap labor, the Europeans turned their eyes to Africa.

There are some discoveries so outrageous they fail to fit any of our preconceived notions of human antiquity. An illustrative example was found not long ago in the Wasatch Mountains of Utah, an area archaeologists assure us was uncivilized until the advent of European settlers less than 200 years ago. Yet, abundant stonework uncovered in a remote region of the Beehive State testifies to the existence of a lively urban center during prehistory. No less intriguing, the identity, origins, and fate of its residents utterly escape the conjecture of even the most speculative cultural diffusionist. Sites such as these serve to remind us that we are far from a thorough understanding of our unwritten past.

Utah's Nameless City of the Clouds
By Wayne May

Archaeologists search forests, deserts, islands, and even beneath the waves for evidence of humankind's ancient past. They naturally presume that no such traces might be found among the mountain goats, stunted vegetation, cold, ice, and thin air of the Rockies. Yet that is precisely where a recent find suggests prehistoric Americans did indeed leave surviving indications of a sophisticated culture radically different from anything produced by Indian tribal peoples. My introduction to this previously unknown site was made possible by its discoverer, who is also one of our subscribers. Due to the vulnerability of the remains, their precise location and the identity of the man who found them will not be disclosed. For purposes of telling his story, I will refer to him as "John." The related sites are all found on posted, private property. He stumbled upon the expanse of stone foundations, broken masonry, and dressed blocks around 1970, while hiking the country as a young man. I first learned of them when visiting his Utah home in 1996.

Collapsed entrance to the lost city of Utah's Wasatch Mountains.

Archaeological Discoveries of Ancient America

Even before he told me about his discovery, I was intrigued by a large and strange-looking stone vessel sitting in his neighbor's front yard. Although serving as a flower box, it more resembled a lidless sarcophagus! But walking up to John's house, I was doubly surprised to see, on either side of his front door, a pair of stone boxes reminiscent of reliquaries used by various cultures in the Ancient Old World for the storage of sacred items, such as holy texts and even cremated human remains. What were they doing here, in Utah? John told me that his neighbor, while hunting among the Wasatch Mountains six years ago, found the stone coffin in an otherwise empty cave. John believes the site must have been a burial site previously looted of its contents.

In any case, the neighbor forgot about hunting, and, with great personal difficulties, dragged the undecorated sarcophagus all the way home. John's own, smaller stone boxes were also found high in the mountains, not far from town. The late Dr. Paul Chessman described similar receptacles in *Ancient Writing on Metal Plates*: "The Dead Sea scrolls were found in large pottery jars. The metal plates of Darius were found in stone foundation boxes.... Over fifty stone boxes have been found in the Americas containing valuable articles, as well as written records. Containers for valuables certainly are varied; however, it is interesting that the burial in stone boxes have a coincidence in the parallel of the Old World and the New." Capitalizing on my amazement, John showed me photographs he had taken of stone ruins high in the Wasatch Mountains at elevations between 8,000 and 9,000 feet (2,438 and 2,743 m). The only comparisons I knew of were the stone "medicine wheels" found between 9,000 and 10,000 feet (2,743 and 3,048 m), and dating back (some of them) to a time contemporary with the final development of Britain's Stonehenge. John's photos were incredible. They depicted ruined walls, paved floors, what appeared to be the doors of tombs, and even man-made mounds. I was anxious to see all this in person, but the press of business made visiting the site impossible at the moment.

The following summer, I returned to Utah from my Wisconsin home, and John escorted me to his discovery in the Wasatch. This range comprises a large segment of the south-central Rocky Mountains, extending southward for some 250 miles (402 km) from the bend of the Bear River in southwestern Idaho to beyond Mt. Nebo, near Nephi, in north-central Utah. It was here, near the southern extent of the Wasatch, east of Salt Lake City, that the stone ruins were found. The ascent was long, but not especially arduous, as pine trees yielded to scrub brush the higher we climbed.

Two hours after setting out, John announced we had arrived at the location. He indicated low, stone walls jutting from the surface of the mountain in a straight line, broken only by apparently deliberate openings before continuing by as much as another 200 feet (61 m). Where the walls did make turns, they occurred at sharp right angles, suggesting building foundations. Numerous smaller structures were more than implied throughout the vicinity in paved floor-space. It took us only about 20 minutes to locate 16 placed-stone floors scattered across the mountainside. Did this group consist of a settlement? We noticed that the stones had been cut identically from one foundation to the next. The edges were actually pecked away around several blocks, leaving no doubt that they had been worked with hammers or other tools.

A few paces from the stone floors, John revealed steps leading into a larger, ill-defined structure. We could trace its foundation, as it zigzagged with right-angle turns to cross a modern fire-lane service road. Pointing to three nearby hillocks, John said he believed they are artificial. Until properly excavated, his conclusion cannot be verified. But after many years of studying such ancient structures in the Midwest, I felt that the suspicious trio of mounds strongly resembled prehistoric earthworks, if only because these specimens found no similar parallels in the surrounding landscape. Moreover, their man-made provenance was reinforced by proximity to masonry and pavements all around us.

Archaeological Discoveries of Ancient America

John led us on to a pair of stone structures he referred to as "tombs." These were collapsed, cave-like depressions in the mountainside with undressed but neatly fitted stone walls and equally unworked but true arches. The openings were approximately 3 feet (1 m) wide at the base and just as high from base to arch, with interiors deepening to less than 4 feet (1.2 m) before fill. He told us that recently the landowner scared off a couple of pot-hunters who were digging into the collapsed entrance of one of the chambers. It had been penetrated by the intruders, who removed edged weapons and metallic tablets covered with an unknown script. Tragically, they escaped with these items, and thereafter the landowner dynamited the underground entrance shut to prevent further looting. John went on to say that there were additional subterranean locations similar to those we saw, but visiting them required another full day of exploration.

Like all the other features at the site, the arched structures have not been properly excavated, and so cannot be yet verified as tombs. That may happen in the near future. John and I have applied for grant funding to engage professional archaeologists and geologists. They alone should be allowed to determine the site's full extent, age and significance through scientific evaluation. One thing at least is certain: The Wasatch stonework is not the result of historic visitors. The local Ute Indians claim to know nothing about the barren area, which they avoided as unlivable.

Were environmental conditions less severe when the people who built the site inhabited it? How long ago was that? And who could they have been? These were only some of the questions that stirred my mind, as John and I descended the mountain. But their answers will be forthcoming, as soon as the experts put tape and trowel to earth among the cut and arched stones of the nameless city in the clouds.

CHAPTER 8

Forgotten Seamanship

ritics of any possibility that pre-Columbian seafarers ever completed transoceanic voyages cite the lack of proper navigational instruments available to mariners before the European Renaissance. But just such a missing piece of the archaeological puzzle has recently come to light, proving that the Norse did in fact possess the means by which to cross great stretches of open sea to America and back.

DID A SUNSTONE GUIDE THE VIKINGS TO AMERICA?

By Earl Koenig

After nearly a century of scoffing denial, even mainstream historians were finally forced to admit that Vikings sailed from Bergen on the coast of Norway to Iceland, continuing to Greenland, eventually landing in America 500 years before Columbus planted the Spanish flag on the shores of El Salvador. But how the Northmen were able to achieve this extraordinarily difficult feat of navigation continued to puzzle conventional scholars. How could the Norse have steered a true course during such long voyages beyond sight of land, especially in the usual bad weather and low visibility of Arctic latitudes?

The North Atlantic run is among the most hazardous open-water crossings on Earth, where even a compass is largely useless, because of close proximity to the magnetic pole. The answer has always been available and cited by cultural diffusionists opposed to stereotypical portrayals of the Norse as skillful, if crude, barbarians. *Hrafnkel's Saga* (circa 1275) tells of a perilous voyage in which "the weather was thick and stormy.... The king looked about and saw no blue sky...then the king took the sun-stone and held it up, and then he saw where the sun beamed from the stone." Other medieval source materials recount the use of "sunstones" as effective navigational devices throughout the Viking Age. But what exactly *were* sunstones? Were they real, or merely legendary?

In 1967, a Danish archaeologist, Thorkild Ramskov, concluded that such objects were not flights of skaldic fancy, but cordierite, a kind of natural crystal with birefringent and dichroic properties that change color and brightness when rotated in front of polarized light, allowing for precise location of the sun's position on an overcast day. Birefringence, or double refraction, is the splitting of a light-wave into two different components: an ordinary and an extraordinary ray otherwise invisible to the naked eye. The color of cordierite will change from blue to light yellow when pointed in the sun's direction.

To back up his conclusion, Ramskov pointed out that cordierite pebbles are found in large numbers along the coast of Norway. Optical calcite, known as "Iceland Spar," works just as well, playing an important role in the scientific discovery and study of polarization. Iceland, of course, was found and occupied by the Norse. Even today, many high-performance polarizers use Iceland Spar. Such stones could have performed even when the sun was several degrees below the horizon, when the atmosphere was still illuminated. Light fog and thin clouds cannot eliminate light polarization, as revealed by optical calcite or cordierite crystal. Only under a thickly overcast sky would sunstones fail to operate.

At first, Ramskov's theory was well received and widely accepted by public and academics alike. Even ordinarily conservative *Scientific American* and *National Geographic* magazines published articles applauding his plausible research. It was not long, however, before the professional deniers began ridiculing any notion of Viking sunstones as just so much "comic-book archaeology." But in early 2007, Hungarian researchers testing cordierite used during the Viking Age (800 to 1200 CE) found that the crystals do in fact reveal the sun's position with a remarkable degree of accuracy, even in bad weather. For more than a month, Dr. Gabor Horvath led a team of investigators from Budapest's Eotvos University recording polarization in the Arctic. They proved that the crystals located the sun's position in foggy or cloudy conditions.

Even 20 years before Ramskov proposed his theory, Norse navigational genius was inadvertently duplicated after nearly a thousand years during the late 1940s, when research technicians at the U.S. National Bureau of Standards (NBS) developed a "sky compass" based on the same principle of polarization so successfully employed by Viking mariners. Based on a "twilight compass" invented by Dr. A.H. Pfund of Johns Hopkins University, an NBS paper for 1949 read, "The principal advantage of the sky compass is during twilight, and when the sun is several degrees below the horizon, as well as when the region of the sky containing the sun is overcast, so long as there is a clear patch of sky overhead. The sky compass is thus of particular value when the sextant is not usable. Since the extent of polarization of the sky's light is greatest at right angles to the incident beam of sunlight, the compass is most accurate in the polar regions, where it is also most useful, because of the long duration of twilight."

Experiments with the sky compass were conducted by the U.S. Navy and Air Force throughout the early 1950s. It was used by pilots of the Scandinavian Air Service (SAS) for several years on polar flights, following in the technological footsteps of their Viking forefathers. Like the Classical Greeks' analog computer taken from an ancient shipwreck near the Aegean island of Antikythera, or Germany's Nebra Disc, an astronomical clock from the Bronze Age, the Norse sunstones prove that our ancestors were not the benighted savages depicted by mainstream scholars, but masters of their natural environment, and world travelers.

Reinoud de Jonge is a theoretical physical chemist and teacher in the Netherlands. His coauthor on this piece, Jay Stuart Wakefield, is a Washington State zoologist who owns a world-class collection of antiquities from around the world. Together, they have tirelessly pieced out a megalithic puzzle that clearly indicates overseas expeditions from Scandinavia centuries before the Vikings launched their first longship.

SWEDEN'S IRON AGE MONUMENT TO TRANSATLANTIC VOYAGES

By Reinoud de Jonge and Jay Stuart Wakefield

The huge megalithic ship monument of Ales Stenar overlooking the Baltic Sea on the south coast of Sweden was known as a "Sun-Ship to the Realm of the Dead." Quadrants at the ends of the vessel both contain 23 menhirs, or standing stones, at 23-degree angles, encoding the 23rd-degree tropic of Cancer, a holy latitude of the ancient sun religion, a numeric feature of all megalithic monuments. Latitudes encoded in the Swedish structure, often based upon the site latitude, show the sailing route used on voyages to Central America, symbolizing the Land of the Dead.

Sweden's megalithic site incorporates Iron Age navigation data to the Americas.

Archaeological Discoveries of Ancient America

Ales Stenar is one of the latest megalithic monuments of Europe, dated to circa 500 BCE. Some archaeologists believe it dates from circa 700 BCE (the Late Bronze Age), and others conclude that a date circa 600 CE (Late Iron Age) is more likely. The site was partially excavated in 1916 and again in 1956, when sand that had blown over the site was removed.

The monument is located near Kaseberga, 9 miles (15 kilometers) east of Ystad, obliquely overlooking the sea on the south coast of Sweden. The port side, or southwest quadrant, faces the sea. Hundreds of ship-like formations are found in southern Scandinavia, but this is reported to be the largest one. Ales Stenar may be the most important megalithic monument in Sweden. It stands in a formation of 58 large menhirs (tall, standing stones erected upright during Paleolithic and Neolithic times), with a length of 220 feet (67 meters) and a width of 62 feet (19 meters). Actually, only 57 are present, because menhir number 46 is missing, although its foundation still exists.

The axis of the ship formation points exactly to 45 degrees northwest of True North. Average diameters of 56 of the menhirs are about 3 feet (1 meter), with heights of 5 feet (1.5 meters). The remaining two menhirs on the axis are larger, with heights of about 10 feet (3 meters). On average, the menhirs are placed about 8 feet (2.5 meters) apart. At least four menhirs of white sandstone (among these, the two big menhirs on the axis) are thought to have been brought a considerable distance, some 25 miles (40 kilometers) down the coast from the northeast, near the town of Simrishamn. The other boulders could have been collected at different spots in South Skane at comparable distances, probably not close to the site. Most of the menhirs have smooth surfaces, but they are not dressed. Their smoothness derives from the working of the ice sheets during Scandinavia glacial epochs.

Inside the northwest end of the formation, and beside the axis, is a small stone. Most likely it was moved from some original position behind the big northwest menhir, making this part of the ship symmetrical with the other end. These two stones are known as keel-stones, and appear at each end of the ship design. Their diameters and heights are only about 1.6 feet (.5 m). Adding these two small posts to the 58 menhirs gives a total of 60 stones. The monument is situated on a flat hilltop, a 121 foot (37-meter) high ridge, about 328 feet (100 meters) from the sea. The latitude of the site is 55.5 degrees North, or rounded off to 56 degrees North.

Ales Stenar is essentially a "sun-ship" sailing toward the west. Solar boat symbolism was of central importance in ancient Egyptian religion, wherein representations of the sacred vessel carried Ra, the sun-god, across the ceilings of tombs dotting the west bank of the Nile River. The name Ales (or Als) signifies "sanctuary" in old Nordic, and Stenar means "of stone."

From the center of the monument, the four cardinal points are occupied by menhirs: north (stone #19), south (#48), east (#12), and west (#41). These four stones may have been originally painted, or perhaps were decorated when the monument was still in use. Similar to the rectangle of the four so-called station stones at Stonehenge, these four "cardinal" stones, erect in a perfect square, mark the equinoxes and solstices observed at the site. Inclusive of the cardinal stones, there are 23 menhirs at either end of the ship. They also form 23-degree angles at both ends.

Modern representations of our planet show the 23-degree tropic of Cancer, a holy latitude of the old solar religion. This latitude is as far north as the sun appears overhead in summer. Also at the latitude of 23 degrees North was located the center of the Egyptians' southern empire, the geographic center of their cult. Where the tropic of Cancer crosses the coast of Africa at 23 degrees North was an early focus for ocean exploration. According to Egyptian belief, the realm of the dead lay in the West, on the other side of the waters, in the land where the sun sets. After death, the human soul was supposed to reunite there with its ancestors, family, relatives, and friends. The Swedish structure memorializes the sailing route that was used to reach the West during ancient times.

Extending the axis of the monument to the southeast at 45 degrees on a globe, observers note it points to the delta of the River Donau at 45 degrees North. By sailing the rivers Wista (in Poland) and Dnister (in Ukraine) to this delta, traders accomplished the first half of the shortest route from the Baltic to the Black Sea and the eastern Mediterranean. The direction from Ales Stenar to the Nile Delta, the center of the northern Egyptian empire, is 60 degrees southeast (60 stones), and the complementary angle, 30 degrees, is the latitude of the Nile Delta at 30 degrees North. Complementary angles are used in megalithic sites to encode large numbers, because this was easier for the ancients than moving large numbers of stones. Think of the labor involved!

The two halves of the ship each contain 30 menhirs, confirming the 30-degree latitude of the Delta. If the three bow and three stern menhirs, which are slightly taller, and the cardinal stones, are excluded, the sides of the ship each contain 26 menhirs, the 26-degree latitude of the whole Egyptian empire, halfway between the tropic of Cancer and the Nile Delta. This latitude marks the center of government in Egypt. The axis of the monument points 45 degrees northwest via the northern tip of Jutland, Denmark, the southern tip of Norway, the northern tip of the Shetland Islands and the Faeroes, to the southeast and west coasts of Iceland, and the east coast of Greenland at 65 degrees North. The 58 large menhirs of Ales Stenar correspond to the north coast of Scotland at 58 degrees North. From this location, mariners may navigate a 45-degree angle via the southwest coast of Iceland to Cape Holm, Greenland, on the Arctic Circle, at 67 degrees North.

Megalithic monuments, such as Stonehenge, or Loughcrew, in Ireland, indicate that Greenland was found by explorers from Iceland at the latitude of 67 degrees. The complementary angle of 23 degrees, 67 degrees, provides this other holy latitude, the Arctic Circle, which was sacred to worshippers of the old sun religion, because it is the northernmost latitude where the sun shines at midwinter. Seen from the center of the monument on the winter solstice, the sun rises exactly behind the large southeastern menhir on the axis.

In total, Ales Stenar consists of 60 stones, which encode the southern and southwestern capes of Greenland at 60 degrees North. Sailing direction from the southwestern cape to the coast of Labrador is 45 degrees southwest, which appeared to ancient sailors as they reached the latitude of 56 degrees North, the same latitude as Ales Stenar, as shown by the 56 menhirs on the two sides of the ship. The southwest side of the central part of the ship, including the cardinal stones, contains 8 stones (#41–#48), encoding the sailing distance of 8 degrees, or 552 miles (888 kilometers). Significant sites always contain their latitudes encoded in the site design, and it appears here in the 60 stones, minus the four cardinal stones. These stones simultaneously encode the 56-degree latitude where an extensive new land was found on the other side of the Atlantic Ocean, which is one of the main reasons why this monument was built, and why it is located where it is.

Note that there are significant parallels with Stonehenge, such as its 56 Aubrey Holes. By dropping off the three bow and three stern menhirs, we find the latitude of important Belle Isle Strait, at 52 degrees North (58–6). So, the sailing route west of Newfoundland is shown to be preferred. Sailing directions from the southwestern cape of Newfoundland to Cape Breton Island are 45 degrees southwest, again shown by the orientation of the ship at 45 degrees. Navigation continues to the south along the east coast of North America. The two large menhirs on the axis encode the south cape of Florida, 2 degrees above the tropic of Cancer, at 25 degrees North (23+2). The same two menhirs provide the sailing distance to Cuba: 2 degrees, or 138 miles (222 km). The four sides at the ends of the ship each contain 11 menhirs, encoding the sailing direction from Cuba to Yucatan, 11 degrees west-southwest. Again, the two large menhirs on the axis provide the sailing distance involved, about 138 miles (222 kilometers).

The 16 menhirs at the central part of the ship image provide the latitude of the culture on the north coast of Honduras, Belize, and Guatemala, at 16 degrees North. Adding the two large menhirs on the axis again gives us the latitude of civilization around the Gulf of Campeche, at 18 degrees North. This is the center of the "Realm of the Dead," the "Land of Punt." Their latitudes are common in late megalithic monuments and petroglyphs. The complementary angle of the monument's 60 stones (90 – 60 = 30) reveals the Mississippi River Delta at 30 degrees North, gateway to the Poverty Point complex, which was of importance for the copper trade with the hinterland.

Ancient Old World visits to Punt took place during the so-called Formative Period in Central America, which lasted from about 1500 BCE to 200 CE. In this period, the most striking characteristics of the civilization developed. Around 500 BCE, the first towns and states are in evidence in several places more or less at the same time. The mouth of the Motagua River, at 16 degrees North, leads south to the Old Mesoamerican civilization, which developed from about 2000 BCE, and flourished after circa 1500 BCE, when permanent villages appeared along the river valleys. The main center formed around Copan, Honduras. Circa 500 BCE, at the time of these visits, a gradual expansion of settlements took place, and the Maya city of Tikal began to develop. The Zapotecs lived further west, and ruled the valley of Oaxaca from Monte Alban ("the Hill of the Jaguar"), which had at least 5,000 inhabitants at this time and possessed interesting petroglyphs indicating cultural diffusion. The Olmec culture flourished from circa 1500 to 300 BCE, famous for its unique art, religion, and calendar. The colossal Negroid stone heads with Egyptian-style helmets found around the ceremonial plazas date from before 500 BCE.

Middle America could also have been reached from Northern Europe via a southern crossing of the Atlantic Ocean. A possible departure point was the Cape Verde Islands at 16 degrees North, again encoded by the 16 menhirs in the central part of the ship. The sailing direction from the Cape Verde Islands to the closest Brazilian shore is 60 degrees southwest, again encoded by the 60 stones. The two ends of the ship each contain 23 menhirs, corresponding to the sailing distance, 23 degrees, or 1,588 miles (2,555 kilometers). A large southeastern menhir on the ship's axis corresponds with the southern Atlantic island of St. Paul at 1 degree North. The four menhirs of the cardinal directions correspond to the two islands of Fernando de Noronha, at 4 degrees South, and together these five correspond with Cape Sao Roque (the "Holy rock"), Brazil, at 5 degrees South.

An alternative return route from Central America to Europe proceeded via the isolated island of Bermuda. The three bow menhirs (#29–#31) correspond to Bimini near Florida, 3 degrees above the tropic of Cancer, at 26 degrees North (23 + 3). The two large menhirs on Ales Stenar's axis encode Bermuda: 2 degrees above the Nile Delta, at 32 degrees North (30 + 2), as well as the initial sailing direction (ISD) from Great Abaco to Bermuda, 32 degrees northeast. Between the cardinal stones in the center quadrants are 12 menhirs (6 + 6), corresponding to the sailing distance involved, 12 degrees, or 828 miles (1,333 kilometers). Bermuda was discovered from the American coast about 2200 BCE, as shown by the Devil's Head petroglyphs in Harmony, Maine. However, from Bermuda to the West Azores is a long sailing distance. Accordingly, most ships sailed along the coast of the eastern seaboard to the north.

The three bow and three stern menhirs encode Cape Hatteras, the East Cape of the North America, 6 degrees above the Nile Delta, at 36 degrees North (30 + 6). It is located at the same latitude as the famous Strait of Gibraltar, at the entrance of the Mediterranean. The main departure point for returning, with the winds and currents, was the east coast of Nova

Scotia, at 45 degrees North, again encoded by Ales Stenar's 45-degree axis angle. They oriented on Cape Race, Newfoundland, 2 degrees higher, encoded by the two menhirs on the axis, at 47 degrees North (45 + 2): the east cape of North America. Ancient mariners focused on finding the western Azores in mid-ocean at 39 degrees North, encoded by adding together the 23 menhirs of the south end of the ship, with the 16 central menhirs (23 + 16 = 39). The mathematical encoding is beautiful in its simplicity. Other encodings are, of course, possible, but less likely.

The three bow menhirs (#1, #2, and #58) symbolize the three-island group of the Azores, which had been discovered by 3600 BCE, as shown in the Tumulus of Gavrinis in the Gulf of Morbihan, Brittany. Excluding these three larger stones, the end of the ship has nine stones at each side of the end, symbolizing the nine islands of the Azores. The nine menhirs on each side add together to the initial sailing direction from Cape Race to the important West Azores, 18 degrees east-southeast, and the sailing distance of 18 degrees, or 1,243 (2,000 kilometers), which is correct. The three bow menhirs and the 30 stones at the southeastern half of the ship encode the terminal sailing direction (TSD) in the neighborhood of the West Azores, 33 degrees east-southeast (30 + 33). The difference between both sailing directions is due to the curvature of the surface of the Earth. The image is striking. The lonely stones of Ales Stenar on the high ridge overlooking the Baltic suggest a small ship sailing the endless ocean.

From the Western Azores, Late Bronze Age seafarers sailed along the other islands to the East Azores. The large, southeast menhir on Ales Stenar's axis encodes St. Maria, East Azores, 1 degree above Gibraltar, at 37 degrees North (36 + 1). The latitude of Gibraltar (at 36 degrees north) corresponds to the ISD from St. Maria to Madeira, 36 degrees southeast. Half the 16 menhirs in the center correspond to the sailing distance to Madeira, 8 degrees, or 522 miles (888 kilometers). The latitude of the eastern Canaries (at 29 degrees North) corresponds to the terminal sailing direction in the neighborhood of Madeira, 29 degrees east-southeast. Ales Stenar's three bow menhirs encode the latitude of Madeira, 3 degrees above the Nile Delta, at 33 degrees North (30 + 3).

All 58 menhirs of the ship correspond to the sailing direction to the eastern Canary Islands, 58 degrees southeast. The 29 menhirs of the southeast half of the ship encode the eastern Canaries, at 29 degrees North. This is the end of a ritual voyage to Central America, the Land of Punt. The entire ship formation at Ales Stenar symbolizes an ancient pilgrimage to the West. The northern menhirs (#2–#29) represent the northern route from the Old World (stern menhir) to the New World (the bow menhir), and the southern menhirs (#31–#58) represent the main southern return route.

Dating the Swedish monument poses real problems. It surely dates back to sometime after the transatlantic discovery of America, circa 2500 BCE, as evidenced by references to America encoded in the structure. It describes the crossing of the Labrador Sea from south Greenland to the North American mainland, indicating a date after 1600 BCE. The formation represents a highly stylized ship, telling a story by reference latitudes, and these show a very late megalithic date, after circa 1000 BCE. It was probably laid out prior to the second Persian rule of Egypt, which lasted from 341 to 333 BCE. Surely, the stones were erected before the Hellenistic Period, which lasted from 332 BCE until 642 CE, when Greek was the official language in Egypt.

The fact that cup marks have been found on many of the menhirs points to origins in the Bronze Age, which ended in Scandinavia circa 500 BCE. However, it has been observed that some of these marks were carved in strange places, some hardly visible. The idea has been put forth that these menhirs were taken from old Bronze Age monuments in the neighborhood. We doubt this, because the stones appear to have been brought to the site over long distances. Generally, sanctuaries were not built by demolishing older sanctuaries. More usually, megalithic monuments were only seriously disturbed during recent centuries. But Ales Stenar is a Scandinavian ship-setting, and these kinds of structures, though much smaller, usually date from the Iron Age, or even later. For all these reasons, we think Ales Stenar dates from the very end of the Late Bronze Age, circa 500 BCE. However, a strong relation with the Egyptian sun-god religion is a typical megalithic tradition. A 500 BCE date implies that Ales Stenar is by far the latest monument of its kind in Europe. The megalithic culture officially ends circa 1500 BCE.

The largest carved rock petroglyph of a ritual boat in Sweden, with a length of 14 feet (4.13 meters), has the same date. It is from Rickeby in Uppland (north of Stockholm), which is situated at the latitude of Cape Farvel, Greenland, at 60 degrees North, and contains six full-sized, dressed rowers, encoding the northwest peninsula of Iceland at 66 degrees North (60 + 6). The entire boat is carried by another figure, the sun god, encoding Cape Holm, Greenland, at the Arctic Circle, 67 degrees North (66 + 1). He carries the ship to the Realm of the Dead in the west. Another petroglyph, dated from circa 3200 BCE, depicts a ship with 67 rowers, showing that it too sailed to Cape Holm at the Arctic Circle. Note the long time span of this megalithic, religious tradition.

Beneath one of the Ales Stenar menhirs, #6, a piece of birch charcoal was found and carbon-dated to circa 600 CE. This result is definitely not in line with previous arguments. We have to presume that the sample was not representative, and recommend further research in this field, if possible, to clarify any conflicting indications.

Denmark's Als (meaning "sanctuary") lies 168 miles (270 kilometers) west of Ales Stenar. On this island, a now famous ship, 62 feet (19 meters) in length, has been excavated and dated to the Iron Age, circa 150 BCE. Its remains contained dozens of iron shields, spears, and swords, but also Roman beakers and dishes, which point to trade with the Roman Empire. Compare this with the monument of Ales Stenar, with its religious orientation to Egypt; the Ales Stenar monument is clearly of a much earlier date.

Rather than construct a huge, laborious monument of a great many stones, the builders of Ales Stenar used a few combinations repeatedly, as an encoding convention. These rules of encoding employed the 60 stones, one end-post stone, the two end-post stones, the four cardinal stones, together with the eight stones of each of the side quadrants, the 23 stones of the end quadrants, and complementary numbers. Clearly, the most important encodings of the monument are the 23-degree tropic of Cancer, and the 60-degree Cape Farvel of South Greenland.

Suggestions of an ancient pilgrimage route from Late Bronze Age Sweden to Central America, the Realm of the Dead, is confirmed by the menhir distances within the monument itself. As an example, we illustrate the main goal of the voyage. The width/length ratio of Ales Stenar at 56 degrees North confirms the latitude of the north coast of Honduras at $(19.1 \text{m}/67.0 \text{m}) \times 56 = 16$ degrees north. This and similar results of other distance/length ratios contribute to the beauty of this ancient, sacred monument. The numbers of such huge menhirs are not happenstance, but were chosen with deliberation.

As in other megalithic sites, astronomical and calendrical meanings appear to have also been built into the Swedish monument. A complex entwining of encodings is particularly clear at Britain's Stonehenge at Salisbury, and at America's Stonehenge in New Hampshire. Given the known level of astronomical expertise displayed at these sites, the encoding of religious pilgrimages and commercial routes in numbers and petroglyphs may be anticipated. Their builders could not write a spoken language. However, they lived outdoors much of the time. They must have been capable of physical exploits in a world full of wildlife. That so much information, both astronomical and geographical, could be encoded in so few stones must have seemed holy, or special to them, as it seems amazing to us.

Humble discoveries sometimes generate radical changes, especially if official notions about the past are based upon fundamentally erroneous suppositions. These flawed preconceptions are therefore particularly vulnerable to even mundane, contrary evidence. A case in point is the long-standing academic position that no Asian mariners could have crossed the vast Pacific Ocean to the Americas before modern times. That Establishment paradigm was dealt a lethal blow, however, when New Zealand scholars presented proof of Chinese impact on pre-Spanish Chile.

AN OLD MAP AND SOME CHICKEN BONES TERRIFY ARCHAEOLOGISTS

By John Gallagher

Did mariners sail from China to the West Coast of America before Spanish explorers claimed California? This question has been argued ever since Chinese anchor-stones were dredged up from the bottom of San Francisco Bay more than 100 years ago. The controversy is currently undergoing renewed debate with the recent discovery of an entirely different kind. It is not made of several tons of stone, but a few grams of paper: a map purchased several years ago from an antique dealer in the People's Republic of China by a local lawyer.

As part of his cartography collection, Liu Gang knew it was old, because the year "1418" appeared in an upper corner. On closer inspection, however, he was able to trace unmistakable references to coastal California, proof that its makers were already familiar with North America. Last January 16, Gang openly discussed his pre-Columbian map for the first time at a packed press conference in Beijing.

Although Chinese scholars are at least open to the possibility of trans-pacific voyages from their country, and have expressed interest in Gang's find, it was immediately pounced upon by British and American archae-ologists as "an 18th-century copy of a European map," according to Geoff Wade, senior research fellow at the University of Singapore's Asia Research Institute. Wade did not actually examine the map, but felt competent enough to dismiss it as a hoax, sight unseen.

He was seconded by Sally K. Church, fellow at the University of Cam-bridge. Wade went on to fault a British magazine, *The Economist*, because its editors ran a balanced, noncommittal article in which arguments both for and against Gang's controversial map were presented. Enraged by such fair play that allowed his myopic views to be challenged, Wade demanded a full retraction from the beleaguered periodical. "That your writer has contributed to the Menzies bandwagon and continuing deception of the public is saddening," he cried. "The support mentioned all comes from Mr. Menzies' band of acolytes, and the claims have no academic support whatsoever. Your writer has been taken in by Mr. Menzies, and you do have a social responsibility to rectify this."

In *1421: The Year China Discovered America,* author Gavin Menzies demonstrated that an Admiral Zhen landed with a flotilla of Chinese ships along the Pacific coasts of North America 71 years before Christo-pher Columbus set sail for the New World. In truth, Admiral Zhen was by no means the discoverer of America, but rather the last in a long series of Chinese voyagers who crossed the Pacific Ocean to California beginning in the early third millennium BCE. In *American Discovery*, Dr. Gunnar

Archæological Discoveries of Ancient America

Thompson abundantly establishes China's deeply prehistoric influence at work in the American Southwest, referred to by the ancient Chinese as *Fu Sang*: "Buddhist historian Kuan-Mei identified the Grand Canyon of Fu Sang as the site of the Chinese observations beginning with the reign of Emperor Hwang-ti, circa 2640 BCE."

Only after reading Menzies's book did Gang realize the real significance of his map, and therefore decided to go public with it. Rather than subject his discovery to a critical, unbiased examination, mainstream archaeologists fulminate against its even-handed discussion, because they are interested only in upholding their disintegrating worldview—not in any evidence that contradicts the Columbus-Was-First dogma.

While trying to patch the leaky boat of their obsolete paradigm after the disclosure of Liu Gang's map, their stricken vessel took on water with more bad news for mainstream historians. According to the latest issue of the *Proceedings of the National Academy of Sciences*, the bones of early-14th- to mid-15th-century chickens, animals not native to the Americas, and previously believed to have been introduced by the Spanish 500 years ago, have been excavated at El Arenal, on the south coast of Chile. Lisa Matisco-Smith, an anthropologist from New Zealand's University of Auckland, stated the obvious by pointing out that chickens were unable to reach South America by themselves and could only have been brought by humans. Genetic material she extracted from the bones showed they belonged to a species of fowl native to Polynesia, not Europe, with a DNA sequence found in chickens from Tonga, Samoa, Niue, Easter Island, and Hawaii. Carbon-14 testing of the El Arenal bones yielded date parameters from 1304 to 1424.

The dates suggest Polynesians beat the Spanish to Chile by 200 years, and they also coincide with Admiral Zheng's voyage to California, as defined in Gavin Menzies's book. The Chinese, en route to America's western seaboard, could have made landfall at Tonga, Samoa, Niue, Easter Island, or Hawaii to replenish their supplies—including chickens—and left the bones of a meal behind at El Arenal. In any case, the Chilean find unequivocally documents the arrival of visitors to South America from across the Pacific Ocean long before modern Europeans set foot on the continent. As such, cultural diffusionists everywhere are gratified to learn that such humble items as an old map and a few chicken bones are sufficient to topple the entrenched Establishment of Official Archaeology that has too long dominated public opinion.

In this, the fifth of his eight articles for Ancient American *magazine, James Grimes shows that seafarers centuries and even millennia before Columbus operated true, oceangoing vessels more than capable of crossing the waves from Europe to our continent.*

THE PRE-COLUMBIAN CONNECTION: ANCIENT TRANSATLANTIC SHIPS

By James P. Grimes

Any discussion of ancient Old World travelers to America seems to bring up the same question: How could they have crossed the Atlantic with the crude ships they had?

Considerable physical evidence, however, suggests, that long before 600 BCE (the advent of Classical Civilization), our ancestors operated oceangoing vessels two and three times the size of Columbus's *Santa Maria*, and far more seaworthy. Direct evidence of their maritime proficiency is found in four primary sources:

1. Graphic images from old paintings, rock inscriptions, pottery art, coins, and so on, although these generally are of little direct help

in determining dimensions, or capacity of the ships portrayed, because the artists made little attempt at scale or even visual accuracy. Their renditions are primarily helpful in visualizing how the ships were built and rigged, while allowing a general conception of their size.

2. Surviving written documents from the Classical era, both texts and inscriptions. Their careful reading provides considerable data about ancient ship-building, although sometimes of a scattered nature.

3. Physical remains, such as Roman Emperor Caligula's first-century CE yacht, dry-dock ruins at Piraeus in Greece, and so on.

4. Detailed analysis of sunken ships. The remains of many Classical-era ships have been found and studied. With the expansion of marine archaeology, much information pertaining to size, building methods, destinations, and cargos is now available. Fortunately, many of the ancient cargo ships carried loads of clay amphora filled with wine or olive oil, staples of the time. These pots and their cushioning packing have not only survived the passage of many centuries, but also in many cases preserved the planking beneath them. Although the rest of the vessel may have rotted away, enough of the hulls and amphorae are still relatively intact.

A major hurdle in reviewing ancient ship capabilities is the definition of the word *size*. The ancients did not have any standard measurements for ships; as a result, we are forced to use a mix of boat length, crew size, and carrying capacity (tonnage), depending on information available. For purposes of comparison, we refer to the *Santa Maria*, *Pinta*, and *Niña*, because these are the earliest-documented transatlantic craft. Although their exact measurements are unknown, the *Santa Maria* was about 75 feet (23 m) from bow to stern, and weighed some 90 tons (82 metric tons). The *Niña* and *Pinta* were each approximately 55 feet (17 m) long and 55 tons (50 metric tons).

The first known ancient sailing ship of any size was a vessel originally dismantled before having been sealed inside a pit at the foot of Egypt's Great Pyramid at the Giza Plateau about 4,500 years ago. When its perfectly preserved 1,200 cedarwood pieces were reassembled in 1982 after their discovery 28 years before, the ship stood at an overall length of 132 feet (40 m). With a crew of 17 men, the barge evidenced graceful lines, was sturdily built, and featured an air-conditioned cabin afforded by moistened palm leaves stowed in an overhead ventilation space. Another Egyptian ship larger by nearly 60 feet, is described in a 1900 BCE inscription that relates that the vessel was wrecked in the Red Sea.

About 400 years later, a relief in the tomb of Queen Hatshepsut portrays a barge 200 feet (61 m) long carrying two 100-foot (30 m) obelisks end to end from Aswan. The same mortuary art represents the return of a fleet from the Land of Punt with ship lengths of 90 to 100 feet (27 to 30 m). These were true oceangoing craft. Punt is believed to be somewhere in East or South Africa, based on the exotic cargo list inscribed—perhaps Somalia, Zanzibar, or even South Africa.

A 14th-century BCE, 50-foot (15 m) merchantman roughly the size of Columbus's *Niña*, and in fairly good shape, was found in 140 feet (43 m) of water off Turkey. Still preserved in its hold were 200 copper ingots, tin, blue glass ingots, gold and silver jewelry, scrap metal, Baltic amber, bronze tools, African exotics, and more. The cargo represented eight cultures: Mycenaean Greek, Minoan, Canaanite, Cypriot, Egyptian, Kassite, Assyrian, and Nubian. Not long after this discovery, a 12th-century BCE wreck of similar size and content was located, also off Turkey, not far from the earlier Bronze Age vessel.

Both ships belonged to a period dominated by Minoans, Etruscans, Phoenicians, Libyans, and early Greeks. These people were the major sea traders of the age, but left few written records of their ships or commerce, though we do know they traveled throughout the Mediterranean and out into the Atlantic at least as far as West Africa and Britain. We also know from their warships, pottery decorations, and inscriptions, that the art of building ships, both in size and seaworthiness, advanced significantly during this time.

Biblical records record that around 900 BCE King Solomon hired Phoenicia's Hiram of Tyre to build freighters capacious enough to access the lucrative Indian Ocean trade. Solomon's chief commercial prospect was "Ophir," which modern scholars have been unable to locate with any certainty, arguing among themselves that it may have been synonymous for Ethiopia, Somalia, or India. In any case, the Israeli king's venture was unsuccessful, as his vessels proved too unwieldy for their sailors. No ship sizes were stated, but they must have been quite large.

The sixth-century BCE relief of a full-hulled trader from Tarshish in Spain indicates a length of 110 feet (34 m) and a tonnage of perhaps 150 (136 metric tons).

First the Greeks and then the Romans found that, with their increased populations, they could no longer feed themselves without massive grain from overseas. They imported wheat by ship from the Black Sea, North Africa, and Egypt, which led to the building of ever-larger grain ships. Records of first 400- (363 metric tons) and then 1,200-ton (1,089 metric tons) and larger grain haulers exist. These were true deepwater transports. A trip from Egypt to Rome with contrary winds took one to three months. Rome had as many as a hundred of these giant ships by the first century BCE. By then, they were importing 150,000 tons (136,078 metric tons) of grain a year.

There were no passenger liners as we know them today in Roman times, but their grain carriers took along as many as 600 passengers. Saint Paul was shipwrecked on a grain ship that carried 276 passengers (Acts 27:37). These must have been very large ships. Surviving third-century BCE records from the Greek island port of Thasos categorize seagoing ships as "small" (80 tons [73 metric tons]), "regular" (200-plus tons [181 metric tons]), and "large" (in excess of 340 tons [308 metric tons]). Athenaeus, a contemporary Greek writer, described what he called the largest ancient sailing vessel ever built (in 240 BCE), the *Syracusia*, a 2,000-tonner (1,814 metric tons), with an overall length of 240 feet (73 m). He also described the Ancient World's largest galley, an oared ship. In 260 BCE, Helenized Egypt's Ptolemy IV commissioned a twin-hulled galley 420 feet (128 m) long. The bow and stern posts were taller than the Great Sphinx. The *Alexandris* took a crew of 4,000 to row her, with as many as eight men per oar. With an additional 400 officers, artillery personnel, cooks, priests, and so on, she could carry as many as 2,800 marines on deck, and must have looked something like an aircraft carrier. Whether or not she used sails is not known. Lesser Greek ships were traveling directly to southern India, using the monsoons, by the second century BCE.

Lionel Casson, the doyen of ancient maritime history, lists 30 pre-Christian shipwrecks that have been found and studied. Four were larger than the *Santa Maria*; one was four times its size. All were solidly built and seaworthy. Hull planks were set edge to edge and held together with mortise and tenons, then pegged for security. This method is very strong, and requires little caulking, but is expensive to build. One of the ships had been in service an estimated 80 years when it sank.

Julius Caesar devoted several chapters in his *Gallic Wars* to an important naval battle in the Atlantic off France in 56 BCE. There, he fought a decisive engagement with 220 warships from France and Britain, and his account provides us with the best-surviving description of the oceangoing ships of his time. Caesar reported that the Celtic vessels, their sails of beaten leather, not more-easily ripped linen, were so large and tall that his own substantial galleys, even with towers, could not reach the enemy's decks. The Celtic ships were oak, with beams a foot thick and iron nails as big around as a thumb, so sturdily built that the Romans could not ram them with any success. He admired their ability to ride heavy ocean swells. Celtic skill in naval affairs greatly surpassed all others.

Unfortunately, Caesar provided no dimensions for his opponents' vessels, other than to add that they were larger than his 180-foot (55 m) galleys. He overcame them only because the wind dropped at an appropriate moment. His own galleys, propelled by oars, were then able to surround the enemy warships one at a time, grapple, and board. Recently, a Celtic ship dated to 200 years after Caesar's victory at sea was found in the western Mediterranean off Marseilles. Its oak beams were 2 feet (61 cm) thick.

By that time, more than 100 Roman ships a year were making the 3,500-mile (5,633 km) direct run from the Red Sea to India for trade. Such trips were farther than Columbus's transatlantic leg from the Canaries to the Bahamas.

Much of the know-how and skills Classical sailors possessed to build such large and sturdy ships was lost during the Dark Ages (500 to 1300 CE) and had to be gradually relearned. Indeed, some of the ancient ship-building capabilities were not matched until the 17th and 19th centuries. An early-17th-century carpenter's plan survives for a Dutch East India merchantman, the largest class of ships then being built. It was a 300-ton (272 metric tons) vessel, about the size of some Greek ships during the sixth century BCE. The first packet to make scheduled trips between New York and London in 1818, the *James Monroe*, was only of 424 tons (385 metric tons). The *Flying Cloud*, the largest clipper ship existent when built in 1851, held the time record for the run from New York to California around the horn of South America for many years. It was a wooden vessel of 1,783 tons (1,618 metric tons) with a length of 229 feet (70 m)—the same size as the similarly designed *Syracusia*, built more than 2,000 years earlier.

Not only did ancient sailors possess the ships, but they also had the seafaring skill to take longer and more difficult organized voyages many centuries before Columbus set out in his little *Santa Maria*. Egyptian tomb paintings and writings affirm they were trading down the Red Sea and into the Indian Ocean before 2000 BCE—voyages as long as Columbus's leg across the Atlantic. Babylonian writings reveal they were traveling to northern India, following the Indian Ocean's northern shoreline during the same period. The Egyptians made regular excursions to Lebanon before 2500 BCE for cedar, which they used extensively. Minoan graffiti, circa 1700 BCE, has been found at Stonehenge, very close to ancient Cornwall, where miners excavated tin, a vital component part in bronze production. The early Phoenicians also left their mark in England and Scandinavia, which they likewise visited for tin and amber.

Herodotus, the Greek Father of History, wrote a detailed description of a Phoenician fleet hired by Pharaoh Necho that made what must be the most extensive voyage of ancient times at about 600 BCE. Hired Phoenician mariners sailed the Red Sea south and circumnavigated Africa's Cape of Good Hope, returning through the Straits of Gibraltar three years later, during which they annually stopped along the African coast to sow crops of wheat. This 13,000-mile (20,922 km) epic journey was many times as long as Columbus's voyage. The Carthaginians sent at least one fleet of colonizers in 60 ships down the west coast of Africa in the fifth century BCE.

In 324 BCE, a Greek scientist, Pythias, circumnavigated Britain, sailing further north from there on a voyage of exploration. Many historians believe his written account credibly documents his travels as far as Iceland before he reached "the frozen sea." Less than 300 years later, the Romans had established direct trade routes to Sumatra and Java for spices, particularly cloves. Shortly thereafter, in 75 CE, the Greek biographer Plutarch accurately described the route across the North Atlantic to what is believed to be Greenland—5,000 stades west of Britain near "the frozen sea" described earlier by Pythias.

Chinese archives record the visit in 166 CE of a Roman ship to the emperor, who complained about the poor-quality gifts he received.

Overseas travel to the Americas long before Columbus has been abundantly documented but less well publicized. For example, heaps of amphoras, or ceramic wine casks, mark the location of Roman shipwrecks off our eastern seaboard. In 1971, a scuba diver from Maine found two amphoras at a depth of 40 feet (12 cm) in Castine Bay. Scholars at the Early Sites Research Society identified the amphoras as Iberic Roman from the first century. A third amphora was recovered from the Atlantic shore near Jonesboro, Maine.

Another ancient wreck was discovered the following year near the coast of Honduras, where many amphoras were seen. They originated, according to scholars, in Roman-era North African ports. But when researchers applied for permission to excavate the wreck, Honduran officials denied their request for fear that further investigations might compromise the glory of Columbus.

In 1976, Brazilian diver Roberto Teixeira found Roman amphoras lying on the seabed near Rio de Janeiro. Archeologist Robert Marx investigated the shipwreck and retrieved several amphoras for scientific analysis. He handed them over to Elizabeth Will, a Classical Greek history professor at the University of Massachusetts, who identified them as Roman-era Moroccan. They had been manufactured at the Mediterranean port of Zillis during the third century CE. Indeed, the retrieved amphoras are remarkably similar in shape to jars produced in kilns at Kouass, on the west coast of Morocco. The Rio specimens appear to be late versions of Kouass examples from 200 to 300 CE.

Marx brought up thousands of pottery fragments from the shipwreck before Brazilian authorities terminated his dives. Further evidence of ancient Roman voyages to South America, they reasoned, might undermine the fame of Pedro Alveres Cabral, who is regarded as the official Portuguese discoverer of Brazil.

In 1982, scuba divers located yet another sunken ship dated to the first century BCE in the waters outside Rio de Janeiro. The vessel's position in a sheltered bay suggests she was deliberately maneuvered there by her crewmembers, who survived the transatlantic crossing. The wreckage contained several hundred long-necked urns with distinctive handles. Such urns were used to carry water, wine, oil and grain on long voyages, and identified the ship as Roman.

Two years later, a similar discovery was made off Venezuela.

Given the exceedingly low probability of any single wreck ever being found, the Brazilian and Venezuelan finds must represent only a small fraction of all the vessels that actually succeeded in sailing from North Africa to South America. Roman civilization lasted about six centuries, so merely a single ship straying off course every few years would have amounted to hundreds of such westward-bound vessels. Even if most of them were lost at sea, at least some would have completed their inadvertent voyage to land on the shores of Brazil and Venezuela.

But just how far did the ancient seafarers travel? Did a Carthaginian ship founder off the Azores, as implied by the discovery of a cache of Punic coins on the island of Corvo? Are there thousands of Phoenician and Roman amphora fragments on Salt Island in Cape Verdes, as reported by Robert Marx? Is the "Rio Wreck" at the bottom of Guanabara Bay near Rio de Janeiro actually a Roman vessel?

Archæological Discoveries of Ancient America

The answers to these questions have explosive potential, because they could forever demolish prevailing notions about the real prehistory of America.

>⊢⟡>⟶O⟵⟨⟡⊢⟨

Gunnar Thompson graduated Magna Cum Laude, Phi Beta Kappa, with High Distinction in anthropology from the University of Illinois, Urbana, in 1968. Despite his impressive academic background, university authorities "invited" him to leave their graduate program, because they found his belief in pre-Columbian contacts between the Old and New Worlds "unacceptable." Forced to change careers, Dr. Thompson earned a PhD in rehabilitation counseling at the University of Wisconsin, in Madison, and then went on to become assistant professor in counselor education at the University of Hawaii, Honolulu.

But he never abandoned his research into prehistory, publishing his first book, Nu Sun: Asian-American Voyages, 500 BCE, *in 1989. Dr. Thompson's most recent book,* Secret Voyages, or True Adventure Stories from the Forbidden Chronicles of American Discovery (2006), *reveals suppressed information detailing transatlantic voyages prior to 1492.*

HOW THE PORTUGUESE
OUT–FOXED COLUMBUS

By Dr. Gunnar Thompson

Standard history books tell of Cristobal Colon's repeated attempts to persuade the king of Portugal to back his "Enterprise of the Indies." Although King John II initially showed interest, a committee of the king's scientific advisors dismissed the scheme as being unrealistic. Next, the Genoese Colon (aka Columbus) took his proposal before John II's arch-rivals, the Catholic Majesties of Spain. Queen Isabella eventually recognized that the persistent mariner might help her achieve one of her foremost dreams: the conversion of millions of heathen Chinese peasants to the True Faith. In order to achieve this divine mission, she even offered her crown jewels to back the Columbus venture. In 1492, Captain Colon sailed away to seek gold and glory in the West.

On his way back from Hispaniola in 1493, Columbus couldn't resist calling upon Portugal's King John to inform him of the successful voyage to Asia. History has left us no account of their meeting, but it seems unlikely that King John II was at all intimidated by the boastful mariner. Indeed, the king might well have chuckled at the cupidity of his guest, for the Spanish commitment to sail west to the Orient actually left the eastern approach squarely in the hands of the Portuguese. That was just fine and dandy, as far as King John was concerned, because the Portuguese had already decided that the best way to reach the Spice Islands was to sail east around the cape of South Africa.

At any rate, John informed his impudent visitor that a new continent was located directly south of the islands in the Caribbean Sea. Furthermore, he advised Columbus that the isles his Spanish expedition had supposedly "discovered" actually belonged to Portugal. So it would seem rather clear that the Portuguese had some detailed intelligence regarding the western isles long before their "official" discovery by the Spaniards. Thus begins a story of political intrigue, commercial espionage, and religious rivalry dating back to the days of Phoenician mariners.

All learned men of the 15th century believed that there was mainland across the Atlantic Ocean from Europe. After all, the world was round; therefore, if one sailed far enough west, there must be land before long. Legends abounded regarding such voyages in ancient times. About 3,000 years ago, Iberians in the Spanish Peninsula and the Phoenicians of North Africa had learned about a huge paradise in the far western Atlantic (according to the testimony of the Sicilian geographer, Diodorus Siculus, in the first century BCE).

During the reign of King Solomon (974 to 937 BCE), the western isles were known to Iberian merchants as "Colchis," "Asqua Samal," "Ophir," and "Bracir." By some accounts, the Western Isles were part of a Far Asian continent, "India Occident"—that is, "India of the West," or "India Superior." Seneca and Aristotle maintained that the distance across the Atlantic to this mainland was within easy sailing range of Roman vessels. Other Greek and Roman scholars envisioned smaller isles across the Atlantic, and these were known as the "Fortunate Isles," or "the Gorgades" and "the Hesperides" in common folklore. Roman mariners sailed in great numbers to India Occident, during the second century BCE.

It is written in Antonio Galvano's 16th-century book, *Discoveries of the World*, that:

> The Romans sent an army into India against the great *Can* of Cathaia, which, passing through the Pillars of Hercules [the Straits of Gibraltar], and running to the northwest, found, right over against the Cape Finisterre, ten islands, wherein was much tin. And they may be those which were called the Cassiterides. And being come to fifty degrees of latitude, they found a straight. And passing through it toward the west they arrived in the empire of India, and fought with the king of Cathay. And so came back again unto the city of Rome. Which thing howsoever it may seem either possible or not possible, true or not true, yet so I find it left to be recorded in the histories of that time.

As the Roman expedition sailed northwest from the Straits of Gibraltar, there is no question that they headed in the direction of America across the North Atlantic. Directly opposite the Atlantic from Cape Finisterre, Spain, we find the region of New England, and farther north between latitude 45°N and 50°N is the Gulf of St. Lawrence. Although "the Cassiterides" ("Tin Isles") are generally thought to refer to the British Isles, it was not uncommon for the same name to be used for a number of locations. In this tale, the "Can" might refer to the Can-ada natives who occupy the Northeastern region of North America.

Farther south, the Romans encountered the Gulf of Mexico, which they named "the Caspian Sea." So, there were at least *two* Caspian Seas in Roman geography. This sea pierces the Eastern coast of India Superior (what we would call Asia) on a Roman map of the fifth century. This map, by Macrobius, is the oldest extant map showing the peninsula of Florida. It is seen again on the Marino Sanudo map of 1320, which accompanied a "book of secrets" by Pietrus Vesconte. Such portrayals of the Asian/Indian mainland with a macro-peninsula (Florida) and a great gulf, corresponded to the actual configuration of mainlands across the Atlantic.

There is absolutely no similarity between this coastline and the coast of modern-day Asia, so we can be quite certain that the gross outline of the American mainland was indicated on these ancient maps. The mistake that Roman geographers made was in assuming that "Seres" (China) was located on this mainland. They might have been confused by similar-sounding names, such as the Canada natives and the *khan* of China. Captain Columbus made a similar mistake in assuming that certain native words confirmed that he had reached the Asian province of Mangi. The Roman concept of a mainland with a southeastern-tending macro-peninsula was repeated in 15th-century Portuguese maps. In the span of some 70 years, Prince Henry the Navigator and later King John II sent numerous expeditions into the western Atlantic to ascertain the distance to mainlands on the other side of the sea.

Maps by Andrea Bianco made between 1436 and 1448 show the approximate locations of Florida, Newfoundland, and Brazil. Bianco's associate, Fra Mauro, prepared a public map in 1459 depicting Asia with a southeastern macro-peninsula; this same peninsula is seen on subsequent maps by Henricus Martellus Germanus (1489) and Martin Behaim (1492). Another Portuguese agent, Paolo Toscanelli, sent a copy of his 1457 map to Columbus—also showing the southeastern macro-peninsula.

The upshot of these public maps is that they all show the Asian coastline with a macro-peninsula reaching toward the southeast. Called "Zaiton," "Mangi," or "India Terza" on the 15th-century maps, this peninsula provided an easy target for ships heading due west along the tropic of Cancer—and that is precisely what Columbus proposed to do. The erstwhile explorer had researched all the maps available in Lisbon, and he believed in their accuracy. Why shouldn't he? Throughout a span of 70 years, such Portuguese navigators as Vincent Dias, Fernao Telles, and Alfonso de Estreito had accurately determined the position of the southeastern tip of Florida at its actual latitude, just above the tropic of Cancer, and within 500 miles (805 km) of its correct longitude. Directly to the east was a large isle (Cuba), which was known to mariners by a variety of names: Antillia, Ophir, or Cipangu.

The public version of this coastline was accurate enough to inspire one so brave as Columbus to dream of gold and glory. His map, which he referred to in his ship's log, was a copy of the most recent, public version of the western Atlantic, as it appeared on maps by Martellus and Behaim. The only problem is that the macro-peninsula that became the target of Columbus wasn't really attached to Asia. It was attached to a New World.

There was another version of the western Atlantic that began as a legend and then became a commercial secret, as Portugal began to rely more and more heavily on espionage and trickery to side-track its arch-rival, Spain.

According to ancient Phoenician accounts well-known to the Portuguese, there was supposed to be an island paradise located in the far-western Atlantic Ocean. This paradise served as a refuge for seven Portuguese bishops during the eighth-century Saracen invasion of Portugal. A legend recorded on the Johannes Ruysch map of 1508 stated that the bishops fled along with their parishioners and assorted farm animals to the western isle. The name given to this overseas refuge was "Antillia," or "the Isle of Seven Cities."

Most 15th-century Portuguese charts of the Atlantic Ocean include two stylized rectangles representing the legendary western isles. Usually, the southernmost isle is called "Antillia," and the northern isle is some variation of "Satanaxio" or "Saluaga." The name "Antillia" has been translated as "isle before the mainland" or "the island opposite Tile" (where Tile represents the Roman Arctic frontier of Iceland). Traditionally, Antillia was situated in the far west at the latitude of the Straits of Gibraltar.

When Portugal's Prince Henry the Navigator inaugurated his campaign to explore the Atlantic Ocean in 1418, finding the lost isles of Antillia and Seven Cities was a major objective. Royal charters issued to eager explorers during Henry's day, and even up to the time of Columbus, clearly stipulate "Antillia or the Isle of Seven Cities" as a principal goal. Even Bristol merchants sought after Antillia, along with another illusive isle in the west: Hybresail.

Andrea Bianco's 1436 map of the Western Atlantic shows the mysterious isle of Antillia in greater detail than is seen anywhere else until Amerigo Vespucci came upon the scene in 1502. The map clearly has an early version of the Florida peninsula attached to the mid-Atlantic isle. This hook-shaped peninsula is similar in shape to another one seen on the Albertin DeVirga map of 1414, which has been attributed to the English Franciscan, Nicholas of Lynn (circa 1360). At any rate, the peninsula is attached to a huge isle or mainland separate from Asia.

When Columbus sailed in 1492, he believed that he might encounter a small isle called Antillia near his direction of sail west along the tropic of Cancer. However, this did not happen. The first isles he sighted were in the region of the "Zaiton Peninsula," or "Mangi" on his map. Nearby, he believed that he found the isle of Cipangu (Japan). However, what he thought was Zaiton turned out to be Cuba; his Cipangu turned out to be Haiti. We are informed by the 15th-century historian Peter Martyr that Columbus had in fact reached isles that were known as the Antilles. That is, Cuba, Haiti, and Florida were part of an island group known to the ancients as the Antillias.

Columbus was convinced that he had reached Asia—because that was what his map indicated. However, he had fallen victim to a Portuguese plot to confuse their commercial rivals. Behaim's own map of 1492 failed to show a continent (South America) below the Antilles. Nevertheless, an account in the *Nuremberg Chronicle* for 1493 reported that Behaim, in company with Jacobus Carnus of Portugal, had crossed the equator to the Antipodes. *Antipodes* (or "opposite land") was a Roman term for a southern continent that was opposite the Old World on the globe.

It was positioned south of the equator on fifth-century maps by Macrobius. It was later identified as the *Mundus Novus*, or "New World," by such 16th-century historians as Peter Martyr and Bartholomew Colon. Eventually, this Mundus Novus came to be called "South America." So it seems that King John II of Portugal had sufficient information regarding the location of this southern continent by 1493 to advise Columbus on his way back from the New World that he would find such a mainland directly south of Hispaniola (Haiti). It is also apparent that Martin Behaim's public globe at Nuremberg did not accurately reflect everything he knew about the layout of the western Atlantic.

Columbus was befuddled by the discrepancy: A journal entry in the Columbus log of 1498 mentions that his expedition to Paria (Venezuela) was to ascertain "what had been the intention of Don Joao II of Portugal who had said that to the south [of Hispaniola] there was mainland."

Bianco's Antillia map was safely hidden away in the royal vault when Columbus planned his Enterprise of the Indies. It was not until 1502 that a spy for the powerful Italian Este family succeeded in bribing a royal Portuguese cartographer into selling a copy of the secret version of the western Atlantic. The so-called Cantino map, which is named after the secret agent, shows the latest version of the New World by Amerigo Vespucci. This map is clearly based on Bianco's 1436 map, for it shows a very similar Antillia with a southeastward-tending macro-peninsula. This peninsula is an early version of Florida—which supposedly wasn't discovered until Ponce de Leon's expedition of 1513. Yet we see it in its full extent on the Cantino map.

Archaeological Discoveries of Ancient America

Who beat Ponce to the Fountain of Youth? Several historical mariners vie for the honor of making the first scientific maps of the northern continent. Amerigo Vespucci sailed past the coast in 1498, and he had sufficient cartographic skills to make such a map. John and Sebastian Cabot were in the region at about the same point in time. However, it is the hook-shape of the Florida peninsula that suggests another ancient mariner, Nicholas of Lynn.

The English Franciscan traveled to the New World for the purpose of making a map between 1330 and 1360. Ferdinand Colon informs us that the friar's travelogue, the *Inventio Fortunatae*, reported isles west of Europe; the account was a significant factor in motivating Columbus to set out on his bold venture in the first place.

At any rate, this concept of a northern mainland with a macro-peninsula on the southeast corner served as the basis for defining the land that eventually became North America. All subsequent maps of the New World in the Lusitano-Germanic tradition of cartography evolved from Bianco's 1436 prototype. Cantino's map expanded the size of the northern land along the Gulf of Mexico; it introduced the Antilles as Isabella (Cuba) and Spagnola (Haiti); and it added most of the coastline of the unnamed, southern continent.

The next map in the series, Nicolo Caveri's 1504 map of the same region, expanded the area of lands along the Gulf of Mexico, as well as the northern coast of the southern continent. By 1507, the German cartographer Martin Waldseemueller named the southern continent *America* in honor of Amerigo Vespucci. This naming was attributed to the fact that Vespucci had proven the existence of a new continent, or "New World," that was separate from Asia.

However, this name for the southern continent did not apply to the emerging continent in the north. Even the name of the southern continent was in doubt after 1513, because Waldseemueller had been forced to recant his support for the heretic Vespucci. Indeed, Amerigo had infuriated orthodox theologians with his deduction that all the new species of animals found in the New World couldn't possibly have fit on Noah's Ark. Meanwhile, the northern continent was generally referred to as the "Western India," "New India," or "the New Land."

In 1538, the Flemish cartographer Gerhard Mercator named the northern continent a second "America." Similar to Vespucci, Mercator was a heretic whose geographical concepts were directly opposed to received wisdom. Thus, he was anxious to honor Vespucci's achievement in proving the existence of a New World. It was principally due to Mercator's great influence in the rising German publishing industry that the name "America" became indelibly linked to both New World continents.

CHAPTER 9

Bones, Skulls, and DNA Rewrite History

*S*keptics of Norse seamanship begrudgingly concede that the Vikings may have sailed as far as L'Anse aux Meadows, in Newfoundland, but certainly no further. Well, here's proof the Northmen went a bit further after all.

INCA SKELETON UNEARTHED IN SCANDINAVIA

By Earl Koenig

The 1,000-year-old remains of an Inca Indian have been found in Norway. Feature writer Rolleiv Solholm reported in the June 26, 2007 edition of *The Norway Post* that the accidental find was made during garden work in the Oestfold city of Sarpsborg.

Archæological Discoveries of Ancient America

Excavators recovered the bones of an infant and a pair of elderly men interred together around the turn of the 10th century CE. The child and one of the adults were identified as Nordic, but the other man's racial provenance was revealed by a telltale genetic flaw in the neck confirming his Andean origins. According to Mona Beate Buckholm, leader of the state archaeologists who conducted the examination, the discovery has prompted her and her colleagues to widen the scope of their diggings in and around Sarpsborg for additional evidence.

The Norwegian find is contemporaneous with the Norse settlement of L'Anse aux Meadows in Newfoundland, from which Viking explorers sailed south along the Atlantic coasts of North America and Mexico, crossing the isthmus of Panama to the Pacific shores of Ecuador or Peru 500 years before the Spanish arrived in the New World. Sarpsborg's skull of the elderly Inca suggests the medieval Scandinavians either captured or befriended an Inca, returning with him to Norway. By the time he died 1,000 years ago, they must have thought highly enough of him to inter his remains with two other Norse.

In any case, the survival of his skull in Norwegian soil proves that the Vikings successfully conducted round-trip voyages from Northern Europe to South America, thereby debunking the paradigm of mainstream scholars who still insist the Northmen never got any further than Newfoundland.

With a background in geology and anthropology from the University of Western Australia, Peter Marsh launched a personal quest to understand the peopling of the Pacific islands. His investigations throughout several years took him to Hawaii, New Guinea, New Zealand, New Caledonia, Niue, Tonga, Samoa, Sumatra, Borneo, and the Philippines. Based on firsthand experience garnered from these extensive

travels, Marsh found and followed a genetic thread into the Andes Mountains of Peru and Bolivia.

GENETICS REWRITE PACIFIC PREHISTORY
By Peter Marsh

The genetic and cultural origins of most Polynesians indicate that they came from Taiwan about 4000 BCE, but spent 3,800 years on the islands off Canada prior to arriving in Hawaii some 22 centuries ago—a straightforward scenario that agrees with all the evidence, and one may be justified in assuming that all questions concerning Polynesian origins have now been answered. If only it was that simple!

Mostly, the genetic trail has established beyond reasonable doubt that Hawaii was the formative homeland of the Polynesians. It was here that they chose to keep some traditions and cast off others, thereby reinventing Polynesian society as we know it today. Their priests retained the traditional robe color of yellow or orange and crescent-crest headgear of their ancestors, seen also among the Tibetans, the 6,000-year-old blood-brothers of the Polynesians.

The Hawaiians created a kingdom based on family genealogies that went back 700 generations, and they invented a dance style that was designed to sexually excite, probably to encourage a rapid build-up of population. They even invented surfing. The Hawaiian archipelago was the perfect environment for developing their seamanship and navigational skills. Their catamaran boat design was clearly developed in response to the large surf conditions found in Hawaii, as catamarans do not broach in the surf like a conventional mono-hull—something modern yacht designers have only recognized in the last three decades.

Inevitably, population growth exerted economic pressure on the island's resources, so the catamaran *Hokulea* went in search of additional living space to find Tahiti, which means "distant land." Further exploration resulted in the discovery of other islands in the southern archipelagos of the Pacific. Places such as Rarotonga ("Sun in the South") and Tonga Tapu ("South Forbidden") only make sense if they were named by people who came from the North: Hawaii. One particular island, Ra'iatea, was called "Sun People White" in honor of its indigenous people. The name seemed particularly appropriate to Captain Wallis, who visited the island in 1767, when he remarked on the high proportion of its pale-skinned natives, many of them red-headed.

Ra'iatea was not the only Polynesian island populated by light-complected, fair-haired residents before the arrival of 17th-century Europeans. After the modern discovery of Easter Island and Tahiti, numerous British and Dutch mariners returned with stories of white people with red hair scattered throughout the native populations of Polynesia. Mendana, who sailed through the Pacific in 1595, visited an island in the Tuamotus. He reported that the chief had "a mass of red and rather curly hair, reaching halfway down his back." After Captain Roggveen's visit to Easter Island in 1722, he recorded that among the first of their hosts to come aboard his ship was a native chief who was "an entirely white man." In fact, all early visitors to Easter Island were surprised not only by the very fair facial features and tall stature of some indigenes, but also by their soft, reddish hair and greenish-blue eyes.

On many islands in southern Polynesia, the native whites were often found to be holding positions of high rank. But in time, however, fewer such sightings were reported. Captain Wallis, who voyaged to Tahiti twice, noted that the paler redheads in Tahiti were succumbing more readily to disease brought by visiting Europeans than the black-haired Polynesians, an observation proving that the ancestry of the Pacific whites was not European.

In 1972, Professor Jean Dausset conducted a study of the Caucasian blue/green-eyed redheads of Easter Island. He found them to have had an ancient strain of Caucasian blood also found among the Basques of Spain, characterized by A29 and B12. His analyses revealed that 39 percent of unrelated Basques and 37 percent of the Easter Islanders were carriers of the HLA gene B12. These were the highest and second-highest proportions tested around the globe. Figures for A29 were similar. The Easter Islanders, with 37 percent, evidenced the highest proportion on Earth, and the Basques were second with 24 percent. Most remarkably, the two genes were found as a haplotype (combined genetic markers) in 11 percent of Easter Islanders and 7.9 percent of the Basques. No other people in the world had remotely comparable figures. In fact, from these tests, the Easter Islanders appear to have been of a more pure ancient Caucasian racial stock than the Basques! Inhabiting one of the most remote islands on the planet undoubtedly played an important part in the preservation of their genetic integrity.

The name of their sun god underwent variations of "Ra," and they belonged to a bird-man cult, a form of which is still practiced by the floating reed-bed people of the Indus River half a world away. The Easter Islanders built reed boats and knew a writing system akin to the ancient Harappa script likewise found in ancient India. They raised Peruvian-style, interlocking stone walls, and buried their dead in circular burial tombs called *tullpa*, similar to the *chullpa* tombs of the Andes' Lake Titicaca. Both Incas and Easter Islanders used the knotted cord called the *quipu* as a mnemonic device for preserving important information. Pacific coastal South America's light-haired Paracas mummies are underscored by regional oral traditions of redheaded culture-bearers, such as the Andean flood-hero, Kontiki-Viracocha. The light-brown and red-haired, green-eyed Araucano, Chile's "Gold People," was South America's only ancestral population to have survived the onslaught of the Incas.

Archaeological Discoveries of Ancient America

How can we account for the undeniable presence of Caucasian populations in the New World and remote Easter Island during premodern times? Dr. Thor Heyerdahl believed he found convincing evidence to show that the "long-eared" maritime traders of the Maldive Islands in the distant Indian Ocean were anciently connected with the Easter Islanders. He had noticed that the Indus Valley written language found its only counterparts among the Cuna Indians of Panama and Easter Island's rongo-rongo. But just who were the literate civilizers of third-millennium BCE India, and how could they have established any kind of a relationship with peoples on the other side of the Pacific Ocean? The Indus Valley Civilization is best known for two of its leading cities: Mohenjo-Daro and Harappa. That ancient Indian epic, the *Rig Veda* ("Praised Knowledge"), recounts that the residents of Harappa were pale-skinned seafarers who arrived on the Indian subcontinent from sunken lands to the south, apparently the Maldives, before sea levels rose to drown the low-lying islands.

Although composed around the close of the Indus Valley Civilization, circa 1500 BCE, it has its roots in the contemporary Andronovo culture of five centuries before. Some Harappa tribal names cited in the *Rig Veda* were the Kurus and Purus, who seem to have reappeared in Pacific coastal South America as the Urus and Puruha, remembered by Peru's Aymara Indians as tall with red or pale curly hair and beards. The mixed descendants of some Urus still live on floating reed beds at Bolivia's Lake Titicaca. Not far from the highest lake on Earth, the Incas conducted the *Inti Raymi*, each winter solstice. This annual "Return of the Sun" paralleled India's Diwali, a festival of light celebrating the return of the sun god, Lord Rama, in the northern Hemisphere.

A general population spread from India into the Pacific and beyond to the shores of South America may begin with native Maori oral history in New Zealand. Folk tradition recounts that 161 generations ago (approximately 1500 BCE), Maori ancestors migrated en masse from a hot country called Irihia in the wake of war. The refugees' principle food supply during the voyage was the sapless, small seed known as *ari*, Hindu for "rice." Moreover, the Maoris' ancestral *Irihia* is an obvious variation of *Vrihia*, an ancient name for India. The migration was said to have taken place around 1500 BCE, the same period that witnessed the bloody collapse of Indus Valley civilization and the sudden abandonment of its chief urban centers, among them, Harappa. Even the Polynesian name *Maori* has roots in the subcontinent.

According to the *Rig Veda*, India's Maurya dynasties flourished in the mid-second millennium BCE. It goes on to report that some Harappans, fleeing the violence of the times, sailed far across the ocean in search of new lands. Some of them, it would appear, ventured as far at least as New Zealand. Material evidence of their transpacific flight was unearthed recently by Professor Matthew Spriggs on the island of Vanuatu, where he and his archaeological team found a 3,500-year-old Lapita pottery site comprising burial urns topped with model birds, designs characteristic of Harappa mortuary practices. Although the Indus Valley voyagers were absorbed by the native islanders, something of them yet survives among the blond-haired Tolai and freckled red-haired people of Missima Island. These mixed Melanesians carry HLA A11 and B40. The only other place in the world where HLA A11 and B40 are found together is among the people of the Indus region, the homeland of Harappa.

Archaeological digs throughout the Pacific suggest the Vedic mariners colonized areas as far eastward as Samoa and Tonga, including Fiji, but disappeared from the archaeological record 800 years before Polynesians entered the Pacific. HLA A11 in Melanesia and Polynesia is undoubtedly one of the few relics left by these ancient mariners. Variations found between HLA A11 clusters in Melanesia and Polynesia reflect the different routes they took to enter the Pacific. Due to their isolation in America and the absence of new influences, they kept their Old World religions and writing system. To more precisely identify the provenance of these fair-complected globe-trotters of the ancient world, geneticist E. Gomez-Casado investigated Spanish Basque genes to discover they belonged to a deeply prehistoric gene pool of Caucasian groups that included blond-haired Berbers and Tuareg in Morocco, dynastic Egyptians, Minoan Greeks, some Palestinians, Lebanese, Kurds, Turks, and trace populations as far east as Iran.

The racial purity of these people 3,500 years ago would have been much greater than it is today. The red-haired Phoenicians and Celts, two great seafaring nations that commanded the Atlantic Ocean, were also part of this gene pool, as was the Haplotype X in North America. Following the DNA trail, Gomez-Casado and his colleagues demonstrated that this branch of Caucasians left the European continent 13,000 years ago, the Celtic branch returning after an absence of 7,000 years. HLA A11 in Celts and Basques is associated with B35 and B52, but is not found in the Pacific, implying that Celts and Basques are not associated with any relic Caucasian populations in the Pacific in the last 2,000 years. A significant trait of ancient Caucasian genes is that they are Rhesus negative. Red hair and blue eyes are also recessive genes, and, as a result, they slowly disappeared into brown-eyed, black-haired populations. Despite this, relic Caucasian genes are still found among the chief families of Polynesia, especially in Raiatea, Huahine, New Zealand, and Easter Island, sometimes with red hair, but with unmistakable Caucasian features, which are still visible after 1,500 years of miscegenation.

When the pre-Polynesian "Long Ears" made their home on Easter Island, they named it *Te Pito O Te Kainga*: "The End of Eating," suggesting the island's poor fishing. They also called it *Te Pito O Te Whenua*, "The End of Land," or "Navel of the World," perhaps indicative of their sense of loneliness. They may have felt they were at the end of the road, the last surviving members of a once great civilization. When the "Short Ear"

Polynesians arrived centuries later, they changed the name of the island to *Rapa Nui*, "Big Rapa." Easter Island oral history recounted that the redheaded Long Ears established a class society, in which the Polynesians served as manual laborers. The arrangement worked for some centuries, but social divisions were exacerbated by the agriculturally stressed island and overpopulation.

When the Long Ears demanded increased productivity from their Polynesian workers, the latter went on a strike that escalated into race war. The fair-skinned Long Ears were exterminated, save for a single male survivor spared by the victorious Short Ears. His name was Ororoina, and it was from him that today's redheaded Easter Islanders trace their direct, if mixed, descent.

One of Easter Island's colossal moai.

>─┤◄►─●─◄►┤─◄

David Hatcher Childress is the publisher of Adventures Unlimited, *and president of the World Explorers Club (Kempton, Illinois). He is also the author of more than a dozen books on alternative history and science. Among the last great world travelers in the tradition of David Livingston or Marco Polo, Childress here addresses one of the strangest, yet most revealing features in all of cultural diffusionism.*

ANCIENT AMERICAN CONEHEADS
By David Hatcher Childress

Readers may remember the old *Saturday Night Live* routine in which Dan Aykroyd and gang played the strange family of "Coneheads" (later made into a feature movie). This bizarre group of comical weirdoes had long, bald heads that were about twice as long as a normal human head, and came to a sharp point at the top—hence the name *coneheads*. As funny and strange as they may have appeared to television viewers, such "cone-heads" did, and do, exist. In fact, conehead remains of various shapes and sizes have been found all over the Americas, from Peru and Mexico to the Pacific Northwest.

Ancient American aristocracy practiced head elongation in imitation of their noble ancestors.

Bones, Skulls, and DNA Rewrite History

I first encountered conehead skulls on a trip to Peru in 1984. At the local museums along the southern desert coast was a wide variety of elongated skulls, and sometimes the complete mummies of these people, often with red hair. On a February 2003, expedition, I had a chance to revisit the museum at the Peruvian town of Ica. It displayed unusual human crania, including the coneheads, with brief explanations in Spanish and English. To the uninitiated, the deformed skulls are rather shocking. They come in all shapes and sizes, some extremely elongated, others rather squarish, instead of pointed. Just exactly who these people were, why they reshaped their heads, and how they created such odd modifications are puzzling considerations.

One explanation suggests that they belonged to the inhabitants of lost Atlantis, where, for reasons unknown, they preferred long, conical-shaped skulls. According to this theory, the head was reshaped in infancy to increase brain capacity. The Atlanteans, in their worldwide journeys, impressed other peoples with their high level of civilization and knowledge of all things psychic and scientific. The natives of Mexico and Peru were so impressed with their ancient colonizers, so the theory goes, that subsequent generations of Mayas and Incas practiced head-binding to achieve cranial elongation in imitation of the intellectual Atlanteans. Indeed, an Atlantean hypothesis may explain why cranial deformation is so widespread. It can be found in ancient Sumer, among the "Watchers" of Kurdistan, and certain members of Egyptian royalty.

This explanation also supports speculation that Mexico's Olmec society plus the Tiahuanaco culture of Peru (and Bolivia), where head-binding was likewise practiced, were remnants of Atlantean civilization, sometimes called the "Atlantean League." The argument goes on to underscore the concept of cultural diffusionism, the arrival in the Americas of ancient seafarers from across both the Atlantic and Pacific Oceans. Such unusual and diverse customs as cranial deformation, turban wearing, jade worship, keystone cuts in megalithic masonry, and trepanning can best be described as having been transferred from one culture to another by prehistoric contact between widely separated societies.

Staunch in their conviction that early man never sailed beyond sight of land, mainstream scientists are at a loss to explain why so many different cultures took up the practice of head-binding. Most scholars concur that it was a universally elitist practice to set a ruling or aristocratic elite apart from the broad masses. Meanwhile, forensic researchers have focused on the procedures used to produce the strange anomalies. It seems that the skulls were deformed while the person was still in an infantile stage of development. For unknown reasons, newborns would have had their heads bound with pieces of wood and rope, or some sort of constrictive cloth, that forced the head to grow in an elongated and unnatural way.

While the plates in a young child's skull have not yet fused together, the skull is bound with materials that are adjusted and tightened as the infant matures. After several years of binding, the head was permanently molded in the desired shape.

By 8 or 9 years (sometimes less), the skull was formed in an elongated fashion that no longer required any binding. From this point on, the head would continue to develop in this unnatural configuration until growth stopped in late adolescence. The person became an otherwise normal adult human, except with a distended skull and nearly double the brain size of other humans. Conventional archaeologists refer to the end result as a *dolichocephalous* cranium, many examples of which may be found in museums around the world. The best collections are preserved in museums in Ica (Peru), Tiahuanaco (Bolivia), and Xalapa (Mexico).

BONES, SKULLS, AND DNA REWRITE HISTORY

In a fascinating article published by *Hera* magazine (Rome, Italy), Editor Adriano Forgione writes that a number of dolichocephalous skulls were discovered in a very ancient underground temple on the Mediterranean island of Malta: "It was known that, until 1985, a number of skulls found in the prehistoric Maltese temples at Taxien, Ggantja and Hal Saflieni were displayed in the Archeological Museum of Valletta. But in the last few years, they were removed and placed in storage, away from public view." He goes on to say that only photographs taken by Maltese researchers, Dr. Anton Mifsud and Dr. Charles Savona Ventura, are all that prove the existence of the strange skulls. He noted, from the Maltese doctors' books, that the skulls exhibit cranial knitting lines, abnormally developed temporal partitions, and drilled and swollen occiputs, as would result from traumas. Most importantly, the pictures showed a strange, large, lengthened skull. Their hypothesis is that the resemblance to similar skulls from South America implies an exceptional discovery: Perhaps the skull was a result of ancient genetic mutation between different races that lived on Malta.

Forgione states that the Mediterranean islands of Malta and Gozo were very important centers in prehistoric times, places where "medical cures" were conducted, oracles were consulted, and ritual encounters with priests of a serpent goddess took place, including many sanctuaries and thaumaturgic centers. Throughout antiquity, the snake was associated with subterranean powers for regeneration, due to the creature's underground habitat and ability to slough off its old skin for a new one. "Perhaps the skulls found in the hypogeum (a subterranean temple) and examined during our visit to Malta," he writes, "belonged to these priests. They present an accentuated dolichocephalous, which is particularly the center of our analysis."

Archæological Discoveries of Ancient America

The long head and drawn features, Forgione writes, must have lent a serpent-like appearance. Furthermore, such deformities would have created ambulatory problems, forcing the person to slither, rather than walk. Without the usual median knitting, the brain could not consistently develop in the skullcap, and was instead forced to develop in the occipital zone of the cerebellum, deforming the cranium and making it appear like a single cap from the frontal and occipital area. This would have caused the person terrible agony since infancy, but probably enhanced visions that were considered proof of a bond with the goddess.

The elongated skulls from Malta might have belonged to a different race altogether. "Even the other skulls we examined presented strange anomalies," Forgione concluded. "Some were more natural and harmonic than the cranium that mostly gained our attention, but they still presented a pronounced, natural dolichocephalous, and we could assume, without fear of refutation, that it is distinctive of an actual race, different to the native populations of Malta and Gozo."

Mifsud and Anthony Buonanno agree with Forgione, despite a lack of decisive C-14 or DNA resting. The Maltese archaeologists conclude that the skulls represent an entirely different race of islanders, which may have originated on neighboring Sicily. They point out that many of the 7,000 human skeletons found by cultural anthropologist Thermistocles Zammit in 1921 at Malta exhibited cranial deformations. Then, 40 years later, a human skull from the same large collection exhumed by British archaeologist Brochtorff Circle demonstrated unmistakable indications of artificial elongation.

Buonanno and Mifsud speculate that ancient peoples practiced head deformation as part of marriage ceremonies, solar rituals, cult initiations, or perhaps as a form of punishment. Other ritual mutilations, such as incisions, perforations, partial or total removals, cauterizations, abrasions, and insertions of extraneous bodies in muscle tissue were undertaken on behalf of magical, medical, or cosmetic purposes. Head elongation differs from these, however, in the lifelong suffering it inflicted on its victims. Perhaps infant skull-binding was intended to make the person resemble the race of serpent priests. In any case, Buonanno and Mifsud point out that it was applied to the architects of Malta's great Earth Mother temples between 4100 and 2500 BCE. Particularly the mid-third-millennium BCE skulls might comprise evidence for the last survivors of a most ancient sacerdotal caste that traveled throughout the Mediterranean and beyond, raising megalithic structures across Western Europe. They do not appear to have intermarried with local populations anywhere, but preserved their line through family unions, a common custom among elite communities. In so doing, however, they impoverished themselves genetically and suffered inevitable pathologies, until this race of serpent-priests finally inbred itself out of existence.

Head-binding continued up until modern times, according to the Australian museum's Website, which displays several photos of living persons with elongated heads. The site explains that head-binding began in Vanuatu approximately a month after birth. Each day the child's head was smeared with burnt paste made from the Navanai-Molo nut. This process softens the skin and prevents "binding rash." The head was then bound with a soft bandage made from the inner bark of a type of banana tree. Over this was placed a specially woven basket made from Nibirip bound around with a fiber rope. This process continued every day for approximately six months to produce the required shape.

The tribesmen practiced cranial deformation because they believed that long-headed people were mentally superior, like the coneheaded culture-bearers of the deep past. The Museum quotes one Vanuatu native as

Archæological Discoveries of Ancient America

saying, "We elongate the heads of our children because it is our tradition, and it originates with the basic spiritual beliefs of our people. We also see that those with elongated heads are more handsome or beautiful, and such long heads also indicate wisdom" (General South Malakulan quotation as translated into Bislama by Kirk Huffinan for the Australian Museum).

The Museum Website also reports that a flat forehead among the Bintulu Malanus Dayak people of Borneo was considered a sign of beauty. The process of flattening the head began during the first month of a new-born's life with an instrument known as a *tadal*. A cushion was placed on the child's forehead with bands placed over the top and around the back of the head. Strings holding the bands in position were adjusted without disturbing the child. In the early stages of the process, only very slight pressure was applied, but gradually the pressure was increased.

The site also mentions that the Mangbetu people of the northeast Democratic Republic of the Congo likewise practiced head-elongation. Infant heads were bound with cloth to create the desired shape. As with adults, the effect was emphasized by wrapping the hair around a woven basket frame, so that the head appeared even more elongated. Curiously, the Museum source points out that, in some parts of Europe, especially France, head-elongation was practiced up until the late 19th century. In the Deux-Sevres area, head-elongation involved wrapping a baby's head in a tight bandage. The binding was left for a period of two to four months, and then replaced with a fitted basket. When the baby was older, the basket was strengthened with metal thread.

Fascinated by the survival of such a practice by a Western culture into modern times, I renewed my search, to find that head-binding gained acceptance with the advancement, during the mid-1800s, of phrenology.

According to the proponents of this pseudo-science, the shape of the head determined human personality attributes; there were criminal shapes, intellectual shapes, and so on. Popular belief led to a fad of head-binding infants to produce the proper shape for what was supposed to be intelligent, well-adjusted growth. The procedure had other offshoots, such as the well-known foot-binding of the Chinese (used up until the 1940s in mainland China). Apparently, the ancient (and modern) Chinese thought that women with small, deformed feet were sexier than women with normal feet; the practice was unfortunately quite common, especially for concubines and upper-class women in Mandarin Chinese society.

In 1976, I resided, as a rental house guest, with the Taiwanese Secretary of the Treasury, a certain General Yi. His wife had had her feet bound in a relatively minor way, which kept her from being able to walk normally. Many of her toes were permanently folded over each other so that her feet could fit into extremely narrow and small shoes. Concubines whose feet had been completely bound and folded over were actually almost incapable of walking, and had to be carried to their masters' beds at night by servants for their weekly trysts.

Similarly, the Mayas believed that cross-eyed women were particularly sexy. They would suspend a small clay or stone ball by a string in front of an infant's eyes, forcing her to stare at the suspended object. In time, the infant girl would become permanently cross-eyed. Her head may have been bound during this period as well. Purposeful deformation of the skull, feet, and eyes can all be part of a culture's fetishes and notions of beauty. The Olmecs and Mayas had dolichocephalous craniums in many cases. Though skeletal material is often difficult to find in tropical areas because of the rapid rate of decomposition, jade figurines attributed to the Olmecs have been found in Costa Rica portraying persons with elongated heads.

Archæological Discoveries of Ancient America

This curious fashion spread from the Andes to the jungles of Panama, Costa Rica, and Nicaragua, to the coasts and mountains of Mexico. It even reached the Pacific Northwest of the United States. The largest freshwater lake west of the Mississippi is Flathead Lake in western Montana, its name deriving from a local tribe known as the Flathead Indians. They were so called because of their elongated, flattened heads. When the first European explorers arrived in the Seattle area, they found local Chinook tribesmen with elongated and flattened skulls. An illustration of the period portrays a native woman with a dolichocephalous cranium. She is holding a child in a deformation cradle on her lap. Curiously, she appears to have unusually small feet, possibly bound when she was an infant, as well as writing-like tattoos on her skin.

Long before, dynastic Egyptians, including Akhenaton, Nefertiti, Tutankhamun, Meritaton, and other members of the heretical king's royal house, had dolichocephalous craniums. Nefertiti was not an Egyptian, but was from Mittani, an area of northern Iraq possibly aligned with the Hittites and ancient India. Although skeletons of Akhenaton, Nefertiti, and their daughters have never been discovered (some researchers, such as myself, believe they would have been cremated in the manner of Hindus and Buddhists), surviving portraits of them and their children show they too had elongated craniums. The mummy of Tutankhamun survives, however, and his skull is decidedly dolichocephalous.

But the big question is: Why did these ancient civilizations, right up until the time of the European conquest, in the case of the Pacific Northwest, practice artificial skull deformation? No one seems to have a good answer.

Some investigators believe that everyone had elongated heads, as it was the style of the day, and the "technology" of deforming craniums was relatively simple; it could be performed by any family that had a newborn infant, a couple of pieces of wood, and some rope. All it really took was some patience and time. But, once again, how could such a bizarre technique ever evolve into a popular style? And how could widely separated cultures have developed this curious fad independently? Or is it evidence of cultural diffusion? Were the ancients imitating a race of beings with naturally elongated skulls? The most credible hypothesis argues that head-binding occurred in emulation of an ancient, long-headed people (either natural or forced) who introduced civilization to our ancestors.

Evidence for this theory may be found among modern folk that still practice head-binding (such as on Vanuatu), as a means of identifying with highly intelligent foreigners who visited their ancestors during the remote past. On a more practical side, the elongated deformation of skulls does almost double the size of the human cranium, allowing the brain to expand beyond normal. Does this mean that people with dolichocephalous craniums had bigger brains, and were therefore smarter or more "psychic" than humans with ordinary crania? It is an interesting question, considering the insistence of some researchers who claim that modern humans are only using a fraction of their intellectual potential. Someone with a larger skull and brain might be making more use of his or her mental capacity, and therefore have an advantage over people with smaller-sized brains.

Then there are the curious holes often cut into human skulls worldwide. The process of drilling or sawing into the skull is called *trepanning*, and this has been found on elongated examples as well as unmodified specimens. Trepanning can result in a round or square hole made with four sawing cuts. That people survived this ancient medical procedure is borne out by many examples still exhibiting calcium growth around the holes. Mainstream scientists explain that trepanning was a type of brain surgery for ancient people with psychological problems. Members of primitive cultures believed that persons suffering from mental illness, such as schizophrenia, were possessed by evil spirits or the like. By cutting a hole in the sufferer's head, the theory went, the demons causing the problem were allowed to escape.

On the other hand, some believe that a hole drilled in one's skull can actually enhance psychic abilities. This notion was first made generally available in popular literature by T. Lobsang Rampa. He claimed that his book *The Third Eye* is a true account of his training at a Tibetan monastery during the 1920s, when, as a young initiate, he had a hole drilled into his forehead to release latent psychic powers. It was made with a crude hand drill, which cored out a 2-inch (5 cm) aperture in his forehead. The hole was then plugged with a piece of "special" wood, and an herbal salve was placed over the entire area. Rampa describes the procedure as a traumatic experience, but claims that he could more easily see patients' etheric auras, and such, after having been trepanned.

In his 1969 book, *More "Things,"* zoologist and author Ivan T. Sanderson wrote of a letter he received regarding an engineer who was stationed on the Aleutian island of Shemya during World War II. While building an airstrip, his crew bulldozed a group of hills, unintentionally excavating what appeared to be an ancient graveyard under several sedimentary layers. The dug-up crania measured from 22 to 24 inches (56 to 61 cm) from base to crown, implying an immense size for a normally proportioned human. Furthermore, every skull had been neatly trepanned. Sanderson tried to gather further proof, eventually receiving a letter from another member of the Seabees unit who confirmed the report. The correspondence indicated that the Smithsonian Institution had collected the remains, yet nothing else was ever heard about the discovery.

Sanderson was convinced that the letters were not part of a hoax, but wondered why the Smithsonian would not release the data. To quote him,

"Is it that these people cannot face rewriting all the text books?" To be sure, a better understanding of the ancient coneheads and their bizarre surgery could force a major revision in our understanding of American prehistory.

Modern forensic scientists not only aid criminal investigations, but are also solving "cold cases" hundreds and even thousands of years old. The fresh evidence being unearthed by these newly equipped researchers unveils a prehistoric scenario more diverse and unexpected than anything hitherto imagined.

Who Were the First Americans?
By Frank Joseph

Although readers of *Ancient American* are familiar with the story of Kennewick Man—the 9,000-year-old skeleton of a Caucasian male found in Washington state—they may be surprised to learn that his are by no means the only such remains discovered in North America. Nor are they the oldest.

That status goes to Penyon Woman III, a specimen at Mexico City's National Museum of Anthropology, found while a well was being dug at the nearby international airport. Inadvertently unearthed was the skull of a Caucasian woman who died when she was 27 years old, between 12,700 and 13,000 years ago.

At that time, according to mainstream archaeologists, Mongoloid peoples migrating out of Asia over a landbridge spanning the Bering Straits into Alaska were the only inhabitants of North America. Their cranial remains are short and broad, similar to those of modern-day Indians. In sharp contrast, the Mexico City example is long and narrow, identifiably Caucasian, according to geologist Silvia Gonzalez.

Archaeological Discoveries of Ancient America

Gonzalez teaches at John Moores University in England, where she received a grant from the British government to conduct her research. Gonzalez wondered if the skull, found back in 1959, was older than its museum designation in the 16th century, and sent it to Oxford University for carbon dating. Testing confirmed that the young woman to whom it belonged was part of a fair-skinned population that resided in the Americas during the last ice age. But Penyon Woman III was not alone.

On October 9, 1933, an Ice Age grave was found in Browns Valley, on the Minnesota border with North Dakota. Although some thousand years younger than the Mexican find, Browns Valley Man is the oldest Caucasian thus far recovered in the United States. Artifacts taken from his grave are not associated with the Yuma or Folsom types that flourished toward the close of the Ice Age, but, for lack of any other explanation, were categorized as "transitional" between the two by conventional scholars. In fact, these grave goods are more likely the products of some foreign, overseas source, a supposition reinforced by the Browns Valley Man's discovery near the eastern bank of the Minnesota River.

A more recent find occurred in 1965, when the remains of a female Caucasian were excavated from another waterway in Colorado. The 9,700-year-old Gordon Creek Woman had a smaller, narrower face than the indigenous people. The remains also displayed alveolar prognathism, which causes the tooth region to jut forward slightly, a characteristic not found in tribal Americans, but typical of modern Europeans.

Interestingly, Gordon Creek Woman's bones and nearby tools had been sprinkled with hematite at the time of her burial. This is a blood-red pigment manufactured in powdered form for funerary purposes by the Red Paint People, unknown mariners who traveled up and down the eastern seaboard of North America 7,000 or more years ago. They appear to be the same race associated with Europe's Old Stone Age.

A no-less-remarkable find was made in 1940, when the excellently preserved body of a 9,400-year-old Caucasian man was discovered inside a Nevada cave. The upper part of his body was partially mummified, and even some scalp and red hair remained on the head. His grave was lined with sagebrush, upon which the corpse was laid, indicating that his people were sophisticated enough to use burial rites. Known as Spirit Cave Man, he had been placed on his left side with the knees flexed upward to the level of the hips—a posture similar to the fetal position (suggesting rebirth) found in pre-Dynastic Egyptian burials. Well-made leather slippers, a rabbit-skin blanket, and mats were still in good condition.

Kennewick Man was found by two men who had come to watch a hydroplane boat race in Columbia Park. Nearly 400 bones and bone fragments were subsequently taken from a 300-foot-square (28 square meters) area at the bottom of the Kennewick River. They formed a skeleton 5 feet, 9 inches (175 cm) tall, much taller and thinner than ancient Indian examples. The 9,300-year-old Caucasian's chest had been crushed, and a projectile point was imbedded in his hip. Perhaps he was one of an unknown race exterminated by the Indians. The Menomonee still have traditions of the Attewandeton, a fierce tribe that, before its own disappearance, was alleged to have hunted down and killed off a premodern, fair-skinned people in the distant past.

Since his discovery in July 1996, Kennewick Man has been at the center of a bitter dispute between scientists who want to learn more about him through further study and the U.S. Army Corps of Engineers intent on turning over his remains to local Indians who are demanding his reburial, even though they are not genetically related to him. A welcome federal court decision recently saved Kennewick Man, and allows for his study by physical anthropologists. The case is an important one, because the physical evidence for Caucasians in pre-Columbian America is being destroyed in the name of political correctness.

Archæological Discoveries of Ancient America

For example, Kennewick Man's contemporary, Spirit Cave Man, disappeared forever after he was handed over to Nevada Indians. Minnesota's 7,800-year-old Pelican Rapids Woman was found in 1938, but eventually presented to local Indians for anonymous internment, even though she displayed Caucasian features. The same fate befell Browns Valley Man. And Gordon Creek Woman, now nearly 40 years after her discovery, has never been DNA-tested.

Nor has the 10-year-old female at Nevada's Grimes Point Burial Shelter been subjected to scientific examination, despite the location's 9,740-year-old origins. Oregon's Prospect Man, more than 6,800 years old, likewise remains untested. Testing, however, is underway on Arlington Springs Woman, a contender for the oldest known inhabitant in the Americas. Her discovery is especially interesting. She was found on an island, Santa Rosa, off the Southern California coast, thereby proving her people's Ice Age maritime skills, contrary to official archaeological opinion.

DNA research is also planned for Nevada's Wizard Beach Man (9,500 years before the present), the Wilson-Leonard Site in Texas (10,000 years before the present), and Montana's 10,800-year-old Anzick Burial of a young child. Such testing is important, not only to determine the racial backgrounds of these individuals, but also in comparing the genetic makeup of the various human population groups that first peopled America, their origins, and their time of arrival.

In summer 2006, Dr. Theodore Schurr told the American Association for the Advancement of Science that DNA research at the Southwest Foundation for Biomedical Research (San Antonio, Texas) was able to trace four major lineages of American Indians to Siberia and northeast Asia; specifically, in Baikal and Altai-Sayan. These findings tallied with conservative theories of Mongoloid peoples arriving in North America over the Bering Straits landbridge before rising sea levels engulfed it.

However, Dr. Schurr and his colleagues were able to trace a fifth, minor lineage with ancestral roots in Europe. Known as Haplogroup X, it was present among some Algonkian-speaking groups, such as the Ojibwa, long before Columbus or even the Vikings arrived here. Haplogroup X comprises about 4 percent of the European population, but also occurs, to a lesser degree, in the Near East. Its discovery by the Southwest Foundation for Biomedical Research was underscored by a University of Michigan team of anthropologists headed by Professor Loring Brace. He said that descendants of the first humans to enter the Americas show no ties to Asia. Yet a second, smaller group of Indians, the Blackfoot, Iroquois, Inuit, and lesser tribes from Minnesota, Michigan, Massachusetts, and Ontario, although mixed with Mongolian blood, nonetheless stem from yet another ancient Caucasian branch that produced the Jomon, the earliest culture-creators in Japan, beginning about 10,000 years ago.

Silvia Gonzalez, who was responsible for the re-dating of Penyon Woman III as the oldest known inhabitant of our continent, concluded, "If this proves right, it's going to be quite contentious. We're going to say to Native Americans, 'Maybe there were some people in the Americas before you, who are not related to you.'"

In reporting these revelations, *The Daily Telegraph* science editor, Roger Highfield, stated that sufficient DNA evidence now exists to show that America was "colonized" by Europeans 30,000 years ago. They did not come over any long-since-sunken landbridges to Asia, but were already in possession of a maritime technology sophisticated enough to carry them across the vast, hazardous stretches of the Atlantic Ocean.

The skulls and skeletons found from Mexico to Minnesota belong to those first discoverers of America, which is more than enough reason to preserve and study their remains. They were the real pioneers, not only of Ancient America, but of the coming New History, of which this book is among its first volumes.

Glossary

antiquarian A person who studies or collects antiques.

archaeology The study of human activity in the past, through recovery of artifacts.

artifact An object that remains from a particular period in history.

authentic Real or genuine.

calamity A disaster.

contemporary Belonging or occurring in the present.

decipher To interpret into an easily understood language.

erroneous Incorrect.

excavate To dig in or remove dirt in order to find hidden items in it.

forgery A fake item, created with the intention to mislead others.

hoax A deliberately fabricated lie, meant to mislead.

linguistic Relating to language and the study of language.

mandala A religious symbol, often a circle or a square, containing the image of a deity.

prehistoric Relating to the period before written records were kept.

skeptic A person who instinctively feels doubt toward knowledge, facts, or opinions.

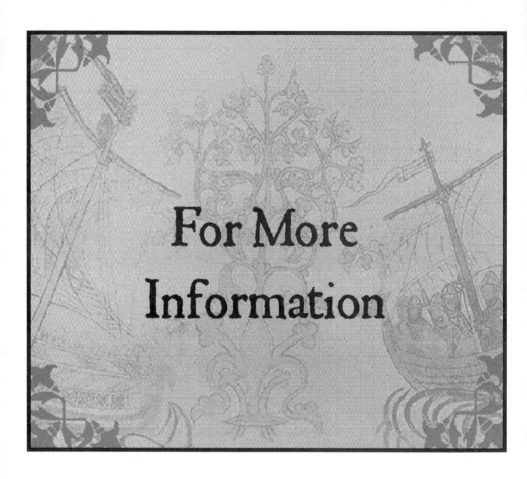

For More Information

American Museum of Natural History
Central Park West at 79th Street
New York, NY 10024-5192
(212) 769-5100
Website: http://www.amnh.org
Science museum that contains artifacts from ancient America and other
places around the globe.

Archaeological Institute of America
Boston University
656 Beacon Street, 6th Floor

Boston, MA 02215-2006

Website: http://www.archaeological.org

North America's oldest and largest organization devoted to the world of archaeology.

Archaeology Magazine

36-36 33rd Street

Long Island City, NY 11106

Website: http://www.archaeology.org

The news magazine of the Archaeological Institute of America. New York, NY 10024

Canadian Archaeological Association

William Ross, President

189 Peter Street

Thunder Bay, ON P7A 5H8

Canada

Website: http://canadianarchaeology.com

Organization that unites archaeologists from across Canada.

European Association for Archaeologists

Institute of Archaeology CAS

Letenská 4, 11801 Praha 1

Czech Republic

+420 257014411

Website: http://www.e-a-a.org

European society that provides a network for archaeologists from around the globe.

Archaeological Discoveries of Ancient America

Society for American Archaeology
1111 14th Street NW, Suite 800
Washington, DC 20005-5622
(202) 789-8200
Website: http://www.saa.org
Society that promotes archaeological study through publication of materials
and providing a network for people working in the field.

Web Sites

Due to the changing nature of Internet links, Rosen Publishing has developed an online list of Websites related to the subject of this book. This site is updated regularly. Please use this link to access the list:

http://www.rosenlinks.com/DAA/Archa

Bibliography

Andersen, Lars. "Hungarians Identify Viking Navigational Device." *Norway Post* 12, No. 9 (2007).

Bartlett, Jonas. "History of Famous Ontonogon Copper Rock Recalled by Society's Outing." *Mining Gazette* 7, No. 11 (1916).

Berlitz, Charles. *Mysteries From Forgotten Worlds*. New York: Doubleday & Company, 1972.

Boder, Thomas Allen. *Schism: The Splintering of Early Christianity*. New York: Putnam & Sons, 1969.

Brackenridge, Henry. *Recollections of Persons and Places in the West*. Temecula, Calif.: Reprint Services Corp., 1989.

Buchanan, Donal. "The Decipherment of Southwest Iberic." *Journal ESOP* 20:2, 1991.

——. "Report on the Morristown Tablet." Early Sites Research Society Bulletin 10, No. 1 (1982): 22.

Budge, E.A. Wallis. *The Book of the Dead: The Papyrus of Ani.* New York: Dover, 1967.

Buergin, Luc. *Geheimakte Archaeologie, Unterdrueckte Entdeckungen, Verschollene Schaetze, Bizarre Funde.* Munich, Germany: F.A. Herbig Verlagsbuchhandlung GmbH, 1998.

Burrows, Russell, and Fred C. Rydholm. *The Mystery Cave of Many Faces.* Marquette, Mich.: Superior Heartland, 1993.

Casson, Lionel. *Ships and Seamanship of the Ancient World.* Princeton, N.J.: Princeton University Press, 1971.

Chessman, Dr. Paul. *Ancient Writing on Metal Plates.* Bountiful, Utah: Horizon Publishers, 1998.

Childress, David Hatcher. *Lost Cities and Ancient Civilizations of North America.* Kempton, Ill.: Adventures Unlimited Press, 1993.

——. *Lost Cities of North and Central America.* Kempton, Ill.: Adventures Unlimited Press, 1992.

Cook, Dr. Warren L. "Vermont's Ancient Sites and the Larger Picture of Trans-Atlantic Visitations to America, B.C." *Proceedings of the Castleton Conference.* Castleton, Vt.: Castleton State College, 1977.

De Jonge, R.M., and G.F. IJzereef. *De Stenen Spreken.* Utrecht/Antwerpen: Kosmos Z & K, 1996.

De Jonge, R.M., and J.S. Wakefield. "The Discovery of the Atlantic Islands." *Migration & Diffusion* 3, No. 11, (2002): 69–109.

——. "How the Sun God Reached America c.2500 BCE: A Guide to Megalithic Sites." *www.howthesungod.com*, 2002 (accessed August 2008).

——. "A Nautical Center for Crossing the Ocean: America's Stonehenge, New Hampshire, c. 2200 BCE." *Migration & Diffusion* 4, No. 15, (2002): 60–100.

——. "The Passage Grave of Karleby: Encoding the Islands Discovered in the Ocean, c. 2950 BCE." *Migration & Diffusion* 5, No. 18, (2004): 64–74.

Deal, David Allen. "Hittite Warriors." *Discovery of Ancient America.* Monumenti-Rosellini, plate CIII. Unknown city, Calif.: KheremLaYah Press, 1984.

——. "Spoken Language: The Connection Between the Old and New Worlds in Pre-Columbian Times." *The NEXUS.* New Zealand, 1993.

Dempsey, Jack. *Thomas Morton of "Merrymount": The Life and Renaissance of an Early American Poet.* New York: Digital Scanning, Inc., 2000.

Dunhill, Alfred. *The Pipe Book.* London: Arthur Barker Limited, 1924.

DuTemple, Octave Joseph. *Prehistoric Copper Mining in the Lake Superior Region.* Unknown city, Ill.: Privately published, 1960.

Eschborn, Archie. *The Dragon in the Lake.* Philadelphia: Xlibris, 2004.

"Explorations in Grand Canyon." *The Arizona Gazette.* April 5, 1909, page 1.

Fell, Dr. Barry. *America, B.C.* New York: Simon & Schuster, 1989.

——. "The Etymology of Some American Inscriptions." *The Epigraphic Society Occasional Publications* 3, Part 2, No. 76, 1976.

Ferguson, William P.F. "Michigan's Most Ancient Industry: The Prehistoric Mines & Miners of Isle Royale." *Michigan History Magazine* 7, No. 5, 1923.

Fitzhugh, William W. *Vikings: The North Atlantic Saga.* Washington, D.C.: National Museum of Natural History, 2000.

Fox, Hugh. "Von Daniken's Gold." *Western World Review,* 2 (1977): 44–50.

Fuson, Robert. *The Log of Christopher Columbus.* Camden, Maine:

Archaeological Discoveries of Ancient America

International Marine Publishing Company, 1987.

Gallagher, Ida Jane, and Warren W. Dexter. *Contact with Ancient America.* Mount Pleasant, S.C.: Sovereign Terrace Books, 2004.

———. "Light Dawns on West Virginia Prehistory." *Wonderful West Virginia* 47, No 1 (1983): 7–11.

Garstang, John. *The Burial Customs of Ancient Egypt.* London: Constable, 1907.

"G.E. Kincaid Reaches Yuma." *The Arizona Gazette.* March 12, 1909, page 12.

Goldberger, David. "'It's a Hoax,' Claims BYU Professor." *Deseret News* 153, No. 12, November 26, 1975.

Graham, Shelia. "Local Treasure Hunter Claims 'Historic' Find." *Olney Daily Mail* 41, No. 3, July 27, 1984.

Grazowicz, Helmut. "Pre-Columbian Christian Refugees in New England?" *Antiquarian Journal* 1, No. 3, fall 1957.

Grimes, James P. *The Incredible Bronze Age Journey.* Philadelphia: Infinity Publishing, 2003.

Hamilton, Ross. *The Mystery of the Serpent Mound.* Berkeley, Calif.: North Atlantic Books, 2003.

Harleston, Hugh, Jr. "Predictions by Precalculations of Archaeological Sites." Mexico City, Mexico: The Uac-Kan Research Group, 1984.

Hemmings, E. Thomas. *West Virginia Antiquities.* New York: Wellington Publishing Company, 1889.

Herandez, Antonio. *Boletin Salesiano* 9, No. 46, May–June 1982.

Hernandez, Oscar. "Archaeologists find City Pre-Inca City." *Lima Times* 29, No. 2, September 7, 2007.

Heyerdahl, Dr. Thor. *Early Man and the Ocean*. New York: Doubleday, 1973.

Highfield, Roger. "Europeans 'Colonized' America 30,000 Years Ago, DNA Shows." *The Daily Telegraph* 49, No. 10, September 3, 2006.

Hill, Adrian, and S.W. Serjeantson. *The Colonization of the Pacific: A Genetic Trail*. Oxford, UK: Oxford University Press, 1989.

Holmes, William H. "Aboriginal Copper Mines of Isle Royale, Lake Superior." *American Anthropologist* 3, No. 12, 1901.

Hunt, Terry L., and Robert M. Holsen. "An Early Chronology of the Hawaiian Islands." *Asian Perspectives* 29, No. 3 (1991): 147–161.

Inman, Mason. "Polynesians—And Their Chickens—Arrived in America Before Columbus." National Geographic News. *http://news .nationalgeographic.com/news/2007/06/070604-chickens.html* (accessed August 2008).

Joseph, Frank. *Atlantis in Wisconsin*. Minneapolis, Minn.: Galde Press, Inc., 1995.

——. *The Lost Pyramids of Rock Lake (Revised Edition)*. Minneapolis, Minn.: Galde Press, Inc., 2003.

——. *Sacred Sites of the West*. Blaine, Wash.: Hancock House, 1997.

Kayser, Manfred, and Gunter Weiss. "Melanesian Origin of Polynesian Y Chromosomes." *Current Biology* 64, No. 8, October 2000.

Koenig, Earl. "Roman Relics Found in Arizona." *Discovering the Mysteries of Ancient America*. Edited by Frank Joseph. Franklin Lakes, N.J.: New Page Books, 2006.

Lehrmontoff, Adrian. *India's Sacred Architecture*. London: Montgomery Publishing, Ltd., 1977.

Archaeological Discoveries of Ancient America

Maclean, J.P. "The Grave Creek Stone Was Real." *One-Horse News* 8, No. 10 (1885): 4, 13.

Mahan, Joseph B. *The Secret: America in World History Before Columbus.* Unknown city, Ga.: Self-published, 1983.

Marsh, Peter. *Polynesian Pathways. www.polynesian-prehistory.com* (accessed August 2008).

Matsuyama, Mary. *New England Antiquities.* Boston: Harvergrove Publishers, 1967.

McCulloch, Huston, Maine. *Journal of the New England Antiquities Research Association,* 22, No. 7 (2000).

McKusick, Marshall, and Eugene A. Shinn. "Bahamian Atlantis Reconsidered." *Nature* 287, No. 11 (2000).

Mertz, Henrietta. *The Mystic Symbol.* Hay River, Wisc.: Hay River Press, 2003.

Muse News 12, No. 3, June 1959. The Museum of Science, Miami.

National Parks Official Website: *www.nps.gov/maca/* (accessed August 2008).

Native American Website: *www.turtle-island.com/customs.html* (accessed August 2008).

Nebenzahl, Kenneth. *Atlas of Columbus and the Great Discoveries.* New York: Rand McNally, 1990.

Nielsen, Richard, and Scott F. Wolter. "The Kensington Rune Stone: Compelling New Evidence." *www.kensingtonrunestone.com,* 2006 (accessed August 2008).

Norona, Delf. *Moundsville's Mammoth Mound.* Charleston, W.Va.: Delf Norona Museum, 1962.

Office of the Surveyor of the Queen's Works of Art, personal communications, London, April 5 and April 30, 1982.

Pálsson, Hermann, trans. *Hrafnkel's Saga and Other Icelandic Stories.* New York: Penguin, 1971.

Pfund, Dr. A.H. "Employment of Crystalline Minerals as Aeronautical Aids." *Bulletin of the U.S. National Bureau of Standards* 26, No. 8, 1949.

Philip Coppens biography. *www.philipcoppens.com/bio.html* (accessed August 2008).

Pomeranz, Irving. *Florida Prehistory.* Pensacola, Fla.: Pensacola Press, 1980.

Ponce, Reginald. *The Collected Correspondence of Cotton Mather.* New York: Hastings Publishing, 1945.

Pourade, Richard. *Ancient Hunters of the Far West.* San Diego, Calif.: Union Tribune Publishing Co., 1966.

——. *Prehistoric Images.* San Diego, Calif.: San Diego Museum of Man, 1982.

Priest, Josiah. *American Antiquities.* Hay River, Wisc.: Hay River Press, 2005.

Ragsdale, Jim. "That Silly Ole 'Runestone.'" *St. Paul Pioneer Press*, December 12, 2006.

Ramskov, Thorkild. *Hedeby.* Denmark: Søndagsuniversitetet Munksgaard, 1962.

Randall, Emilius O. *Serpent Mound, Adams County, Ohio.* Whitefish, Mont.: Kessinger Publishing, 2003.

Rebikoff, Dimitri. "Underwater Archeology: Photogrammetry of Artifacts Near Bimini." *Explorers Journal* 19, No. 2, September 1979.

Sanderson, Ivan T. *More "Things."* New York: Pyramid Books, 1969.

Schiff, Bernard. *Encyclopedia of Rock Art.* Atlanta, Ga.: Wonderful Press, 1990.

Archaeological Discoveries of Ancient America

Shinn, E.A. "Atlantis: Bimini Hoax." *Sea Frontiers* 13, No. 4 (1978).

Smart, George. *The Knights Templar: Chronology*. New York: Authorhouse, 2005.

Smith, Anita. *An Archaeology of West Polynesian Prehistory*. Australia: Pandanus Books, Research School of Pacific and Asian Studies, Australian National University Canberra, 2002.

"Soil and Ecosystem Development Across the Hawaiian Islands." *ftp://rock.geosociety.org/pub/GSAToday/gt9709.pdf* (accessed August 2008).

Solholm, Rolleiv. "Archaeological Sensation in Oestfold." *The Norway Post. www.norwaypost.no/cgi-bin/norwaypost/imaker?id=87357* (accessed August 2008).

Sora, Steven. *The Lost Treasure of the Knights Templar*. Rochester, Vt.: Destiny Books, 1999.

Spencer, Herbert. *A Theory of Population*. London: Transfiguration Press, Ltd., 1962.

Spriggs, Mathew. "The Lapita cultural complex—origins, distribution, contemporaries and successors," in "Out of Asia: Peopling of the Americas and the Pacific," edited by R. Kirk and E. Szathmary. *Journal of Pacific History* 12, No. 2 (1985): 185–206.

Sykes, Edgerton. "Atlantis in America." *The Atlantean Journal* 12, No. 8 (1969).

Thompson, Dr. Gunnar. *American Discovery: The Real Story*. Seattle, Wash.: Argonauts Misty Isles Press, 1994.

——. *The Friar's Map of America–1360 A.D.* Seattle, Wash.: Radio Bookstore Press, 1996.

Toma, Bill. "New Discovery of Ancient Maps Puts Phoenicians in America." *Ancient American* 3, No. 16 (1997).

BIBLIOGRAPHY

Topographic map of Blythe, California: *www.mindbird.com/blythe 100.htm.*

Trochner, Phillip. *The Constellations and Their Astrological Equivalents.* London: Quill Press, Ltd., 1983.

Turolla, Pino. *Beyond the Andes.* New York: Random House, 1981.

Wall, Alban. "An Ancient Greek Historian's Sailing Directions to North America." *Ancient American* 6, No. 37 (2001).

Weber, Joseph. *Church Triumphant, 600 A.D.* Chicago: Regnery Press, 1978.

Will, Elizabeth Lyding. *Archaeology Odyssey* 33, No. 6 (2000).

Wilson, Ian. *The Columbus Myth: Did Men from Bristol Reach America Before Columbus?* New York: Simon & Schuster, 1991.

Winchell, N.H. "Ancient Copper Mines of Isle Royale." *Engineering and Mining Journal* XXXII, July to December, 1881.

Zalar, Michael. "Examinations of the So-Called 'Kensington Rune Stone.'" *Journal of the New England Antiquities Research Association* 19, No. 7 (1999).

Zink, Dr. David D. "The Poseidea Expeditions: A Summary," *Explorers Journal* 22, No. 3, Winter 1991.

——. *The Stones of Atlantis* (New and Revised). New York: Prentice Hall Press, 1990.

Index

A

Adena Stone, 94
Adena, the, 46, 53
Ales Stenar, 211-222
Alexander the Great, 108
Alexandris, 229
America BC, 142
American Antiquities, 22
American Discovery, 21, 223
Ancient American, 13, 14, 26, 39, 109, 143-148, 161, 177, 198, 225, 265
Ancient Writings on Metal Plates, 204
Andean Civilization, 199
Andros Platform, 149, 153
Antillia, 239, 240, 241
Antony, Marc, 112
Apenzeller, Tim, 117
Aptuxcet Rock, 94
Arainism, 77-78
Arenal, El, 224
Arius, 77
Arriaga, Jose de, 66
Artake, Kihachiro, 144
Atlantic Ocean, 148-157
Atlantis, 255
Atlantis, Temples of, 88

Augustine, Saint, 78
Aztalan, 167

B

Bahamas, 150, 153
Banco Central, Museo de, 57-58, 63-66, 71, 73
Baranowski, Mark T., 186-187
Barton, Jared G., 132
Basil, Saint, 78
Bat Creek Stone, 47
Behaim, Martin, 238, 240
Berassi, Padre Virgilio, 68
Berlitz, Charles, 73, 87-88
Bes, 131
Biano, Andrea, 238, 239-240, 241
Biggs, Thomas, 52
Bimini Road, 148-157
Biscaynehenge, 84
Blessed Mother Mary, 79-80
Blythe, 191-196
Book of the Dead, The, 17, 18
Borobudor, 27-28
Boroto, Richard, 58
Brace, Loring, 269
Brackenridge, Henry, 200-201
Brazil, 199-200, 232-233

INDEX

Brewer, John, 134-139
Brickell Point Site, 84
Brown, Elsie, 151
Brown, Krista, 151
Browns Valley Man, 266
Buchanan, Donal, 51
Buckholm, Mona Beate, 246
Buddha, 29-30
Buddhists, 24-30
Buonanno, Anthony, 258-259
Burgin, Luc, 105
Burrows Cave, 103-113, 131, 132-139
Burrows, Russell, 103-113

C

Cabot, John, 241
Cabot, Sebastian, 241
Cabral, Pedro Alveres, 233
Caesar, Julius, 229-230
California Archaeology: 1940 to 1960, 195
California desert, 191-196
Caligula, 112, 226
Cardozo, Licenciado Rene, 58
Carmody, Dr. Pat, 24, 26
Carnus, Jacobus, 240
Carr, Robert S., 85, 88
Casson, Lionel, 229
Cat Island, 152-153
Catlett, Peter B., 53
Caveri, Nicolo, 243
Celtic America, 30
Cerne-Abbas Giant, 192
Ceylon, 27-28
Chachapoyas, the, 198-199
Champlion, 23
Cheesman, Dr. Paul, 55-57, 67, 71, 134, 136, 204
Chicago World's Fair, 20
Childress, David Hatcher, 128-131, 254
Chile, 194, 222-225
Chinese foot-binding, 261
Church, oldest Christian, 75-82
Church, Sally K., 223
Ciboney, the, 150
Clavijo, Dr. Ezequiel, 61
Clemens, Dr. James W., 51-52, 53
Cleopatra, 112
Cliff Mine, the, 121-122
Cole, John, 55
Colon, Bartholomew, 240
Colon, Cristobal, 234-235, 238
Colon, Ferdinand, 241-242
Colossus of Rhodes, 120
Columbus, Christopher, 19, 29, 31, 44, 54, 82, 103, 108-109, 208, 231, 232, 234-235, 238, 240-242, 269
Coneheads, 254-265
Connecticut, 75-82
Constantine, 32

Constantinople, 77
Constantius II, 142
Constellations, 92-93
Cook, Dr. Warren, 54, 112
Coppens, Philip, 103, 113
Copper, 113-123, 125
Copts, 31-37
Cordero, Yniguez Juan, 63
Cortes, Hernando, 200
Crania Americana, 52
Cranial deformation, 259-261, 263
Creighton, A.O., 97
Crespi Collection, the, 54-74
Crespi, Padre Carlo, 54-74
Cuba, 240, 242
Cuenca, 54-74
Cuevas, Mariano, 22-24

D

Dark Ages, 230
Dausset, Jean, 249
Davenport Tablet, 94
Davis, E.H., 46, 189
Deal, David Allen, 30
"Decipherment of Southwest Iberic, The," 51
Decius, 77
Dempsey, Steve, 171
Deneb, 174
DeSoto, 202
Destruction of Atlantis, The, 186, 187
Detzer, Dr. Jordan, 195
DeVirga, Albertin, 240
Dexter, Warren W., 56, 57, 73
Dezter, Warren, 64
Diamond Lake, 15, 17-18, 19-20
Dias, Vincent, 238
Dighton Rock, 90-94
Diocletian, 77
Diringer, David, 51
Discoveries of the World, 236
Discovering the Mysteries of Ancient America, 132
Disease, 201-202
Donato, William, 148
Donnie's Stone, 151
Dunhill, Alfred, 178
Dycke, Kassandra, 95

E

Easter Island, 249-250, 253
Ecuador, 54-74
El Puente Pyramid, 162
Elephant Pipe, 181
Eschborn, Archie, 160, 173
Estreito, Alfonso de, 238
Etzenhouser collection, 33
Extirpacion dfe la Idoltria, 66

Archaeological Discoveries of Ancient America

F

Fell, Dr. Barry, 22, 49, 55, 67, 94, 142-143
Fields, Donnie, 151, 155, 156
Figuig, 76
Flaaten, Nils, 40
Flood of Noah, 33
Flores Haro, Padre Luis, 59, 61, 62, 63, 65-68, 72
Florida, 82-89, 238, 240
Flying Cloud, 230-231
Foot-binding, 261
Forgione, Adriano, 257-258
1421: The Year China Discovered America, 223
Frontier, 103
Fu Sang, 224
Fue, 29-30

G

Gallagher, Ida Jane, 49
Gallagher, John, 75
Gallic Wars, 229-230
Galvano, Antonio, 236
Gang, Liu, 222-224
Geiseric, 78
Germanus, Henricus Martellus, 238
"Giant Etchings on California Desert Sands," 193
Gold of the Gods, 62-63
Gomez-Casado, E., 252
Gonzales, Miguel Angel, 23
Gonzalez, Silvia, 265-266, 269
Gordon Creek Woman, 266
Gossage, Douglas, 159
Goya, Drancisco de, 69
Gran Pajaten, 198
Gran Saposoa, 197-199
Grand Canyon, 123-132
Gratianus, 142
Grave Creek Mound, 45-49, 52
Grave Creek Tablet, 45-53
Great Pyramids, 119, 120
Great Serpent Mound, 183-191
Great triangle, 171, 172
Greenwood Group, 169
Grimes, James, 225

H

Haiti, 240, 241, 242
Halley's Comet, 35
Hanson, Evan, 33
Haplogroup X, 269
Harleston, Hugh, 170
Hatshepsut, Queen, 227
Hawaii, 247-248
Hayes, John, 121-122
Head-binding, 259-261, 263
Hebrews, pre-Columbian, 182-183
Heinerman, Dr. Robert, 136-138

Heliod, Alexander, 106, 112
Hemmings, E. Thomas, 46
Henry the Navigator, Prince, 238, 239
Hepburn, Charles, 56-57
Herodotus, 19, 231
Heyerdahl, Dr. Thor, 250
Hidden Mountain, 33
Hieroglyphs, 16, 22, 127, 131
Highfield, Roger, 269
Historia de la Nacion Mexicans, 22-23
Histories, 19
Ho Chunk, 170
Hoffman, David, 199
Holand, Hjalmar R., 42
Hold, Dr. Olaf, 64
Hoover Dam, 191, 192
Hope, Joan, 101
Hopewell Culture, 13, 178-179
Hopi Indians, 188
Hornbostel, Jr., Lloyd, 39
Horvath, Dr. Gabor, 209
Hrafnkel's Saga, 208
Hubbard, Harry, 108, 112
Huffinan, Kirk, 260
Huneric, 78

I

Iberian-Runic alphabet, 92-94
Iceland Spar, 209
Illinois, 13-24, 102-113
In Plain Sight, 30
Inca Empire, 56, 198, 245
India Occident, 236
Inventio Fortunatae, 241-242
Iowa, 181
Isabella of Spain, 31, 235
Iseki Point, 144
Isle Royale, 24-30, 117-118, 120, 123

J

James Monroe, 230
Java, 27-28
Jecas, Nelson, 141-143
Jennings, Dr. Jesse, 136
Jesus Christ, 79-81
John II of Portugal, 234-235, 238, 240-241
Jonge, Reinould de, 210, 211
Jordan, S.A., 125-129, 131
Joseph, Frank, 24, 123, 161, 167, 265
Juba II, 112-113
Justinian, 78

K

Keefe, Bill, 156
Keller, George, 132-134
Kennedy, John, 159

Index

Kennewick Man, 265, 267-268
Kensington Rune Stone, The, 44
Kensington Runestone, 40-44
Kentucky, 163-165
Kimura, Masaaki, 143-148
Kincaid, G.E., 123-132
Kincaid's Cave, 131
Knights Templar, 95-96, 101
Knohls, Max Gene, 159
Koenig, Earl, 132, 197, 207

L

Lake Superior, 24-30, 113-123
Land of Punt, 216, 219, 227
Lapham, 173
Lemuria, 143
Leon, Ponce de, 85, 241
LeTourneau, Jack, 171
Little, Dr. Greg, 149-154
Little, Dr. Lora, 149-154
Livingston, David, 254
Lone Eagle, 132-134
Long Man of Wilmington, 192
Los Angeles, 191, 192
Los Barriles, 33
Lost Cities and Ancient Civilizations of North America, 128
Lost Outpost of Atlantis, The, 86-87
Lova, Pedro, 69
Lovelock Cave, 139

M

MacLean, J.P., 47
Macrobius, 237, 240
Mahabodhim Temple, 28-29
Mahan, Joseph P., 108
Maio, Dr. Benigno, 69
Malta, 257-259
Mammoth Cave, 163-165
Mandan Indians, 188-189
Manicheanism, 77
Marsh, Peter, 246-247
Marshall, Harry, 97
Martyr, Peter, 240
Marx, Robert, 232, 233
Mary, 79-80
Masinissa Plaque, 55, 70, 71
Massachusetts, 90-94
Matheny, Dr. Ray, 136
Mather, Cotton, 89, 91-92
Matisco-Smith, Lisa, 224
Mauretania, 131-132
Mauritania, 112
Mauro, Fra, 238
May, Wayne, 13, 26, 109, 177, 202
Mayas civilization, end of the, 194
McCulloch, Huston, 46

McGinnis, Daniel, 96-103
Megis, 166-167
Menorah petroglyph, 182
Menzies, Gavin, 223-224
Mercator, Gerhard, 242-243
Mertz, Henriette, 31-32, 34
Metlakatla, 195-196
Miami, 82-89
Miamihenge, 82-89
Michigan solar eclipse tablet, 31-37
Michigan tablets, 47
Michigan, 24-30, 31-37, 113-123, 182-183
Micmac, 22
Micrite, 154-155
Mifsud, Dr. Anton, 257-259
Minnesota, 40
Mojave Indians, 193
Money Pit, the, 96-103
Montanism, 77
More "Things," 264
Moreno, Gabreil Garcia, 73
Moricz, Juan, 63
Morristown Tablet, 49
Morton, Dr. S.G., 52
Morton, Thomas, 202
Mundud Novus, 240
Museo del Banco Central, 57-58, 63-66, 71, 73
Mysteries From Forgotten Worlds, 87-88
Mystery Cave of Many Faces, The, 109
Mystic Symbol, The, 31

N

National Geographic, 209
Nazca Desert of Peru, 191-196
Nazca Lines, 194
Nebra Disk, 210
Necho, 231
Necho, II, 19-20
Necho, Wehimbre, 19-20
New Jersey, 141-143
New Ross, 101-102
Newfoundland, 245-246
Nibley, Dr. Hugh, 136
Nicean Council, 32, 34-35, 77
Nicholas of Lynn, 240
Nielson, Richard, 40, 43-44
Nile Valley, 13-24
Nina, 226-227
Noah's Flood, 33
Nolan, Fred, 100
Norse, 39-44, 207-210, 245-246
North Africa, 76-77, 94
Nova Scotia, 96-103
Nu Sun, 234

O

O'Connor, Father, John, 82
Oak Island, 96-105

Oak Island Association of Truro, 99
Oak Island Eldorado Company, 97
Oak Island Treasure Company, 99-100
Ohio Decalogue Stone, 47
Ohio Valley, 178-181, 183-191
Ohmann, Olof, 40-42
Olmec culture, 216
On SITE, 34
Onslow Company, 97-98
Ophir, 228
Ophites, the, 188
Osiris, 17

P

Pacific Islands, 246-253
Pahana, 188
Patton, George S., 193
Pelagianism, 77
Pelican Rapids Woman, 268
Penyon Woman III, 265-266, 269
Pepi II, 21
Peru, 191-196, 197-199, 255
Pfund, Dr. A.H., 209-210
Philip IV, 96
Pinta, 226-227
Pipe Book, The, 178-181
Pitblado, James, 98-99
Pizzaro, Francisco, 198
Plutarch, 232
Pohl, Frederick J., 76-77
Polo, Marco, 254
Polynesians, 246-253
Portugal, 234-243
Pourade, Richard, 193
Pre-Columbian Hebrews, 182-183
Pre-Columbian oceanic travel, 111-112, 207
Pre-Columbian times, 22, 29, 77, 175, 267
Prehistoric Images, 193
Priest, Josiah, 22
Proctor's Road, 149, 150-151, 153-154, 155
Ptolemaeus I, 112
Ptolemy IV, 229
Puritans, the, 90-91
Pyramids, Great, 119, 120
Pythias, 231-232

R

Ragsdale, Jim, 43
Rampa, T. Lobsang, 264
Ramskov, Thorkild, 208-209
Rasmussen, Donald, 56-57
Rebikoff, Dimitri, 151, 154, 155
Rebikoff's Pier, 154-156
Red Paint People, the, 118, 119, 266
Reinoso Hermidia, Dr. Gustavo, 64, 70
Renaissance, 207
Rig Veda, the, 250, 251

Ritual mutilations, 258
Rock Lake Research Society, 160, 171, 173, 175
Rock Lake, 157, 161-176
Rockies, the, 132-139, 163, 203, 205
Roggveen, Captain, 248
Rose, Howard, 142
Rosslyn Chapel, 96, 101
Ruysch, Johannes, 239
Rydholm, Fred, 109, 111, 113

S

"Sacred Duality," 172
Sacred Sites of the West, 194
Sacred Sites, 185-186
Saint Paul Mounds, 170, 174
Saite, 16, 18, 19, 20
Salcedo, Dr. Carlos Ramirez, 61
Sanderson, Ivan T., 264-265
Santa Maria, 225, 226-227, 229, 231
Sanudo, Marino, 237
Savoy, Gene, 198
Savoy, Sean, 198
Sawinski, Herbert, 150
Schaffranke, Paul, 108, 112
Scherz, James, 24-30, 111, 159, 160, 166
Schock, Robert, 147-148
Schoolcraft, Henry R., 52
Schurr, Dr. Theodore, 268-269
Scientific American, 117, 209
Sea Peoples, 190-191
Secret Voyages, or True Adventure Stories from the Forbidden
    Chronicles of American Discovery, 234
Secret, The, 108
Selene, Cleopatra, 112
Selenite, 163
Serrano, Dr. Alfonso, 56-58
Setzler, F.M., 129
Shamans, 180-181
Shanaberger, Richard, 35
Shatter cones, 186
Shaw, John, 116
Shinn, Eugene, 156-157
Sierra Club, 89
Sinclair, 102-103
Sinclair, Henry, 96, 101-103
Sky compass, 209-210
Smith, Ron, 152-153
Smith's Cove, 98, 101
Smithsonian Institution, 42, 46, 89, 123, 124, 126-
    129, 264
Smoking pipes, 177-181
Snake Clan, the, 188
Solheim, Rolleiv, 245
Solomon, 228, 236
Spain, 94
Spencer, Herbert, 37
Spirit Cave Man, 267, 268
Spriggs, Mathew, 251

INDEX

Squier, Ephraim George, 52
Stonehenge, 214, 221
Summer Triangle, the, 174-175
Sunstones, 207-210
Sweden, 210-212
Sykes, Edgerton, 88
Syracusia, 229, 231

T

Tallegewi, 31
Taylor, Victor, 159
Teixeira, Roberto, 232
Telles, Fernao, 238
Temple Mount, 95
Temples of Atlantis, 88
Tennessee, 177-181
Tenochtitlan, 200
Tequesta Indians, 82-89
Third Emergence, the, 188
Third Eye, The, 264
This Land, 13
Thompson, Dr. Gunnar, 21-22, 28, 223-224, 234
Thrasamun, 78
Tolonen Medallion, 24-30
Tolonen, Paul, 26
Tomlinson, Abelard, 52, 53
Toral, Hernan Crespo, 71
Toscanelli, Paolo, 238
Totem worship, 179
Transatlantic ships, ancient, 225-234
Trepanning, 263-264
Trinity Stones, 155
Truro Company, 98-99
Turollo, Pino, 68-69
Tutankhamun, 18, 107
Twain, Mark, 20
26th Dynasty, 16, 18, 19, 20

U

Unsolved Mysteries, 160
Upper Michigan, 113-123
Ushabti, 17, 19
Utah, 132-139, 202-206

V

Valdivia, 64
Valens, 142
Valentine, Dr. J. Manson, 86-87
Valentinianus I, 142
Valerian, 77
Vandals, 78-79, 82
Vandre, Armand, 171, 172
Venezuela, 233
Ventura, Dr. Charles Savona, 257
Vesconte, Pietrus, 237
Vespucci, Amerigo, 239, 241, 242

Vikings, 29-44, 76, 207-210
Vikings, 43
Von Daniken, Erich, 62-63
Voyager, 35

W

Wade, Geoff, 223
Wahlgren, Erik, 42-44
Wakefield, Jay Stuart, 210, 211
Waldseemueller, Martin, 242
Wallis, Captain, 248
Wampanoag tribes, 94
Ward, Jack, 112
Wasatch Mountains, 202-206
Wasson, R. Gordon, 195
Watts, Doyle, 187
Welling, Captian, 100
Westford Knight. 102
Wharton, J.E., 51, 53
White House of Uffington, 192
White, Dr. John, 181
Will, Elizabeth, 232
Wilmington Trust, 47
Wilson, Claude, 159
Wilson, Lee, 159
Wingate, Richard, 86-87
Winnebago Indians, 158, 170
Wisconsin, 157-160, 167-176
Wizard Beach Man, 268
Wollin, Elmer, 171, 172
Wolter, Scott, 41, 43, 44
Woodward, Arthur, 193
World Explorers Club, 128
World War II, 193

Y

Yi, General, 261
Yin-yang, 172
Yonaguni "Monument," 145-146

Z

Zalar, Michael, 43
Zink, Dr. David, 154, 156

About the Author

Frank Joseph began as editor-in-chief of *Ancient American* magazine with its first issue in 1993. His 20 books in as many foreign editions resulted from worldwide investigations into the riddles of prehistory. Joseph's research has been honored by organizations in the United States and overseas, including Japan's Savant Society and Ohio's Midwest Epigraphic Society. He lives with his wife, Laura, and son in Colfax, Wisconsin.